COMPUTER BOOK SERIES FROM IDG

Windows NT™ Netw... For Dummies®

Cheat Sheet

Here's a list of the most important Windows NT 4.0 utilities, with the name of the tool on the left, the menu sequence to launch it in the middle, and a brief explanation on the right. Enjoy!

Windows NT 4.0 Utilities

Tool	How to Start It	What It Does
Add/Remove Programs	Start⇨Settings⇨Control Panel	Add and remove server software
Administrative Wizards	Start⇨Programs⇨Accessories⇨Administrative Tools	Wizards help you add users, manage groups, manage file and folder access, add printers, add and remove programs, install modems, administer network clients, and check licenses
Backup	Start⇨Programs⇨Accessories⇨Administrative Tools	Back up data from hard drives to tape
Date/Time	Start⇨Settings⇨Control Panel	Set system date and time
Devices	Start⇨Settings⇨Control Panel	Start and stop hardware device drivers; maintain hardware profiles
DHCP Administrator	Start⇨Programs⇨Accessories⇨Administrative Tools	Manage the Dynamic Host Configuration Service; adjust IP address pools, subnet masks, and related settings for client workstations
Disk Administrator	Start⇨Programs⇨Accessories⇨Administrative Tools	Perform disk maintenance: disk partitioning, formatting, and hard drive analysis
Event Viewer	Start⇨Programs⇨Accessories⇨Administrative Tools	Display System, Application, and Security logs
License Manager	Start⇨Programs⇨Accessories⇨Administrative Tools	Use to adjust Windows NT licenses
Network	Start⇨Settings⇨Control Panel	Add and configure network components and services (especially network device drivers and protocols)
Network Client Administrator	Start⇨Programs⇨Accessories⇨Administrative Tools	Install and update network client workstations
Network Monitor	Start⇨Programs⇨Accessories⇨Administrative Tools	Monitor network traffic; show transmission rates for bits, frames, and overall utilization
ODBC	Start⇨Settings⇨Control Panel	Add and remove ODBC drivers; configure and remove database resources
PC Cards — PCMCIA	Start⇨Settings⇨Control Panel	Add and remove PC Cards
Performance Monitor	Start⇨Programs⇨Accessories⇨Administrative Tools	Monitor low-level OS behavior

(continued)

...For Dummies: #1 Computer Book Series for Beginners

Windows NT 4.0 Utilities *(continued)*

Tool	How to Start It	What It Does
Ports	Start⇨Settings⇨Control Panel	Control COM port settings
Printer Folder	Start⇨Settings	Add and configure printers
Remote Access Admin	Start⇨Programs⇨Accessories⇨ Administrative Tools	Manage RAS, including user access and start/stop service
SCSI Adapters	Start⇨Settings⇨Control Panel	Install and remove SCSI adapters
Server	Start⇨Settings⇨Control Panel	Display server activity, including users connected, available shares, resources in use and who's using them, replication settings, and alerts
Server Manager	Start⇨Programs⇨Accessories⇨ Administrative Tools	Manage Windows NT Servers and Workstations; add or remove domain member workstations, synchronize domains, and promote or demote domain controllers
Services	Start⇨Settings⇨Control Panel	Configure startup parameters for installed services; start and stop services
Sounds	Start⇨Settings⇨Control Panel	Map sounds to system events
System Policy Editor	Start⇨Programs⇨Accessories⇨ Administrative Tools	Set policies for computers in a domain, add or remove policy templates, and modify registries on remote computers
System Properties	Start⇨Settings⇨Control Panel	Configure performance, environment, user and hardware profiles, and startup and shutdown policies
User Manager	Start⇨Programs⇨Accessories⇨ Administrative Tools	Add or remove user accounts and groups; set access privileges for users and groups
Windows NT Diagnostics	Start⇨Programs⇨Accessories⇨ Administrative Tools	Display system information, including memory, drives, display, environment, resources, services, and network
Windows NT Explorer	Start⇨Programs	Manage the file and directory system, set access permissions for files and directories, map network drives, and control sharing
WINS Manager	Start⇨Programs⇨Accessories⇨ Administrative Tools	Start and stop WINS service, show WINS statistics, define scopes, and configure WINS

IDG BOOKS WORLDWIDE™

Copyright © 1996 IDG Books Worldwide, Inc.
All rights reserved.
Cheat Sheet $2.95 value. Item 015-5.
For more information about IDG Books,
call 1-800-762-2974.

...For Dummies: #1 Computer Book Series for Beginners

®

References for the Rest of Us!®

COMPUTER BOOK SERIES FROM IDG

Are you intimidated and confused by computers? Do you find that traditional manuals are overloaded with technical details you'll never use? Do your friends and family always call you to fix simple problems on their PCs? Then the *...For Dummies*® computer book series from IDG Books Worldwide is for you.

...For Dummies books are written for those frustrated computer users who know they aren't really dumb but find that PC hardware, software, and indeed the unique vocabulary of computing make them feel helpless. *...For Dummies* books use a lighthearted approach, a down-to-earth style, and even cartoons and humorous icons to diffuse computer novices' fears and build their confidence. Lighthearted but not lightweight, these books are a perfect survival guide for anyone forced to use a computer.

"I like my copy so much I told friends; now they bought copies."

Irene C., Orwell, Ohio

"Quick, concise, nontechnical, and humorous."

Jay A., Elburn, Illinois

"Thanks, I needed this book. Now I can sleep at night."

Robin F., British Columbia, Canada

Already, hundreds of thousands of satisfied readers agree. They have made *...For Dummies* books the #1 introductory level computer book series and have written asking for more. So, if you're looking for the most fun and easy way to learn about computers, look to *...For Dummies* books to give you a helping hand.

™

IDG BOOKS WORLDWIDE

7/96r

WINDOWS NT™ NETWORKING FOR DUMMIES®

by Ed Tittel,
Mary Madden,
and
Earl Follis

IDG Books Worldwide, Inc.
An International Data Group Company

Foster City, CA ♦ Chicago, IL ♦ Indianapolis, IN ♦ Southlake, TX

Windows NT™ Networking For Dummies®

Published by
IDG Books Worldwide, Inc.
An International Data Group Company
919 E. Hillsdale Blvd.
Suite 400
Foster City, CA 94404
http://www.idgbooks.com (IDG Books Worldwide Web site)
http://www.dummies.com (Dummies Press Web site)

Copyright © 1996 IDG Books Worldwide, Inc. All rights reserved. No part of this book, including interior design, cover design, and icons, may be reproduced or transmitted in any form, by any means (electronic, photocopying, recording, or otherwise) without the prior written permission of the publisher.

Library of Congress Catalog Card No.: 96-77265

ISBN: 0-7645-0015-5

Printed in the United States of America

10 9 8 7 6 5 4 3 2

1A/SV/RR/ZW/IN

Distributed in the United States by IDG Books Worldwide, Inc.

Distributed by Macmillan Canada for Canada; by Transworld Publishers Limited in the United Kingdom and Europe; by WoodsLane Pty. Ltd. for Australia; by WoodsLane Enterprises Ltd. for New Zealand; by Longman Singapore Publishers Ltd. for Singapore, Malaysia, Thailand, and Indonesia; by Simron Pty. Ltd. for South Africa; by Toppan Company Ltd. for Japan; by Distribuidora Cuspide for Argentina; by Livraria Cultura for Brazil; by Ediciencia S.A. for Ecuador; by Addison-Wesley Publishing Company for Korea; by Ediciones ZETA S.C.R. Ltda. for Peru; by WS Computer Publishing Company, Inc., for the Philippines; by Unalis Corporation for Taiwan; by Contemporanea de Ediciones for Venezuela. Authorized Sales Agent: Anthony Rudkin Associates for the Middle East and North Africa.

For general information on IDG Books Worldwide's books in the U.S., please call our Consumer Customer Service department at 800-762-2974. For reseller information, including discounts and premium sales, please call our Reseller Customer Service department at 800-434-3422.

For information on where to purchase IDG Books Worldwide's books outside the U.S., please contact our International Sales department at 415-655-3172 or fax 415-655-3295.

For information on foreign language translations, please contact our Foreign & Subsidiary Rights department at 415-655-3021 or fax 415-655-3281.

For sales inquiries and special prices for bulk quantities, please contact our Sales department at 415-655-3200 or write to the address above.

For information on using IDG Books Worldwide's books in the classroom or for ordering examination copies, please contact our Educational Sales department at 800-434-2086 or fax 817-251-8174.

For press review copies, author interviews, or other publicity information, please contact our Public Relations department at 415-655-3000 or fax 415-655-3299.

For authorization to photocopy items for corporate, personal, or educational use, please contact Copyright Clearance Center, 222 Rosewood Drive, Danvers, MA 01923, or fax 508-750-4470.

LIMIT OF LIABILITY/DISCLAIMER OF WARRANTY: AUTHOR AND PUBLISHER HAVE USED THEIR BEST EFFORTS IN PREPARING THIS BOOK. IDG BOOKS WORLDWIDE, INC., AND AUTHOR MAKE NO REPRESENTATIONS OR WARRANTIES WITH RESPECT TO THE ACCURACY OR COMPLETENESS OF THE CONTENTS OF THIS BOOK AND SPECIFICALLY DISCLAIM ANY IMPLIED WARRANTIES OF MERCHANTABILITY OR FITNESS FOR A PARTICULAR PURPOSE. THERE ARE NO WARRANTIES WHICH EXTEND BEYOND THE DESCRIPTIONS CONTAINED IN THIS PARAGRAPH. NO WARRANTY MAY BE CREATED OR EXTENDED BY SALES REPRESENTATIVES OR WRITTEN SALES MATERIALS. THE ACCURACY AND COMPLETENESS OF THE INFORMATION PROVIDED HEREIN AND THE OPINIONS STATED HEREIN ARE NOT GUARANTEED OR WARRANTED TO PRODUCE ANY PARTICULAR RESULTS, AND THE ADVICE AND STRATEGIES CONTAINED HEREIN MAY NOT BE SUITABLE FOR EVERY INDIVIDUAL. NEITHER IDG BOOKS WORLDWIDE, INC., NOR AUTHOR SHALL BE LIABLE FOR ANY LOSS OF PROFIT OR ANY OTHER COMMERCIAL DAMAGES, INCLUDING BUT NOT LIMITED TO SPECIAL, INCIDENTAL, CONSEQUENTIAL, OR OTHER DAMAGES.

Trademarks: All brand names and product names used in this book are trade names, service marks, trademarks, or registered trademarks of their respective owners. IDG Books Worldwide is not associated with any product or vendor mentioned in this book.

is a trademark under exclusive license to IDG Books Worldwide, Inc., from International Data Group, Inc.

About the Authors

Ed Tittel is the author of numerous books about computing and, with Mary Madden, is a columnist for *Windows NT Magazine*. He's the coauthor of three other *...For Dummies* books, including *NetWare For Dummies* (now in its second edition, with a third edition due by the end of 1996; coauthors: Deni Connor and Earl Follis), *HTML For Dummies* (also in its second edition), and *MORE HTML For Dummies* (both HTML books were cowritten with Stephen N. James). For IDG Books, he's also coauthored two books on CGI programming, including *Foundations of WWW Programming with HTML and CGI* and *Web Programming Secrets*, as well as books on Java and VRML.

In a previous life, Ed was Director of Technical Marketing for Novell, Inc. where he was responsible for the technical content of Novell's trade shows and developer conferences. Today he works as a full-time freelance writer and consultant, with a focus on networking and Internet technologies. He's also a member of the NetWorld + Interop Program Committee and a consultant to SoftBank for their Interop.Com trade show.

Ed is a principal at LANWrights, Inc., a networking consultancy based in Austin, TX. You can reach Ed at etittel@lanw.com or through his Web site at http://www.lanw.com.

Earl Follis has worked in the computing industry for nearly 15 years and has been a network administrator for several major corporations and state agencies in Texas. He has also worked as a network trainer and training manager at Thomas-Conrad Corporation, and is currently the Principal Engineer at Zora Consulting, a networking consultancy based in Pflugerville, TX. A bona-fide networking consultant, Earl is a Master CNE and is pursuing his credentials to become a Certified Microsoft Technician.

Earl is a coauthor of *NetWare For Dummies*, and has contributed articles to numerous networking publications, including *The NetWare Advisor*, *Computerworld*, and *NetWare Solutions* magazine. In his spare time, Earl's an amateur pilot and a devotee of Vietnamese pot-bellied pigs, which he raises at the Pflogiston Ranch, in Pflugerville, TX. You can reach Earl at efollis@io.com and on CompuServe at 71022,47.

Mary Madden has worked in the computing industry since 1988, during which time she's been a network administrator for Texaco Chemical Corporation and Huntsman Corporation. A true networking aficionado, Mary is a Certified NetWare Engineer (CNE) and is currently pursuing Microsoft NT Certification.

Mary has contributed to many networking books and projects, most recently as a writer for the *PC Networking Handbook* (by Ed Tittel, Academic Press Professional, 1996), for *The WWW Encyclopedia*, a CD-ROM project for Charles River Media (1995), and for the forthcoming IDG book entitled *Running a Windows NT Web Server*. She was also the technical editor for *Encyclopedia of Networking* (2nd Ed., Werner Feibel, Network Press/Sybex, 1996) and for *PC Roadkill* (Michael Hyman, IDG Books Worldwide, 1995), among other titles.

You can reach Mary at mtm@io.com or through the LANWrights Web site at http://www.lanw.com.

Authors' Acknowledgments

We have too many people to thank for this book to fit onto a single page, so we'd like to start by thanking everybody who helped us with this project that we don't mention by name. We couldn't have done it without you!

Ed Tittel — As always, I have lots of thanks to give, starting with my family: Thanks to Suzy, Austin, Chelsea, and Dusty — you are the greatest! Second, a talented crew of people helped me on this project, including my coauthors, Mary Madden and Earl Follis, but especially Dawn Rader and Michael Stewart, both of whom were instrumental to this book. Third, we'd like to thank the folks at Microsoft and *Windows NT Magazine* for all their support, especially Jenny Lysaker (one of my favorite people). Finally, I'd like to thank my mom and dad, for making this whole wild adventure possible.

Mary Madden — My first round of eternal thanks goes to Ed for inviting me to join in the writing of this book. You showed me the ropes while helping me avoid the burns! You're a great friend for whom I have tremendous respect. Second, many, many thanks to Dawn Rader for turning my run-on sentences into grammatically correct ones, and to Michael Stewart for helping me find my way around the Internet. Third, love, hugs and thanks to my friends JoAnne Holm, Sherif Ahmed, Nancy Starnes, Jim Huggans, and Cathy Gianaras, who always keep me going! And last but certainly not least, thanks to my mother, who's been a great inspiration to me!

Earl Follis — My first and most heartfelt thanks go to my lovely wife and best friend, Kaye. Without her patience and support, my modest contributions to this tome wouldn't have been possible. Thanks also to Matt, Haley, and Karly for their patience and understanding. I promise (perhaps unfortunately?) you'll see more of me in the next 50 years than you did in the last six months. Thanks to Mom and Dad for their continued love and support — though I noticed that the last few birthday cards contained no money! Thanks to the best guitarist I know, Sanjay Vrudhula, for his patience and willingness to postpone our other projects while I slaved on this one. Thanks to the fine folks at Waterside and IDG for their efforts on my behalf. Thanks also to Larry Koff and his uncle Sid (oy!) for their considerable inspiration in the face of adversity. Last but not least, many thanks to Ed Tittel. Without his support and tutelage, I wouldn't be writing these or any of the other words in this book.

As a threesome, we'd all like to thank the many vendors who lent us hardware, software, and support during the research of this book, including Microsoft, O'Reilly, AOL, Iconovex, InContext, Beverly Hills Software, US Robotics, and APC. We also have to thank the outstanding editorial staff and contractors at IDG Books, including our editor, Susan Pink; our technical reviewer, Garrett Pease; the Editorial Manager, Mary Corder; the acquisitions editor, Gareth Hancock; and the proofreader, Jennifer Overmyer.

Please feel free to contact any of us in care of IDG Books Worldwide, 919 East Hillsdale Boulevard, Suite 400, Foster City, CA 94404. Check the "About the Authors" section for our email addresses and Web pages. Drop us a line sometime!

ABOUT IDG BOOKS WORLDWIDE

Welcome to the world of IDG Books Worldwide.

IDG Books Worldwide, Inc., is a subsidiary of International Data Group, the world's largest publisher of computer-related information and the leading global provider of information services on information technology. IDG was founded more than 25 years ago and now employs more than 8,500 people worldwide. IDG publishes more than 275 computer publications in over 75 countries (see listing below). More than 60 million people read one or more IDG publications each month.

Launched in 1990, IDG Books Worldwide is today the #1 publisher of best-selling computer books in the United States. We are proud to have received eight awards from the Computer Press Association in recognition of editorial excellence and three from *Computer Currents'* First Annual Readers' Choice Awards. Our best-selling *...For Dummies*® series has more than 30 million copies in print with translations in 30 languages. IDG Books Worldwide, through a joint venture with IDG's Hi-Tech Beijing, became the first U.S. publisher to publish a computer book in the People's Republic of China. In record time, IDG Books Worldwide has become the first choice for millions of readers around the world who want to learn how to better manage their businesses.

Our mission is simple: Every one of our books is designed to bring extra value and skill-building instructions to the reader. Our books are written by experts who understand and care about our readers. The knowledge base of our editorial staff comes from years of experience in publishing, education, and journalism — experience we use to produce books for the '90s. In short, we care about books, so we attract the best people. We devote special attention to details such as audience, interior design, use of icons, and illustrations. And because we use an efficient process of authoring, editing, and desktop publishing our books electronically, we can spend more time ensuring superior content and spend less time on the technicalities of making books.

You can count on our commitment to deliver high-quality books at competitive prices on topics you want to read about. At IDG Books Worldwide, we continue in the IDG tradition of delivering quality for more than 25 years. You'll find no better book on a subject than one from IDG Books Worldwide.

John J. Kilcullen

John Kilcullen
President and CEO
IDG Books Worldwide, Inc.

Eighth Annual
Computer Press
Awards ≥1992

Ninth Annual
Computer Press
Awards ≥1993

Tenth Annual
Computer Press
Awards ≥1994

Eleventh Annual
Computer Press
Awards ≥1995

IDG Books Worldwide, Inc., is a subsidiary of International Data Group, the world's largest publisher of computer-related information and the leading global provider of information services on information technology. International Data Group publishes over 275 computer publications in over 75 countries. Sixty million people read one or more International Data Group publications each month. International Data Group's publications include: **ARGENTINA:** Buyer's Guide, Computerworld Argentina, PC World Argentina; **AUSTRALIA:** Australian Macworld, Australian PC World, Australian Reseller News, Computerworld, IT Casebook, Network World, Publish, Webmaster; **AUSTRIA:** Computerwelt Osterreich, Networks Austria, PC Tip Austria; **BANGLADESH:** PC World Bangladesh; **BELARUS:** PC World Belarus; **BELGIUM:** Data News; **BRAZIL:** Annuario de Informática, Computerworld, Connections, Macworld, PC Player, PC World, Publish, Reseller News, Supergamepower; **BULGARIA:** Computerworld Bulgaria, Network World Bulgaria, PC & MacWorld Bulgaria; **CANADA:** CIO Canada, Client/Server World, ComputerWorld Canada, InfoWorld Canada, NetworkWorld Canada, WebWorld; **CHILE:** Computerworld Chile, PC World Chile; **COLOMBIA:** Computerworld Colombia, PC World Colombia; **COSTA RICA:** PC World Centro America; **THE CZECH AND SLOVAK REPUBLICS:** Computerworld Czechoslovakia, Macworld Czech Republic, PC World Czechoslovakia; **DENMARK:** Communications World Danmark, Computerworld Danmark, Macworld Danmark, PC World Danmark, Techworld Denmark; **DOMINICAN REPUBLIC:** PC World Republica Dominicana; **ECUADOR:** PC World Ecuador; **EGYPT:** Computerworld Middle East, PC World Middle East; **EL SALVADOR:** PC World Centro America; **FINLAND:** MikroPC, Tietoverkko, Tietoviikko; **FRANCE:** Distributique, Hebdo, Info PC, Le Monde Informatique, Macworld, Reseaux & Telecoms, WebMaster France; **GERMANY:** Computer Partner, Computerwoche, Computerwoche Extra, Computerwoche FOCUS, Global Online, Macwelt, PC Welt; **GREECE:** Amiga Computing, GamePro Greece, Multimedia World; **GUATEMALA:** PC World Centro America; **HONDURAS:** PC World Centro America; **HONG KONG:** Computerworld Hong Kong, PC World Hong Kong, Publish in Asia; **HUNGARY:** ABCD CD-ROM, Computerworld Szamitastechnika, Internetto online Magazine, PC World Hungary, PC-X Magazin Hungary; **ICELAND:** Tolvuheimur PC World Island; **INDIA:** Information Communications World, Information Systems Computerworld, PC World India, Publish in Asia; **INDONESIA:** InfoKomputer PC World, Komputek Computerworld, Publish in Asia; **IRELAND:** ComputerScope, PC Live!; **ISRAEL:** Macworld Israel, People & Computers/Computerworld; **ITALY:** Computerworld Italia, Macworld Italia, Networking Italia, PC World Italia; **JAPAN:** DTP World, Macworld Japan, Nikkei Personal Computing, OS/2 World Japan, SunWorld Japan, Windows NT World, Windows World Japan; **KENYA:** PC World East African; **KOREA:** Hi-Tech Information, Macworld Korea, PC World Korea; **MACEDONIA:** PC World Macedonia; **MALAYSIA:** Computerworld Malaysia, PC World Malaysia, Publish in Asia; **MALTA:** PC World Malta; **MEXICO:** Computerworld Mexico, PC World Mexico; **MYANMAR:** PC World Myanmar; **NETHERLANDS:** Computer! Totaal, LAN Internetworking Magazine, LAN World Buyers Guide, Macworld Netherlands, Net, WebWereld; **NEW ZEALAND:** Absolute Beginners Guide and Plain & Simple Series, Computer Buyer, Computer Industry Directory, Computerworld New Zealand, MTB, Network World, PC World New Zealand; **NICARAGUA:** PC World Centro America; **NORWAY:** Computerworld Norge, CW Rapport, Datamagasinet, Financial Rapport, Kursguide Norge, Macworld Norge, Multimediaworld Norge, PC World Ekspress Norge, PC World Nettverk, PC World Norge, PC World ProduktGuide Norge; **PAKISTAN:** Computerworld Pakistan; **PANAMA:** PC World Panama; **PEOPLE'S REPUBLIC OF CHINA:** China Computer Users, China Computerworld, China Infoworld, China Telecom World Weekly, Computer & Communication, Electronic Design China, Electronics Today, Electronics Weekly, Game Software, PC World China, Popular Computer Week, Software Weekly, Software World, Telecom World; **PERU:** Computerworld Peru, PC World Profesional Peru, PC World SoHo Peru; **PHILIPPINES:** Click!, Computerworld Philippines, PC World Philippines, Publish in Asia; **POLAND:** Computerworld Poland, Computerworld Special Report Poland, Cyber, Macworld Poland, Networld Poland, PC World Komputer; **PORTUGAL:** Cerebro/PC World, Computerworld/Correio Informático, Dealer World Portugal, Mac*In/PC*In Portugal, Multimedia World; **PUERTO RICO:** PC World Puerto Rico; **ROMANIA:** Computerworld Romania, PC World Romania, Telecom Romania; **RUSSIA:** Computerworld Russia, Mir PK, Publish, Seti; **SINGAPORE:** Computerworld Singapore, PC World Singapore, Publish in Asia; **SLOVENIA:** Monitor; **SOUTH AFRICA:** Computing SA, Network World SA, Software World SA; **SPAIN:** Communicaciones World España, Computerworld España, Dealer World España, Macworld España, PC World España; **SRI LANKA:** Infolink PC World; **SWEDEN:** CAP&Design, Computer Sweden, Corporate Computing Sweden, Internetworld Sweden, it.branschen, Macworld Sweden, MaxiData Sweden, MikroDatorn, Nätverk & Kommunikation, PC World Sweden, PCaktiv, Windows World Sweden; **SWITZERLAND:** Computerworld Schweiz, Macworld Schweiz, PCtip; **TAIWAN:** Computerworld Taiwan, Macworld Taiwan, NEW ViSiON/Publish, PC World Taiwan, Windows World Taiwan; **THAILAND:** Publish in Asia, Thai Computerworld; **TURKEY:** Computerworld Turkiye, Macworld Turkiye, Network World Turkiye, PC World Turkiye; **UKRAINE:** Computerworld Kiev, Multimedia World Ukraine, PC World Ukraine; **UNITED KINGDOM:** Acorn User UK, Amiga Action UK, Amiga Computing UK, Apple Talk UK, Computing, Macworld, Parents and Computers UK, PC Advisor, PC Home, PSX Pro, The WEB; **UNITED STATES:** Cable in the Classroom, CIO Magazine, Computerworld, DOS World, Federal Computer Week, GamePro Magazine, InfoWorld, I-Way, Macworld, Network World, PC Games, PC World, Publish, Video Event, THE WEB Magazine, and WebMaster; online webzines: JavaWorld, NetscapeWorld, and SunWorld Online; **URUGUAY:** InfoWorld Uruguay; **VENEZUELA:** Computerworld Venezuela, PC World Venezuela; and **VIETNAM:** PC World Vietnam.   10/22/96

Cartoons at a Glance

By Rich Tennant • Fax: 508-546-7747 • E-mail: the5wave@tiac.net

page 7

page 85

page 294

page 287

page 129

Publisher's Acknowledgments

We're proud of this book; please send us your comments about it by using the Reader Response Card at the back of the book or by e-mailing us at feedback/dummies@idgbooks.com. Some of the people who helped bring this book to market include the following:

Acquisitions, Development, and Editorial

Project Editor: Susan Pink

Assistant Acquisitions Editor: Gareth Hancock

Copy Editor: Suzanne Packer

Technical Editor: Garrett Pease of Discovery Computing

Editorial Manager: Mary C. Corder

Editorial Assistant: Chris H. Collins

Production

Project Coordinator: Regina Snyder

Layout and Graphics: E. Shawn Aylsworth, Brett Black, Cameron Booker, Linda Boyer, Elizabeth Cárdenas-Nelson, Tyler Connor, Todd Klemme, Jane Martin, Drew R. Moore, Anna Rohrer, Brent Savage, Kathie Schutte, Gina Scott, Kate Snell, Michael Sullivan

Proofreaders: Jennifer K. Overmyer, Michael Bolinger, Rachel Garvey, Nancy Price, Robert Springer, Carrie Voorhis, Karen York

Indexer: Anne Leach

Special Help

Gwenette Gaddis, Stephanie Koutek

General and Administrative

IDG Books Worldwide, Inc.: John Kilcullen, CEO; Steven Berkowitz, President and Publisher

Dummies, Inc.: Milissa Koloski, Executive Vice President and Publisher

Dummies Technology Press and Dummies Editorial: Diane Graves Steele, Vice President and Associate Publisher; Judith A. Taylor, Brand Manager

Dummies Trade Press: Kathleen A. Welton, Vice President and Publisher; Stacy S. Collins, Brand Manager

IDG Books Production for Dummies Press: Beth Jenkins, Production Director; Cindy L. Phipps, Supervisor of Project Coordination; Kathie S. Schutte, Supervisor of Page Layout; Shelley Lea, Supervisor of Graphics and Design; Debbie J. Gates, Production Systems Specialist; Tony Augsburger, Reprint Coordinator; Leslie Popplewell, Media Archive Coordinator

Dummies Packaging and Book Design: Patti Sandez, Packaging Assistant; Kavish+Kavish, Cover Design

◆

The publisher would like to give special thanks to Patrick J. McGovern, without whom this book would not have been possible.

◆

Contents at a Glance

Table of Contents

Introduction

. . . .

*W*elcome to *Windows NT Networking For Dummies,* the book that helps anyone unfamiliar with Windows NT Workstation, Windows NT Server, or networks in general find his or her way into and around the wonderful world of networks. In a wired world, networks provide the links that tie us all together. Even if you're not using a network already, you will someday!

Although a few fortunate individuals may already be acquainted with Windows NT and networks, a lot more of us are not only unfamiliar with networking, but downright scared of it. To those who may be worried about the prospect of facing new and difficult technologies, we say "Don't worry." Using a network is not beyond anybody's wits or abilities — it's mostly a matter of using language that ordinary people can relate to.

That's why this book talks about using Windows NT and networks using everyday — and deliberately irreverent — terms. Nothing is too highfalutin to be made fun of, nor too arcane to be put into basic English.

This book focuses on you and your needs. You'll find everything you need to know about Windows NT and networking to find your way around — without having to know lots of jargon and without obtaining an advanced degree in computer science along the way. We want you to *enjoy* yourself. If networking really is the "next big thing," it's important that you be able to get the most from it. We sincerely want to help!

About This Book

This book is designed so that you can pick it up at any point and begin reading — like you would read a reference. In Parts I through III, each chapter covers a specific topic about networking or Windows NT — networking basics, the two primary flavors of Windows NT, setting up and using shares to access networked drives and printers, running networked applications (such as file management utilities), and the like. Each chapter is divided into freestanding information modules, all related to the major theme of the chapter. The chapter on LAN technology, for example, contains the following collection of information:

- The concept of a network service and why it's important
- How independent computers can share network services as peers (called — surprise! — peer-to-peer networking)
- The rules of etiquette when sharing with fellow users on a network
- Learning how to find and use network services, because asking for them isn't the same as getting them
- A discussion of what network servers are for and how they are used
- Which tools are available and which ones make sense to use

You don't have to memorize stuff in this book. Each section supplies just the facts you need to make Windows NT networking easy to learn and use. On some occasions, you may want to work directly from the book to make sure you get things straight.

How to Use This Book

This book works like a reference. Start with a topic that interests you. You can use the table of contents to identify general areas of interest or broad topics. The index, however, works best to pinpoint detailed concepts, related topics, or particular Windows NT capabilities, tools, or controls.

After you find what you need, you can close the book and tackle the task you've set for yourself — without having to grapple with unrelated details. Of course, if you want to learn additional information about your topic, you can check the cross-references. If you've never worked on a network, it's a good idea to read Part I. Otherwise, just dig in wherever your fancy strikes first!

When you need to key in something, you'll see the text like this: TYPE THIS. You're expected to type the line at the keyboard and then press the Enter key. Because typing stuff can be confusing sometimes, we always try to describe what it is you're typing and why you need to type it.

This book occasionally suggests that you consult the Windows NT online documentation or printed manuals for additional information. In most cases, though, you'll find everything you need to know about a particular topic right here — except for some of the sometimes bizarre details that abound in Windows NT Workstation and Server and information about applications that run in this environment. If there's a topic we don't cover, we suggest that you look for a book on that subject in the *...For Dummies* series, published by IDG Books Worldwide. We also provide information so that you can get help when you need it, even if you choose not to investigate other *...For Dummies* titles.

Who Are You, Anyway?

We're going to go out on a limb and make some potentially foolish assumptions about you, our gentle reader. You have or are thinking about getting a computer, a network, and at least one copy of Windows NT (be it Workstation or Server). You know what you want to do with these things. You might even be able to handle all these things yourself, if somebody could just show you how. Our goal in this book is to decrease your need for such a somebody, but we don't recommend telling him or her that out loud — at least not until you've finished this book!

How This Book Is Organized

This book is divided into four major parts, each of which is divided into four or more chapters. Each chapter covers a major topic and is divided into sections, which discuss particular issues or concerns related to that topic. That's how things in this book are organized, but how you read it is your choice. Choose a topic, a chapter, a section — whatever strikes your fancy or fits your needs — and start reading. Any related information will be cross-referenced in the text to help guide you through the whole book.

Part I: Introducing Local Area Networks

Part I contains networking basics, including fundamentals of technology, operation, usage, and etiquette. If you're not familiar with networks, this section should come in handy. If you're already a seasoned networker, it's optional. Look here for discussions about networking terminology, such as client, server, NIC, and topology.

Part II: The Wonder of Workgroups

Part II covers the entry-level version of Windows NT, known as Windows NT Workstation. It is a peer-to-peer networking product, so this part of the book includes information about the basics of using the software: its requirements, its tools and capabilities, administering a Windows NT Workstation network, and deciding whether it's what you want or less than what you really need.

Part III: Networking with Windows NT Server

In Part III, we cover the latest Microsoft client-server network operating system, known as Windows NT Server (NTS). This part starts with a history lesson to explain what Windows NT is, where it came from, and where it's going. Then we talk about rules for running Windows NT Server, NT networking and communications, protocols, naming services, the NTFS file system, network security, printing, backing up and restoring networked data, and lots more. You'll find most of the real meat of the book in this part, especially for those who already have Windows NT Server and want to get down and dirty right away.

Part IV: The Part of Tens

The last part follows the grand tradition of the ...*For Dummies* books — namely, it provides lists of information, tips, and suggestions, all organized into short and convenient chapters. This supplemental information is supposed to be helpful and is supplied at no additional charge.

Icons Used in This Book

The icons used in this book point you to important (and not so important) topics.

This icon lets you know that you're about to be swamped in technical details. We include this information because we love it, not because we think that you have to master it to use networking or Windows NT. If you aspire to apprentice-nerd status, you probably do want to read it; if you're already a nerd, you'll want to write us letters about stuff we left out or other information we should put in!

This icon signals that helpful advice is at hand. We also use it when we provide insight that we hope will make networking or Windows NT more interesting or easier to use. For example, when you add a new piece of equipment to your computer, make sure you unplug it before cracking open the case!

Oh gosh, I'm getting older — I can't recall what this one means. Maybe you should check one out and see whether it's worth your time!

This icon points out sites to visit on the World Wide Web.

This one means what it says — you need to be careful with the information it covers. Nine times out of ten, it's warning you not to do something that can have particularly nasty or painful consequences, as in "Have you ever played Bet Your Job?"

Where to Go from Here

With this book at your beck and call, you should be ready to wrestle with networking and take on even the most advanced version of Windows NT. Find a subject, turn to its page, and you'll be ready to jam! Feel free to mark up this book, fill in the blanks, dog-ear the pages, and do anything that might make a librarian queasy. The important things are to make good use of it and to enjoy yourself in the process!

Part I
Introducing Local Area Networks

The 5th Wave   **By Rich Tennant**

"I DON'T THINK OUR NEWEST NETWORK CONFIGURATION IS GOING TO WORK. ALL OF OUR TRANSMISSIONS FROM OHIO SEEM TO BE COMING IN OVER MY ELECTRIC PENCIL SHARPENER."

In this part . . .

1n this opening part of the book, we provide some background material about local area networks, or LANs. We present the essentials: how computers communicate with one another, why that's such a good idea, and what makes networking happen. We also cover vital topics such as proper network etiquette, the hardware and software that make up a network, and networking terms that you may not have heard before (but everyone assumes you already know). We even perform the "dance of the seven veils" as we reinterpret a standard but ho-hum model for the way networking *really* works.

We present each chapter's material in small, easy-to-understand sections. If information is really technical (mostly worth skipping, that is), it's clearly marked. Nevertheless, we hope you find this information useful — and even a bit entertaining!

Chapter 1

A Network Is Just Like Tin Cans and String — Only Better!

*I*f you have ever built a tin-can-and-string telephone, you know more about networking than you might think. If not, we can't help you recover your childhood, but we can cover the networking bases anyway. (If you're feeling nostalgic or adventurous, you could build one today. Go ahead — give it a try!)

What's a Network?

What is networking about, anyway? Why is it such "hot stuff"? What's a network interface? Why do you have to worry about what kind of network you're using? All these topics are important. If you understand them, you'll be better able to connect your computer to a network. Let's start with some definitions.

A *network* is a collection of at least two computers linked together so that they can communicate with each other. Most networks are based around a cable (typically, copper wire of some sort) that links computers through a connection. That connection permits the computers to talk (and listen) through the wire. More than just hardware is involved, though. Cables and connections are essential to networking; without computer software to use them, however, they're purely decorative.

Primitive communications or time warp?

To make a tin-can-and-string telephone, attach two cans by a string. One person yells into the open end of a tin can, and the other one holds the open end of her tin can up to her ear and strains to hear what the other person is saying. Here are the two secrets to building a good tin-can-and-string telephone:

1. Make sure the knots at the ends of the string completely plug the holes the string is threaded through.

2. Stretch the string tightly between the yeller (the sender) and the yellee (the receiver).

Two other essential elements are using string that is capable of transmitting sound and letting only one person talk while the other one listens.

An electronic network is far more reliable than a tin-can-and-string telephone. It's also much more efficient and precise. You don't need to yell, although it can help sometimes, especially when things don't work like they're supposed to.

As an electronic device, a networked PC is a lot like a telephone handset or a household intercom. Continuing our tin-can-and-string metaphor, a network requires that computers be able to listen or talk to each other over a common connection. That's all a computerized network consists of, though it may seem more mysterious. When a computer network doesn't work, it consists of even less!

We hope that we've debunked some of the glamour of networking so that you can relax and enjoy this chapter. It provides a gentle introduction to networking, where you'll learn the basics that lay the groundwork for the rest of the book.

A simple-minded view of networking recognizes only three requirements:

- ✔ **Connections** include the gear needed to hook up a computer to the network, along with the wires and other stuff — called the networking *medium* — that's used to carry messages from one computer to another. Because the gear that attaches a computer to a network acts as an intermediary between the computer and the network, that gear is called the *network interface*. (Attaching a PC to a network requires an add-in board known as a *network interface card,* or *NIC.*) Sans physical connections, computers can't communicate.

- ✔ **Communications** establish rules for how computers talk to each other and what things mean. Because one computer often runs different software than other computers, this requirement means that computers must speak a "shared language." Without shared communications, computers can't exchange information, and they remain isolated.

- ✔ **Services** define the things computers can talk about. Put differently, services are things that computers can *do* for each other, including sending or receiving files or messages, looking up and managing information, and talking to printers. Without services, a computer cannot respond to requests from other computers or formulate requests for what other computers can provide. Unless they're able to do things for each other, computers must also remain isolated.

Prehistoric networking

Networks originated in the days of yore, when computers were really big and filled large rooms. Computers were also quite expensive — most cost more than a thousand times an average worker's annual wages. Because computers were so scarce and costly, no one expected them to be widely available or easy to use. People communicated from dumb terminals to a computer, often called a mainframe. The terminals acted just like they sound — they had no brains of their own. Without a mainframe to round them up and make them work, nothing happened.

Most aspects of networking have changed radically since those early days, but the concept of sharing remains the key justification for networking. Networking makes it possible to share scarce or expensive resources, but those resources aren't computers any more — the brains for computers have become so cheap that most office workers have at least one on their desk. It's the cost of the other stuff attached to the network — the plotters, modems, and printers — that adds up. You might say, "Whoa there, a printer doesn't cost *that* much." But in a large organization, the bill to put a printer on every desk is huge. Electronically speaking, networking remains the method of choice to unite people and resources.

Making Networks Work

The three fundamentals of networking — connections, communications, and services — must combine harmoniously for a network to function. But what *really* makes networks work?

First, the connections must operate so that any computer can send or receive electrical signals (called data) across the physical medium that links computers. Without a connection, nothing happens. A computer on a network is like a telephone at the phone store, sitting on a shelf. It's perfectly capable of working once you attach it to the phone system, but it can't do anything without a connection.

Second, communications must function so that when one computer sends a message, the others can listen to and understand the message. Without communications, nothing has meaning. The phone system analogy works here, too. Put yourself in a place where you don't understand the local language and no one speaks your language. Although you can try to talk to other telephone users, including the operator, you can't have a meaningful conversation. (You can't understand what anyone is saying and they can't understand you.)

Third, the computers must be capable of working together so that one asks only for things that the other can deliver, and vice versa. Without a common set of services, neither computer can do anything for the other. Without common services, nothing can happen. It's like trying to buy tires at a flower shop, or flowers at a tire store. Even though everyone knows what flowers and tires are, what you want isn't what they have.

Networking depends on being able to talk (through a working connection), being able to understand what other speakers say (sharing communications), and having something useful to say or do (sharing services). All these components must work for the network to function. As you learn more about networks, you'll realize that no one really notices when things are working, but when something breaks, *everyone* notices that things aren't working.

What Do Computers Say to Each Other?

If we look closely at the details of how computers communicate with each other, the analogy to a telephone conversation breaks down. The basic principles are still there — unless you're talking to a teenager, and then all bets are off. Table 1-1 shows the striking similarities between the ways humans talk to humans and computers talk to computers.

Table 1-1	How Humans and Computers Converse
Human Conversation	*Computer Conversation*
Hello, this is Bob.	Computer states name and address of sender.
Is Mary there?	Computer states name and address of receiver.
May I speak to her, please?	Computer asks for and sets up connection, and establishes access to receiver.
Mary, do you want to buy some insurance?	Computer requests or offers services.
Mary, I can offer you a whole-life plan for only $100 a year.	Computer makes specific request or provides specific service.
Thanks for your time.	Computer closes service.
Good-bye.	Computer breaks connection.

On the surface, human and computer conversations don't look too different — the basic components are reasonably alike. When you look at the content of each piece, however, you realize that humans communicate using sounds with specific but flexible meanings, and that computers communicate using electronic bit patterns (for now, let's ignore the way they move across the medium) that have specific and highly inflexible interpretations. The important things to remember still originate with the two cans and the string: For every message, you have a sender and a receiver, and connections and media let them communicate.

Computers send the following when they talk: a small amount of data, which establishes the connection; the bulk of the information, which relates to a specific service or request; and a small amount of data, which breaks the connection so others can use the network. This process sidesteps the nitty-gritty details but captures the stages of communications.

What's Normal? Network Industry Trends

Now that you've seen how networks work and what computers say to each other, it's time to examine a typical network. This, however, is an exercise in abstraction because there are so many kinds of networks, because they come in so many sizes, and because of the wide differences among their users. Our ideas about what is typical are based on industry statistics (and you know what statistics are worth). Here goes, anyway.

It's estimated that at least five million PC networks are in use today, and that a Windows NT server of one kind or another is in use on some 15 percent of those networks. This figure fits Microsoft's claims, made in 1996, that it sold more than two hundred thousand copies of Windows NT Server in the first quarter of that year. It also fits the company's claims that somewhere between 10 and 20 million individuals use some kind of Windows NT server regularly, a number that's growing almost too fast to keep up with.

If the numbers don't lie — or at least don't stretch the truth too far — most networks are small and simple. The trend, however, is toward ever-increasing size and complexity. The number of individual networks per company, including all sizes of businesses, is up from a modest 0.78 in 1988 to a more aggressive 2.02 in 1996, and it continues to grow.

According to the U.S. Bureau of Labor Statistics, 95 percent of all businesses fall on the small end of the continuum. Because less than half these businesses are networked (courtesy of the same source), over half the networks in use today are in the 5 percent of businesses that qualify as medium-sized or large. Because that 5 percent is already networked, and small businesses are starting to network with increasing frequency, small business is predicted to be the biggest growth market for networking in the next ten years.

Here's the picture that emerges from the numbers:

- An average network handles a modest number of users, at or under 15.

- An average network uses a small amount of dedicated networking equipment, including a server, one or two printers, and a small amount of other gear.

- Most networks are too small to justify hiring networking specialists, which means average folks — like you — end up running them.

It's an interesting world to find yourself in, and an increasingly common one. Because you're reading this book, you probably are pretty well described by these numbers. If you're not, take a look at the networking in your immediate vicinity: it should still fit this model. As you'll learn, large, aggregated networks usually break down into collections of small, individual networks. When it comes to understanding what's up, your own immediate neighborhood is always the most important one to know well.

Touring the Facilities

If you take a tour of a statistically average network, you'll find several classes of equipment and a variety of software in use. If you make an inventory list of these pieces and parts as you take the tour, you can use the list to try to figure out what's out there and what the components are for.

Networks travel in threes

There are three basic categories of network software: *host/terminal*, *client/server*, and *peer-to-peer*. All three reflect types of networked communications.

Host/terminal networks are old-fangled networks that you access through a terminal. In a host/terminal network, dumb terminals (computers without processors) communicate with a host (a large computer with a brain). The host parcels out parts of its intelligence to workers at their terminals. The terminal can either send information from the user to the host or display information sent from the host to the user. Sounds dumb, huh? It is, but when the cost of a mainframe can break the bank at Monte Carlo, it's kind of smart, too. Lots of people still work this way!

A *client/server* network is made up of a collection of smart machines. One of these machines — the server — is equipped with massive stores of data and runs software that allows it to serve other machines exclusively. The machines that the server interacts with are called clients. You've probably heard of client/server networks, or server-based networks as they're sometimes called, if you're using Windows NT Server. Novell's NetWare and Banyan's VINES are also client/server networks.

A *peer-to-peer* network is one in which true equality in networking holds. Here, all machines are equal: They can act as servers, or clients, or both. Unlike client/server networks, no dedicated machine controls operations; everyone is expected to be a good networker and share information willingly with others. If you use the built-in networking included in Windows NT Workstation, Windows 95, or Windows for Workgroups, you already know what peer-to-peer networking is.

First stop: your desktop

One of the beauties of networking arises from taking the perspective that what you do at your desk — and we hope, for your sake, that it's best described as "work" — is extended by adding a network. From that perspective, adding a network to your bag of tricks connects you to resources and other things that are otherwise unavailable or much less affordable.

For convenience, we'll call the computer that you work at your *desktop computer,* or simply, your *workstation*. It's where you do the bulk of your work and perhaps some play. One of the key goals of networking is to take all of an organization's desktops, whether they use DOS, Window 95, Windows NT, OS/2, UNIX, or Macintosh OS, and connect them so that they can communicate and share resources, such as large disk drives, expensive laser or color printers, and access to a CD-ROM or the Internet.

In networked environments, it's normal to find user-to-desktop ratios close to one-to-one. Put another way, every user has access to, if not exclusive possession of, a workstation attached to the network. Because workstations are typically the source of requests for resources and services, it's reasonable to call a workstation a *client on the network*, or simply, a *client*. Calling it a workstation focuses on its role in supporting an individual working at a desk; calling it a client focuses on its connection to the network. Whatever you call it, it's still the same thing — the machine you sit in front of when you're working.

Next stop: servers do the servicing

As you've learned, networking without access to a shared set of services can be a sterile exercise. Because networks aren't useful unless you can *do* something with them, access to services is critical.

You use a server to get a resource or to get something accomplished. When you want to access a networked printer, it's safe to assume that a print server is operating somewhere in the background. When you want to save or retrieve files from a networked drive, it's okay to assume that a file server is involved.

This is true for most networked services, including electronic mail and database management systems. For every service, there's some kind of server that can deliver that service. But the server may not be dedicated solely to the needs of that one service. Sometimes one server provides many services; other times, a server is dedicated to one service exclusively.

So, even though a service may not be handled exclusively by a single computer — and this is seldom the case these days — it's useful to think of the computers that provide services as *servers*. A server's job is to listen for requests for its particular services, and to satisfy all the legal requests it receives. You will spend a great deal of time pondering this idea as you read the rest of the book.

Final stop: the glue that binds it all together

It's fashionable to talk about "infrastructure" — the system of roads, bridges, highways, and other modes of transportation that links our country into a working whole called the highway system. From a networking standpoint, the pieces of equipment that hook computers into a network, the wires or other media that make up the network, and the specialized pieces of hardware and software used to control a network make up its infrastructure.

By the same token, it's reasonable to call this collection of connections, cables, interfaces, and other stuff the "glue" because it's what binds computers together into a network. But just as highways are useless without cars and trucks moving across them, networks are useless without computers to send and receive traffic across their links and pathways.

At this level, you might worry about what kind of wiring to use — or what kinds of wireless technologies, if applicable. You also might be concerned about what kind of networking to use, the software that provides networking services, and the pieces that make the network fit together. Because networking is invisible when it works correctly, it's also one of the easiest components of the puzzle to overlook, even if it is the most common source of problems.

Figure 1-1 shows a simple diagram of a typical network. Notice that clients (desktops) outnumber servers and that the infrastructure must be everywhere in order to connect everything together. Networking follows the rules of supply and demand — the more clients you have, the more servers you need and (we hope) the more work is accomplished.

Figure 1-1:
A typical network with desktops, servers, and "glue."

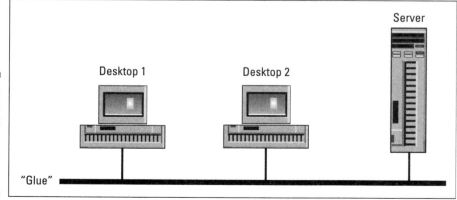

How Software Uses the Network

The critical ingredients for using a network include the necessary hardware to make a physical connection, at least one other computer on the network to communicate with, and a shared set of services that represents what the network can do for you. With all these requirements in place, what must actually happen so that your computer can use the network? The answer is that your computer must know *how* to ask for services from the network and precisely *what* to request.

Asking for services isn't asking for favors

Knowing how to ask for network services requires the capability to tell the difference between what's local to and immediately available from your own machine and what's available from the network. Determining this is the key to handling networks properly, and depends on some specialized software.

In modern operating systems, such as Windows NT, networking is built into the system itself. Right out of the box, NT understands the difference between local resources, which are directly attached to the computer, and network resources, which must be delivered or accessed through the network. Thus, the specialized software that handles networking is part and parcel of what NT does. The same is true for Windows for Workgroups, Windows 95, the Macintosh OS, and OS/2, as well as that old warhorse, UNIX.

But for DOS and Windows 3.x, software that keeps track of what you own and control on your own machine versus what's available across the network is used to discriminate between local requests and network requests. Because this piece of software takes requests for service and redirects any that cannot be delivered by your own computer to a service provider on the network (also known as a server), it's called — surprisingly enough — a *requester,* or sometimes a *redirector.* Using a requester is a pretty common way to handle network access from a desktop.

You'll hear the words *requester, redirector,* and *shell program* thrown around interchangeably. That's because Novell and Microsoft changed their minds. What originally was a tidy little program called the redirector changed to the requester when Microsoft changed DOS to include network access. To make things more complicated, this program is also called the NetWare shell by NetWare users — it sits between the workstation operating system and the network, and shells out DOS requests to the local machine and network requests to the network. Only real byte-heads need to know the difference, but if you want to impress those around you, it helps to use the correct technical terms. Most versions of Windows use a built-in network requester.

A local computer's main control program usually is called its *operating system* because it's the program that lets the computer operate and run the programs you use to get things accomplished. The operating system sometimes gets a special augmentation to incorporate "network intelligence" with an understanding of what's happening locally on the desktop.

A typical network server runs a special operating system (sometimes called a *network operating system*) to provide network services to its users. This operating system includes built-in network sharing functions along with basic file, print, and application services. In Microsoft's Windows NT Server environment, clients that use DOS (with or without Microsoft Windows 3.*x*), Windows 95, Windows NT, OS/2, UNIX, or the Macintosh operating system can request services from a Windows NT Server.

It's becoming increasingly common for computer operating systems to include built-in networking. A requester or a shell does not need to be added to obtain networking intelligence, because these operating system programs already understand networking and include it as part of their core functions. This is how Macintosh OS, UNIX, Windows for Workgroups, Windows 95, and Windows NT Workstation provide networking capability.

Whatever the network operating system, or the kind of network access it needs, the point is that a set of network services is defined, and a way to use the network is made available. Now you will want to figure out how to use this capability.

What services are available?

For a computer to use network services, it must know how to ask for them. But knowing *what* to ask for is equally important. In most cases, applications supply the knowledge about the network services they seek to use, either through information supplied by a requester or within intelligence built into so-called networked applications. Electronic-mail and remote-control software are good examples of programs built to use networking capabilities directly.

Sometimes, all that's needed to add network know-how to your computer is software that augments local applications or commands to make them network-aware. Extending directory listings or other file-handling commands (such as those provided in the Windows 95 or Windows NT Explorer program) to talk to networked drives is a classic example, as are other basic commands, such as printing and sharing data files.

Working through a specific command or a particular kind of program also means that you're working with a well-developed understanding of what you want the network to do. This understanding helps users interact with the network.

Whether you treat the network as a basic part of your desktop or look at it as an extension of your local world, you can interact with it only as long as you know exactly what you're trying to do. This statement may sound incredibly basic, but the crucial aspect of defining a common service is to work from a shared and explicit understanding of what that service is and what it does. Nothing less will do.

Whether this process happens is a function of your networking software and how it is set up. For example, when you print a file at a local printer, you can watch the machine so you'll know when it has finished. For networked printer services, it's common to send a message to users when their print jobs are finished so they'll know when to pick up their output. But even though all flavors of Windows NT can notify users when a print job is finished, they won't do so unless they're configured that way. (Don't worry — there's more on this subject in Chapter 22.)

This discussion doesn't really capture all the nuances of how programs talk to the network, but it does capture the basics: knowing about a service, requesting that service, providing the information to handle the request (in this case, the file to be printed), and waiting for a reply (the optional notification that the file has finished printing).

TECHNICAL STUFF

How networking works is . . . magic!

When a program — a spreadsheet, for example — is running and you want to print a copy to a networked printer, the sequence of actions is something like this:

1. Request print services from the spreadsheet.

2. The program formats the spreadsheet and then builds a print file for the printer.

3. The spreadsheet program sends the file to the printer.

4. The local networking software (whether it's a requester or a built-in operating system extension) recognizes that the chosen printer isn't local and ships the print file to a print server somewhere else on the network.

The network knows how to get to the print server and how to ship it the required print file.

5. The print file gets copied across the network to a holding tank for the chosen printer, where it gets in line behind any print files that arrived before it and have not yet been printed.

6. The print file gets printed when its turn comes.

7. In this optional step, the user may get notified when the file has finished printing (so that you don't have to wait around the printer for your stuff to come out).

Let's continue with our printing example. Every make and model of printer is a little different. To format output the way it's supposed to look, a program must translate the information you're trying to print from its internal representation to an external format tailored for the specific printer you're printing to (or at least to a standard format such as PostScript). This is where service delivery has to get to the device level — from a program to a particular printer — and where the real magic of networking comes into play.

Sharing Resources Is the Greatest Good

Our discussion of printing (see the sidebar entitled "How networking works is . . . magic!") paints a good picture of how network resources are used — by asking for them and by providing the right details so that services can be supplied. Because many users can send files to be printed on the printer in this example, it's also a classic illustration of how to share a resource. Sharing is the key to networking. After you've mastered this idea, everything else makes more sense.

The secret to sharing is making sure that everyone gets a shot at what needs to be shared. For the printer discussed in the sidebar, sharing access to the printer requires a "stand-in-line" mechanism so that print files can hang around until it's their turn to be printed; sharing access to the printer also provides a dandy mechanism for keeping track of who goes next.

This kind of waiting in line is called "first come, first served" because whoever gets in line first gets first crack at the printer. It's analogous to buying groceries — whoever is in line first is checked out first. Other services may take a different approach to fulfilling requests, but they all have to have some way to keep track of who has asked for what, and in what order, so that they can handle requests from multiple users in some kind of reasonable way. Cutting in line is sometimes permitted, but isn't that what sharing is all about?

The most important job a server performs is keeping track of the requests for service it receives, controlling access to its resources, and acting on valid requests as soon as it possibly can. The mechanisms that make that delivery possible also make sharing possible. Ain't it grand? Next, please. . . .

Chapter 2

Making Connections, or Lost in the Wires

*C*hapter 1 describes the three fundamental components of networking: connections, communications, and services. In this chapter, you look more closely at connections by untangling the wires and other media that tie your network together.

Connections are the wires or other media that move electronic signals from computer to computer, along with the interfaces that hook up the computers to the media.

Your network wiring is analogous to the pipes that make up a plumbing system. By following the "pipes" that move data around, you can see where the pipes go and what they do. In this way, you can better understand how things work — and why they sometimes don't work — on your network.

Oh, What a Tangled Web We Weave . . .

Working connections are essential for the transmission of information across the network. This networking axiom is also the most common source of problems and failures. If your network starts acting twiggy, it's time to track down "loose connections."

Take Bruce in accounting, for example. He — and his chair — bound around his office as he answers a never-ending stream of questions from upper management. Bruce races from one set of files to another, compiling the arcane statistics that keep the boss happy. So what if he runs over a few cables hanging from the back of his PC — they still *look* okay. But are they?

Looks may be everything for Bruce, but looking good is meaningless when it comes to network connections. As long as connections work correctly, no one cares what they look like; when they don't work correctly, *everyone* cares. On some networks, one faulty cable means the whole network goes down.

This scenario may seem artificial, but it doesn't even begin to capture all the wild and wonderful ways that loose connections can occur. In the truth-is-stranger-than-fiction department of wiring, we have heard things like the following (we are not making this up):

- "I needed to tie up a package."
- "Why can't I unhook my computer from these wires whenever I want to?"
- "I borrowed that cable to hook up my VCR."
- "I didn't even know we had a network!"
- "The electrician said that these wires weren't important. And anyway, they were in his way."

Beginning to get the idea? Here it is in a nutshell: No wires means no network. Break or damage the wires, and you break the network.

What's This Cable Here?

Before we go into detail about how cables can be arranged and used on a network, let's look at the types of wires typically used in networks.

These days, three basic kinds of cable are used in networks:

- Twisted pair
- Coaxial
- Fiber optic

Look, Ma — no wires!

You can also have a network with no wires. This is called — surprisingly enough — *wireless networking.* This type of network typically uses a broadcast frequency that can range from infrared for short-range or special-purpose connections, to radio frequencies for spread-spectrum devices, all the way to microwaves for high-speed LAN-to-LAN links.

These days, cellular telephone modems and battery-powered laptops supply the foundation of wireless networks in which everyone can stay connected while they're on the go.

Wireless networking is still too expensive to be a good choice for everyone, but it's definitely an emerging trend. When it becomes more commonplace, you'll never be able to get away from the office! You probably can't wait.

Twisted-pair cabling: TP or not TP

As you can see in Figure 2-1, *twisted-pair* wiring (TP) lives up to its name. TP comes in two flavors: shielded (STP) and unshielded (UTP). STP has a foil or wire braid wrapped around the individual wires that are twisted around each other in pairs; UTP does not.

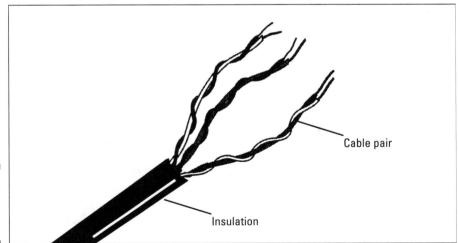

Figure 2-1:
The inside of twisted-pair cabling.

Cable pair

Insulation

Watch that wire!

Because TP is similar to the cabling used for telephone systems, its strength is also its greatest weakness. Because TP is everywhere, it means that there's a nearly irresistible temptation to recycle telephone wiring for LANs as well as for telephones. Although recycling unused telephone wiring has the appeal of saving money — the biggest single expense for most new networks is cabling costs — and the recycled wiring works perfectly well for today's voice-grade phone lines, it doesn't always work well for networks.

Recycling is a fine idea, as is preserving your bottom line. Even so, if you're thinking about reusing already-installed TP wiring for your LAN, it will pay to have your TP wiring system tested by a technician before blithely assuming that it will work for your LAN. It's much less expensive to build a network in the first place than to have to rebuild one. An ounce of testing is worth a pound of unnecessary expense. It might also be worth your job.

For better or worse, TP is the wiring system of choice for network connections; it is safe and usable, if the wiring is up to snuff.

Be aware that silver satin telephone cable (its name comes from the silvery, smooth outer covering) is also sometimes called twisted-pair. Don't be deceived: there's nothing twisted about silver satin, including the pairs. Real TP wire is actually cheaper than silver satin, especially in the quantities you'll need to cable up your network. If you get wrapped up in silver satin anyway, remember that it may work just fine for up to four nodes. As your network grows, however, problems will creep in due to the non-twisted pairs.

A spec for every spot

There are as many cabling specifications as there are types of cable; most networks use twisted-pair cabling of Category 3, 4, or 5. For fast networks, running at 100 megabits per second, you need Category 5 (Cat 5) cable.

The upside of TP is that the wiring and its connectors are cheap, it's easy to install new cable, and existing telephone equipment can be used for networking needs. If your company is big enough to have a network, you're probably already using TP.

One of TP's downsides is that it requires specialized hardware, called *hubs,* to connect more than two computers. This adds to the cost of the network. Hubs do have an upside, though. They generally provide better cable monitoring and management, and they can often reconfigure themselves to block out failing cables or connections.

Another downside of TP is that it's more susceptible to interference from electrical sources, such as motors and radios, than other media is. Also, it can handle only short distances between the hub and the desktops it has to reach. The distance varies with the type of cable used, but 100 feet from hub to desktop is a good rule of thumb for maximum TP reach. (And that's 100 feet not as the crow flies but as the cable runs.)

Coaxial cable

Coaxial cable consists of a two-element cable: A solid or stranded center conductor is wrapped by an insulator, which is wrapped by an outer conductor (usually a wire braid), which in turn is covered by still more insulation.

Coaxial cable, or *coax,* can handle many signals across a broad range of frequencies, so it's also used for cable TV. Look at it this way: Even though each TV channel uses a chunk of spectrum, a single coax cable can carry as many as 200 channels. So it's no sweat for coax to handle networking. If that doesn't clear things up, check out Figure 2-2. (We ran into a network manager who used cable TV media to wire part of his network. When data started colliding with refrains from 4 Non-Blondes, even he knew something was wrong.)

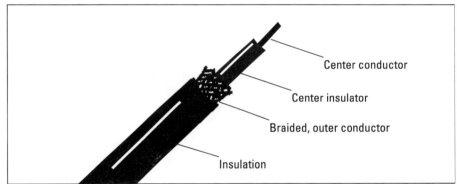

Figure 2-2:
Coaxial
cable
internals.

Center conductor

Center insulator

Braided, outer conductor

Insulation

The downside of coaxial cable is that it's thick and stiff compared to TP. It also requires expensive, specialized connectors and well-trained, knowledgeable installers. Coax is much stronger than TP, but it is also more difficult to repair.

The upside of coax is that it's moderately resistant to electrical and magnetic interference, and can be used to build networks that span much larger areas than TP. Again, the maximum length per cable varies with the kind of cable, but the range for coax is 500 to 1500 feet. Many networks use both TP and coax: TP is used on a per-floor basis to run wires out to individual desktops, and coax is used to wire multiple floors together. Who says you can't have the best of all possible worlds?

Another plus for coaxial cable is that it's often already in your walls from computing prehistory, when SNA-based equipment ruled the roost. This cable is called RG-62 coax, and can be reused for ARCnet networks. (Networks use RG-58 or RG-62 media.)

Coax is worth considering even for very small networks because you can buy prefabricated cables of varying lengths. You can hook up your network quickly and easily, and can change things around with equal ease. We're writing this book on a LAN cabled with Thin Ethernet (a.k.a. 10Base2). Its biggest attraction is that you can go to the electronics store and buy everything you need to cable up a small network for about $30 per workstation (not including each computer's network interface card).

Fiber-optic cable

Not much is metallic about *fiber-optic* cable, unlike twisted pair and coax. Fiber optic is more flexible than typical coaxial because its core is made of glass fibers, which are thin enough to be flexible. (Handle it with care.) In Figure 2-3, the internals of fiber-optic cable may look a lot like that of coax, but they're similar only on paper.

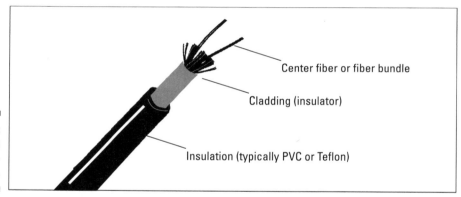

Center fiber or fiber bundle

Cladding (insulator)

Insulation (typically PVC or Teflon)

Figure 2-3:
The innards
of fiber-
optic cable.

Fiber-optic cable runs can range from 1/2 to 20 miles per cable, depending on the kind of fiber-optic cable and network. If you're running cable between networks in different buildings, fiber-optic cable is the only way to go.

As another plus, fiber-optic cable is immune to environmental interference, short of a black hole in your neighborhood. Fiber's biggest advantage is its *bandwidth*, which is the amount of information it can carry. It can handle thousands of times more data than twisted pair or coax.

On the downside, fiber is the most expensive of the three cable types. The costs of the cable aren't that different, but installation costs for fiber are by far the highest. This is because each end of a fiber must be polished for maximum light transmission, and the best polishing is still accomplished by a human technician, one cable at a time. Experienced fiber-optic installers are scarce and charge premium rates.

Never hire a cable installer who cannot provide multiple references. Always check those references, too.

Installation costs are the main reason why fiber still costs at least twice as much as a coax or twisted-pair network. The interface costs are also high. If you aren't prepared to amortize the cost of a fiber-optic network over the long run, fiber isn't worth it.

Home of the Brave: Tips for Do-It-Yourselfers

If you're going to mess around with wiring, either in extending an existing LAN or building a new one, here are a few things to keep in mind:

- ✔ Observe local, state, and federal building codes. If you're planning to run cable, some of it will probably be in the ceiling. If that area (called plenum airspace or plenum air return) is used also for A/C ventilation, fire codes require that you use non-toxic, nonflammable cable — Teflon-coated cable. It costs more, but it doesn't release toxic fumes if the place catches on fire.

- ✔ The buy-versus-build decision is worth reviewing for coaxial and UTP cable, but not for fiber. If you decide to build your own copper cables, buy the best cable and connectors you can afford. Then, whether you can afford one or not, buy a professional crimping tool. These tools rarely go for less than $100 a pop, and they require special dies for each specific cable and connector diameter. (A cheap crimping tool can cost as little as $20, but it will screw up your work every time.)

- ✔ If you're using TP, which is marginal stuff to begin with, buy the best cable you can afford. (Cat 5 is the best.) With any kind of TP, better quality means better conduction.

- ✔ No matter how much cable you have to lay — and especially if you are using TP cable — check the building's electrical plans before starting. More than one LAN installation has been botched by running cable next to large motors or transformers (elevators are a common culprit here), which interfere with transmissions.

- ✔ If you plan to lay any cable yourself, be prepared for slow, dirty, backbreaking work. Check whether your budget can allow for some help. At the least, hire an experienced installer to review your installation plan and help you get started.

- ✔ Above all, plan and keep a stiff upper lip when things get weird — as they always will. If you have a good plan and a good estimation of your own abilities, you will know when to move ahead and when to ask for help. Good luck!

Now that you've taken a look at the wiring itself, it's time to examine the wiring layout.

It's a Topology, Not a Wiring Layout

The term used to describe wiring layouts comes from the sick minds of mathematicians, who love to create arcane terminology. Mathematically speaking, any arrangement of lines can be called a topology, so that's what network-savvy folks call the different kinds of networking schemes. A *topology* is simply the shape of the network: Some look like bean poles and others are gently curved — much like the folks who use them.

Network wiring can be laid out in many ways. Figure 2-4 shows the two most common layouts — the star topology and the bus topology. A *ring topology* is a wiring pattern laid out in a circle.

Topologies can cross-pollinate just like flowers. If you add a star topology network to a bus topology network, you end up with a distributed-star network, which is also known — to use another plant analogy — as a hybrid. Most networks are hybrids, but many networks work better if you stick to the simple stuff. When in doubt, do as the cable masters do.

Now starring . . .

A *star topology* consists of separate wires that run from a central point (called the hub) to devices, such as computers, on the end of each wire. A *bus topology* is a single cable to which all the computers on a network (or on part of a network) are attached. If you break a wire in a star, only one link is affected; if you break a wire on a bus, everything connected to it is affected.

In a star topology, the hub of the star acts as a relay for computers attached to its arms, like this:

1. **The sending computer sends a chunk of information across the wire to the destination computer.**

2. **The hub, positioned between the computers, passes the message either to the destination computer — if it's attached to the same hub — or to another hub.**

3. **The hub to which the destination computer is attached sends the message to the destination computer.**

On a large network, the middle step can be repeated several times, as your data jumps across hubs between the sender and receiver until you reach the receiver's hub and, finally, the destination computer.

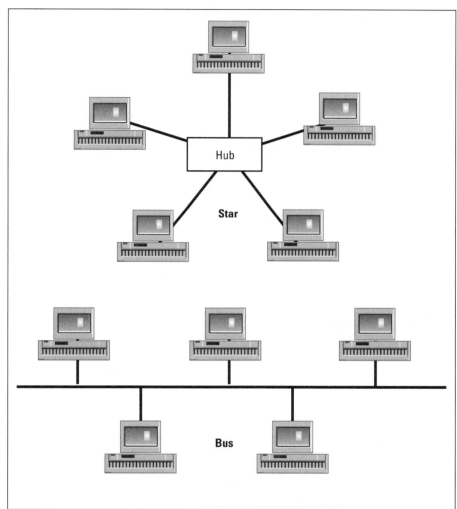

Figure 2-4:
Layouts of
star and bus
wiring.

On or off the bus

With a bus topology, every computer on the wire sees every message sent. If the sender and receiver are on the same wire, called a *segment*, messages are delivered very quickly. If the sender and receiver are not on the same wire, a special message-forward computer, called a *bridge*, passes the message from the sender's wire to the receiver's wire by copying the message and retransmitting it.

Just as you might have to forward a message through multiple hubs in a star topology, you can forward a message through multiple bridges on a bus topology.

Ring around the network

While we're on the subject of topology, let's look at ring topology. Real rings are seldom built because they tend to fail frequently. You often end up with a ring, however, over a bus or a star or in the form of a redundant ring with multiple cables and pathways in an attempt to improve the odds that the ring will keep running. Some network access methods, including ARCnet (bus and star) and token ring (star), work by mapping a ring onto a star or a bus.

Buses and rings are attractive because they keep track of who gets to send a message by circulating an electronic "permission form," or *token*, around and around the network. The token prevents workstations from sending messages at the same time, which can greatly improve network availability. A computer must wait for the token to come around before it can send a message. Every computer waits the same amount of time, on average, to send a message. This allows the network's available bandwidth to be used more fully before the network starts slowing down.

It's important to distinguish between a network topology and an access method. The topology identifies a network's wiring scheme. It describes how communications move around and among the computers and other devices that send and receive information across a network. The *access method* identifies how the network behaves. It describes the network's electrical characteristics, the type of signaling it uses, what the connectors look like, how the interfaces work, how large a message can travel across the media, and everything else necessary to build a working environment. Topology deals with network layout; access method deals with how the network operates. Put another way, a topology describes a wiring layout, and an access method is what you buy to make it work.

Logical versus physical

Networking topologies can be physical or logical. The physical topology of token rings is a star, but the way data is passed from one computer to another is a ring. ARCnet, too, can physically be a bus or a star, but logically, it's a bus. Not even Ethernet is exempt from the confusion. When it's wired as a bus, it acts like a bus. But when it's wired as a star, it still acts like a bus.

By the same token

Networks use sets of rules to communicate with one another. Some use tokens to control communications. Others opt for a free-for-all, in which any computer can send data at any time, with the luckiest getting through. Networks that send tokens are called token-passing networks — the rule, or *protocol,* they use to regulate access to the media is the token-passing protocol.

Networks that let multiple computers send data whenever they want are called *Collision Sense Multiple Access with Collision Detection* (CSMA/CD); they use the CSMA/CD protocol. In these networks, computers listen to the media to see whether electrical signals, representing data, are present. If the computer doesn't hear anything, it goes ahead and sends data. When the computer has "misheard," data collides and all computers hear the collision.

The kinds of networks we've mentioned — token ring, Ethernet, and ARCnet — are different implementations of token-passing protocols (ARCnet and token ring) and CSMA/CD protocols (Ethernet). These names that describe how networked computers access media are also called *access methods.* People often confuse topologies with access methods, but now that we've got it straightened out, the details of the access methods will become clearer.

Brand X Basics

The hundreds of different kinds of networks can be broken down into five categories. You can distinguish one from another by answering the following questions:

- ✔ What kind of access method, protocol, and topology does the network use?
- ✔ How does the network work?
- ✔ What are the network's technical pros and cons?
- ✔ What kinds of media does it support?
- ✔ How business-friendly (cost, availability, reliability, and that sort of thing) is this network?

These basic concerns are discussed in the following section. Then the mystery candidates are compared and contrasted. After that, we make some admittedly biased recommendations.

Introducing the Contestants

When you talk about kinds of networks, you're talking about the access method around which the network hardware is built.

For the purposes of this book, there are four access methods (but that's a gross oversimplification, as you'll see):

- ✔ Ethernet
- ✔ Token ring
- ✔ ARCnet
- ✔ Fiber Distributed Data Interface (FDDI)
- ✔ Other

Count 'em yet? Five, not four! The first four access methods are the important ones, but there's enough left over in the "other" category to make it worth mentioning.

Entertaining Ethernet

Ethernet is the most well-known, widely used, and readily available networking technology today. As network access methods go, it has been around longer than most, since the mid-to-late 1970s. It was the brainchild of Xerox's Palo Alto Research Center (PARC) and adopted by Digital, Intel, and Xerox (which is why the old-fashioned, 15-pin D connectors for thick-wire Ethernet are called DIX connectors), but it has long since passed into commodity status.

Ethernet uses the CSMA/CD protocol. The sidebar titled "Ethernet: network bumper cars" explains what this stuff means in everyday English, insofar as the subject allows — which isn't in so very far.

The easiest way to think about how Ethernet works can be summed up as follows: "Listen before sending. Listen while sending. If garbage happens, quit and try again later."

Strengths and weaknesses

Ethernet's strengths are as follows: It is robust, reliable, and comes in a broad, affordable range of flavors. Its weaknesses are collisions and more difficult troubleshooting. In addition, Ethernet's speed of 10 Mbps is on the slow end for emerging high-volume applications such as real-time video or multimedia.

Ethernet: network bumper cars

The acronym that describes Ethernet is CSMA/CD, which stands for *Carrier Sense Multiple Access with Collision Detect.* Echoes are the auditory equivalent of a collision, and a collision means that you must repeat everything that was just said. The following list provides a definition for each term in this acronym:

✔ **Carrier sense:** Everyone attached to the network is always listening to the wire, and no one is allowed to send while someone else is sending. When a message moves across the wire, an electrical signal called a *carrier* is used. By listening to the wire, you know when it's busy because you *sense* that signal.

✔ **Multiple access:** Anyone attached to the network can send a message whenever he or she wants, as long as no carrier is being sensed. This means multiple senders can begin at roughly the same time — when they think things are quiet — so it's called *multiple access.*

✔ **Collision detect:** If two or more senders begin sending at roughly the same time, sooner or later their messages have a *collision:* they run into each other on the wire. Collisions are easy to recognize because they produce a garbage signal that bears no resemblance to a valid message. Ethernet hardware includes circuitry that recognizes this signal and immediately stops all sending; each sender must then wait a random amount of time before listening to the wire and trying to send again.

Ethernet does not perform well for these applications or for networks that have heavy traffic. In fact, Ethernet's CSMA/CD access method means that its real ceiling is between 56 and 60 percent of total bandwidth (5.6 to 6.0 Mbps), because that's the level of use at which collisions result in a significant network slowdown.

Don't abandon all hope, though; two 100-Mbps Ethernets — 100BASE-VG and 100BASE-T — are sold for those with higher bandwidth needs. In addition, special switching hubs for Ethernet let it run faster than its more customary ceiling by creating and managing multiple 10-Mbps connections as they're used — this is called fast-switched Ethernet or fast switching.

All flavors are available

Ethernet comes in all the basic flavors. It can run over all the major cabling types — twisted pair, coaxial cable (thin and thick), and fiber optic — and works with both bus and star topologies.

Ethernet devices to mix and match these cable types are readily available, so you can use Ethernet to build networks of just about any size and for even the most hostile environments.

Getting down to business

In spite of, or maybe because of, its age, Ethernet is the most widespread and popular networking technology. Twisted-pair leads the pack for new Ethernet cabling, but a lot of coax is still out there. Fiber-based Ethernet is usually limited to networks in campus environments, where long distances and electrical interference issues are greatest, but you'll also find it used in elevator shafts to connect multiple floors in a single building. (Remember what we said about elevators shafting your networks?)

The main reasons for Ethernet's continuing popularity are as follows:

- **Affordability.** Cabling is cheap, and interfaces range from less than $50 for desktops to less than $250 for servers. Ethernet may not be the cheapest of all the network access methods, but it's close.

- **Choice.** Ethernet supports all cabling types and offers a lot of gear for building hybrid cabling setups. In addition, many manufacturers offer Ethernet-based hardware. If there's a specialized need for networking gear, chances are that an Ethernet variant is on a retailer's shelf or someone's drawing board.

- **Experience.** Ethernet's longevity means Ethernet-savvy people are easy to find and there are many training courses, books, and other resources to help you or your colleagues, should you run into problems.

- **Continuing innovation.** At 10 Mbps, Ethernet isn't the fastest networking technology. But vendors make special high-speed network switches for Ethernet, as well as the 100-Mbps varieties previously mentioned. That speed should help Ethernet survive the climb to the next level of networking, where far-out things such as real-time video and multimedia are on everyone's desktop.

Let's talk token ring

Token ring has gained a substantial foothold in the marketplace, even though it hasn't been around in commercial form as long as Ethernet or ARCnet. Token ring is based on technology refined and originally marketed by IBM, so it is more commonly found in places where IBM is entrenched. When personal computers started taking desktop space away from the dumb terminals connected to IBM mainframes, IBM took action. They developed token ring as a way of tying all those new PCs to their mainframe computers.

Token ring uses the *token-passing* protocol, a collection of individual point-to-point links that happen to make a circulating pattern. *Point-to-point* means one device is hooked to another; for token ring, that typically describes a computer attached to a hub, which may itself be attached to other hubs or computers.

Token ring is fair to everyone who participates, and it guarantees that the network won't be overwhelmed by traffic. It's fair because it constantly passes an electronic permission slip, the *token,* around the network. To send a message, a user must wait until he or she has possession of the token. The token isn't released until the message has been delivered (or until it's obvious that it cannot be delivered). Everyone gets the same shot at using the token.

The easiest way to think about how token ring works is as follows: If you want to send a message, first wait for a token. When the token comes by, tack your message onto the token. When the token comes around again, strip off your message and send the token to the next user.

Strengths and weaknesses

Token ring's strengths are equal opportunity and guaranteed delivery capabilities. Token ring works predictably and reliably, even when it's loaded to capacity. Token ring is available in two speeds. The lower (and older) version runs at 4 Mbps. This is 40 percent of the purported speed of Ethernet, but only slightly slower than Ethernet's actual speed. The higher (and newer) version, 16-Mbps token ring, runs at 160 percent of Ethernet's purported speed, but it really runs much faster through the simultaneous use of multiple tokens and because, unlike Ethernet, it can use 100 percent of its total bandwidth. Waiting in the wings is full-duplex token ring, which works similarly to switched Ethernet. For higher speeds, IBM is considering a 100-Mbps variant.

We hear you thinking, "If token ring is so great, why does anyone buy anything else?" Token ring has weaknesses that have less to do with technical considerations than with inflexibility and expense. Its major downside is that it requires expensive hub-like devices, called *multistation access units* (MAUs), and the use of double-stranded cable from computer to hub (one for the outbound trip and the other for the return trip). These requirements add to the expense as well as reducing the maximum distance between computer and hub. Token ring is also more complicated and, depending on the media type you use, requires fancier connectors than Ethernet or ARCnet.

All flavors are available

Token-ring implementations for TP and fiber are available, but TP is by far the most common implementation, and it's the most likely medium for tying desktops to hubs. Fiber is the cable of choice for spanning longer distances and daisy-chaining MAUs. Only limited amounts of shielded twisted-pair are used for token-ring networking these days. Because of individual cable-length limitations and maximum ring-size limitations, cabling a token-ring network takes more planning and number-crunching than does cabling either ARCnet or Ethernet.

Getting down to business

From a cost-benefit perspective, there's not enough upside in the reliability, fairness, and guaranteed performance of token ring to offset its higher costs. At present, token ring costs between 75 and 150 percent more than Ethernet without

---

Type cast

Token-ring cables are classified by the terms *categories* and *types*. You'll hear about Type 1 cable — that's the thick, shielded twisted-pair cable, originally used for 4-Mbps token ring. Type III corresponds to Category III wire, but the phrase often refers to Category III, IV, or V. If you are using 4-Mbps token ring, Category III wire is fine. If 16-Mbps token ring is more your idea of fun, opt for Category V wire.

---

necessarily providing significant performance or reliability advantages. Although there are two schools of network thought on this issue — "Token ring: Don't do it" and "We're token-passing bigots. What's Ethernet?" — we're not about to go out on either limb. If someone is giving token ring away at a price that's too good to pass up, or if that's what you're told to use, go ahead and use it. It works just fine. We just don't recommend it as the technology of choice for starter networks.

Arguing ARCnet

ARCnet, which stands for Attached Resource Computer Network, was originated by Datapoint Corporation of San Antonio, Texas. ARCnet is used in more than 6 million computers worldwide — a lot of computers, but that number is not as large as it could have been. Whereas the groups responsible for Ethernet and token ring pushed for their technologies to become engineering standards (losing control over the technologies in the process), Datapoint tried to maintain exclusive control over ARCnet to get the fullest financial advantage from it. The irony is that the other companies, by letting go, benefited far more than Datapoint, which elected to hold on.

ARCnet is a *token-bus technology,* in which the wires act like a bus — everything is broadcast to everyone at more or less the same time — but a token-passing protocol is used to control when a computer is permitted to transmit information.

Just as token-ring implementations typically map a ring topology onto a star configuration, ARCnet typically maps itself onto a star. ARCnet also supports coax buses, TP daisy chains (in which each machine hooks to each of its neighbors on a separate cable), and a variety of other configurations. From a cabling standpoint, ARCnet is the most forgiving and flexible of all the networking access methods covered in this section.

Strengths and weaknesses

We can recommend ARCnet only for existing installations, where its low cost, high flexibility, and ease of use will find a niche. Of all the major access methods commercially available, ARCnet remains the cheapest. Ethernet interfaces range from less than $50 to over $250; equivalent ARCnet interfaces range from less than $30 to $150. ARCnet's prefabricated cables and other components let you put together a robust, reliable, home-baked hybrid network. It's also easy to mix and match components and cable types without having to figure out all the details in advance. Finally, ARCnet has the least restrictive cable-length limits — from 300 to 2,000 feet per segment — and a capacious total network span of 20,000 feet (which can be increased at the cost of reduced network speeds).

ARCnet's primary downside is a function of the technology's age: a speed limit of 2.5 Mbps, only one-fourth of Ethernet's official rating and roughly one-half to one-seventh of token ring's. Even so, ARCnet works well for basic business applications such as word processing and spreadsheet use. It bogs down, however, for the more demanding applications on today's business horizons.

All flavors are available

Like Ethernet and token ring, ARCnet is available for TP, coax, and fiber-optic cable, with plenty of hubs for linking together any or all of these wiring types. ARCnet's flexibility and forgiving nature make it ideal for small networks or for networks that have a lot of additions, moves, and changes.

Getting down to business

From a small-business perspective, ARCnet is as much of a good investment as Ethernet. Despite its bandwidth limitations, ARCnet is as fair as token ring, and it also guarantees delivery. ARCnet is the least expensive of all the access methods discussed in this section. Because ARCnet appears to be stuck in its current design — Datapoint tried to promote a design for a 20-Mbps version called ARCnet-Plus, but it never went anywhere — it doesn't have as much room to grow into the twenty-first century as the alternatives.

Here are some considerations in approaching ARCnet:

- ✔ If you already have ARCnet, keep using it. It's even okay to add more, but do so judiciously.

- ✔ If you're not forced to go with ARCnet, choose Ethernet or token ring (or something even faster). ARCnet is no longer the right place to start out.

Proprietary, like ARCnet used to be

A variant of ARCnet, called TCNS, comes from a company just up the road from Datapoint. Thomas-Conrad, which also makes ARCnet cards, makes this 100-Mbps version of ARCnet. Although Thomas-Conrad hasn't given the specs for TCNS to anyone else (maybe the company should learn from Datapoint's experience), TCNS is a popular choice for those megahungry, power-gobbling applications you'll soon see on your desktop. Thomas-Conrad claims to have sold nearly as many TCNS cards and hubs as there are FDDI equivalents.

Fabulous FDDI

Fiber Distributed Data Interface (FDDI) is about as fast a network access method as you can get and still be able to order it through the mail. It was designed in the mid-1980s — at least 10 years after the other options covered in this chapter — to provide a high-speed, fiber-based, token-passing network. A successor, FDDI II, has already been designed that adds video, image, and voice data support to conventional network traffic. You don't have to remember the Roman numerals, though; both versions are lumped together and called FDDI.

One of the authors of this book pronounces FDDI using the letters — "eff dee dee eye." Another pronounces it "fiddy" — which rhymes with "giddy" or "Liddy" (as in G. Gordon). We don't care how you pronounce it, but it's safest to use the letters for clarity. (Guess which author wrote this?)

FDDI was originally designed as a kind of superhighway for network data to tie together multiple networks. Its data rate is a brisk 100 Mbps — 40 times faster than ARCnet and 8.5 times faster than fast token ring. Figure 2-5 covers all these comparative numbers for you in a way we think is easy to understand. The figure also gives you a good idea of how all the access methods discussed here stack up.

One of the best uses of FDDI is as a networking *backbone*. Just as your backbone ties the rest of your body together and carries important neural information throughout your body, a network backbone provides a special-purpose, high-speed link tying lots of networks together. All FDDI networks aren't backbones, though, nor is every backbone an FDDI network.

FDDI uses the token-passing protocol. FDDI cabling uses a real ring topology, but it consists of two rings. One ring transmits messages clockwise; the other transmits messages counterclockwise. If either ring breaks, the other ring automatically functions as a backup. If both rings get cut at the same place — look out for the guy with a backhoe — the two rings automatically splice together to form a ring about twice the length, but still capable of functioning.

Although FDDI functions well as a network that services other networks, it can also be used as a high-speed LAN access method to hook computers together. At present, it's used far more as a backbone technology, but its LAN applications are growing. We expect that it will show up in more and more LANs as applications become more demanding and the technology gets cheaper.

Strengths and weaknesses

FDDI's biggest advantage is speed — and lots of it — but there are other plusses, too. It supports rings as much as 200 kilometers in circumference (that's roughly *124 miles,* for you non-metric types). FDDI can also support as many as 500 active devices on a single cable segment, which is considerably more than any other access method discussed here. Speed, distance, and coverage — what more could you want?

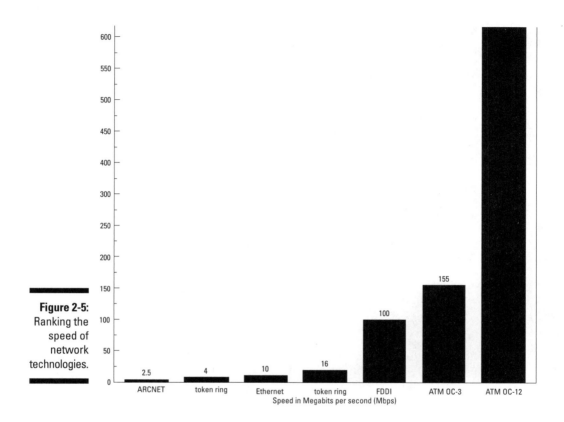

Figure 2-5:
Ranking the
speed of
network
technologies.

On the downside, FDDI requires fiber-optic cable for runs of any length. There's a CDDI (*C* stands for copper), but it doesn't support cable runs longer than 75 feet and isn't yet widely available.

Cost is another negative. Fiber optics makes for higher cost cables and expensive installation, and FDDI adapters range from $800 to $2000 per computer. FDDI will look better and better as the technology gets cheaper.

Getting down to business

For widespread use, FDDI is still a little ahead of the business curve. Not many operations are willing to shoulder the cost of running fiber everywhere and spending upward of a grand per networked desktop. Plenty of companies are working toward FDDI, though, and some of them are using FDDI backbones.

What else is there?

If you have to ask, "What else is there?" you're probably wondering why this book doesn't mention *your* networking access method. We hate to be the bearer of sad tidings, but if you're not using one of the four access methods already covered — Ethernet, token ring, ARCnet, or FDDI — you're networking the hard way. Sorry.

There are hundreds of other kinds of networks in use. There's probably something for all the letters of the alphabet between *A* for AppleTalk and *W* for wireless.

Exotic networking access methods can be a problem for NT Server too. If you're involved with an exotic network access method, you should find out whether NT Server works with it before you spend any money on the software. The good news is that Windows NT runs over a reasonable subset of available networking technologies. The bad news is that you'll have to do some research to find out whether your stuff is in one of those subsets. The worst news is that you'll have to work harder to do basic stuff that more commercial methods take for granted, and you may have to forgo more exotic options, such as LAN-attached printers.

An emerging star in the area of high-speed networking is ATM, which is short for Asynchronous Transfer Mode. In the last year, several companies have started building LAN equipment based on ATM. The long-distance phone companies already use ATM implementations that run at 155 (OC-3) and 622 (OC-12) Mbps, and current ATM specifications include speeds of 1.2 (OC-24) and 2.4 (OC-48) gigabits per second (Gbps) as well.

ATM is a fast-switching technology that requires a hub-like switching device and network interfaces for each computer. You can expect to spend at least $2000 per workstation (including allocated switch and fiber-optic cable costs) to bring ATM to your LAN.

The best way to find out what's what is to get online and ask the collective wisdom on Microsoft's electronic forums on CompuServe, MSN, and the Internet: "Does my QuackNet work with NT Server?" (For instructions on using CompuServe, MSN, or the Internet, see Appendix B.) Chances are, you will get the right answer in a day. If you don't have access to CompuServe, MSN, or the Internet, ask around. With so many users worldwide, you shouldn't have to look far to find someone who can help you.

The Polls Are In!

If you have to make a choice for a new network access method today, with no constraints, go for Ethernet. It's the only widely available technology whose 100-Mbps versions leave significant room for growth. Token ring is worth considering only for new networks if an IBM mainframe or minicomputer operating system is in the picture somewhere, or if other considerations — such as company policy — dictate it. ARCnet is a bottom-feeder's choice for new networks today. But if money is a major concern, it can be the difference between networking or not.

Chapter 3

Message in a Bottle: Mastering the Art of Protocols

. . . .

In This Chapter

▶ Figuring out how protocols work

▶ Learning the language that lets computers speak

▶ Moving messages

. . . .

*C*hapter 1 describes the three fundamental components of networking: connections, communications, and services. In this chapter, you leave the wires and interfaces behind and go inside the network to take a look at communications — how senders and receivers field messages moving across the network.

Communications rely on a shared set of rules for exchanging information and for defining things at the most rudimentary levels, such as how to present digital data — what's a one and what's a zero? The rules also determine the format and meaning of network addresses and other essential information.

In this chapter, we stick with the plumbing metaphor. You've already looked at the pipes; now it's time to look at what the pipes carry — messages and data that computers send to each other. This should help you better understand how computers communicate on your network — and why they occasionally don't.

How Do Computers Talk to Each Other?

Table 1-1 compared a computer conversation to a human conversation, and showed that any communications between humans or machines have much in common. A trivial difference is that computers use ones and zeroes to communicate and humans use words. There are also some real differences, however. Understanding those will help you understand networking.

DWIM — do what I mean!

In human communication, what's being said is always interpreted and often misunderstood. What one person says is not always what the other person hears. Human communication, like the communication of computers over a network, relies on shared rules and meanings and a common frame of reference.

Computers, however, are linear. They can do only what they're told to do. For computers to exchange information, every piece of that information must be explicitly supplied; computers are not strong on picking up implications and subtlety. To communicate, computers have to begin in complete agreement about the following issues. (The questions are phrased from a computer's point of view.)

✔ What's my address? How do I find it out? How do I find out other computers' addresses?

✔ How do I signal another computer that I'm ready to send or receive a message? That I'm busy? That I can wait if it's busy?

These are the fundamentals, but they are only the tip of a large technological iceberg. Before computers can communicate with each other, *everything* must be completely mapped out and implemented in software that supplies all the answers to these questions in a way that all the computers know and understand. These answers form the basis of a set of rules for computer communications, rules the computers use to handle networking.

Standardized rules

Building a complete set of communications rules is time-consuming and picky and would bore most people out of their skulls. In the early days of the computer industry, individual companies or groups put a bunch of programmers to work building programs to do whatever they needed to have accomplished. As time went on, this process resulted in many different ways of doing such things as networking, none of which would work with the way talented programmers over at another company did the same things.

These incompatibilities were not a big deal (or so it seemed) in the beginning. As networks became a more common part of the business landscape, however, it seemed natural for people who bought computers from companies A and Z to wonder, "Well, gee, if my company A computers can talk to each other and my company Z computers can talk to each other, why can't the As talk to the Zs and vice versa?"

Why not, indeed?

Uncle Sam played an important role in bringing order to this potential network chaos. When the government tried to get their A and Z computers to talk to each other, they learned that they had a monster compatibility problem. A consensus emerged that a set of rules was absolutely necessary for networking. The industry also learned that networking was difficult, if not impossible, when everyone didn't share the same set of rules.

If this story had a happy ending, it would be: "Nowadays there's only one set of networking rules, and everyone uses the rules wisely and well." Unfortunately, there's no happy ending. Although the chaos has been reduced, there's still plenty to go around, and vendors trying to stay in the vanguard seem to be inventing more rules as they go.

According to Protocol

Just to keep things simple, these "sets of networking rules" are usually called networking *protocols* — they're also referred to as networking standards, or even as standard networking protocols. You get the drift.

In diplomacy, protocol is the code of correct procedures and etiquette that representatives from sovereign governments follow to prevent all-out war. For example, protocol is the reason why diplomats refer to screaming matches as "frank and earnest discussions" or to insoluble disagreements as "exploratory dialogue." Political double-talk aside, the word *protocol* nicely captures the flavor of rules for network communications.

The concept of the networking protocol is based on the premise that any two computers must have an identical protocol in common to communicate; that is, the computers are peers in any communication. The particular protocol defines the language, structure, and rules for that communication.

Suites for the . . . never mind!

Although this book is about Windows NT Server and focuses its attention on the Microsoft protocols, you should be aware that these protocols are just one of a large number. Microsoft has become surprisingly catholic in its support for protocols, including support not only for government standards (TCP/IP) but also for the Novell IPX/SPX protocols. That may be because IPX/SPX was built to enable desktop computers, including PCs, to communicate and also because there are more PCs on the nation's desktops than any other kind of computer. And, too, the government's finger is in many pies, and the Internet uses the same protocols, so it is not surprising that NT Server supports today's most popular networking protocols.

Raising the standards

An interesting — not to say confusing — thing about networking rules is that both vendors and standards groups call their stuff a "standard." Some vendors expend a lot of hot air talking about the difference between *de facto* and *de jure* standards. *De facto* means "It ain't official, but a lot of people use it, so we can call it a standard if we want." *De jure* means "It's a standard because XYZ (a standards-setting group) has declared it to be so and has published this foot-high stack of documentation to prove it."

Behind the sometimes heated discussion of what is or is not a standard is a control issue. Purists — including academicians, researchers, and techno-weenies — flatly assert that only a standards-setting group can be "objective and fair," and, therefore, only they can adequately handle the job of selecting the very best that technology has to offer by putting it in their standard — thus making this the best of all possible worlds (and everything in it a necessary evil).

The other heat source comes from vendors' desperate race to keep up with the market and customers' demands by heroically struggling to get their products off the drawing board and out the door. "Of course we have to be in control of our technology," they say. "It's the only way we can keep up!" The objectivity, fairness, and leading-edge characteristics of most standards are not disputed, but establishing standards involves groups of individuals who must agree on them, which takes time. In the meantime, technology continues to evolve and nothing goes stale faster than leading-edge technology.

Whether networking technologies are standards or not, or *de facto* or *de jure* doesn't matter: The action is where the markets are. Vendors must be involved on both sides of the debate to some extent because they cannot afford to miss any of the technology boats leaving port. Some astute vendors have published their "standards" and given customers and industry people sufficient documentation and input to both keep things working and keep up with the development of the technology.

Some standards bodies have been wise enough to realize that a standard is a good thing only when it's widely implemented, and have given vendors opportunities to deal with the real-world concerns of getting products to market. The winners in both camps are the protocols that are used the most.

One last remark on protocols: They rarely, if ever, occur in the singular. Most networking protocols consist of a named collection of specific message formats and rules for interaction rather than a single set of formats and rules. For that reason, protocols are also called *protocol suites,* not because they like to lounge around on matched collections of furniture, but because they travel in packs.

A protocol's work is never done

So now you know that your computer cannot talk to another computer without sharing a common protocol. Where does this protocol stuff come from? Put differently, who decides which protocols are used?

Protocols cover networking capability from software to hardware. The programs that let your computer access the network must use a protocol. This protocol holds all the way down to the edge of the hardware, where the computer says "send this message" to talk to the network, or "give me the message," depending on what the hardware is telling it.

Protocols come a little from here and a little from there. For example, most protocols don't care which kind of network they're talking through; in most cases, they don't even notice if it's an ARCnet, Ethernet, or token-ring network. This is because part of the software that provides network capability comes from a *LAN driver* and part of it comes from other sources.

The LAN driver on a computer tells it exactly how to talk to the network interface in your machine. If you're lucky, you use a network machine such as a network-ready PC or a Sun workstation. Otherwise, you have to locate and install a LAN driver on your computer so it can talk to the network.

Some applications may know how to directly communicate with a network through a special kind of software interface. Applications with this kind of savvy used to be scarce, but they're becoming more common as networks become more widespread. Other applications may use standard computer system access and end up talking through the network, totally unaware that the network is being accessed.

The key to network access from applications or from a computer's operating system is a collection of software that implements the *protocol suite* being used. The operating system, such as DOS or Windows 95 on a PC, is a program that keeps the computer running and capable of doing the jobs you ask it to perform.

If an application or operating system is network-savvy, the vendor may supply all or part of the network access software, including the LAN driver.

For Windows NT Server, for example, Microsoft supplies software for most of its desktop clients: Windows (in all its many flavors), UNIX, OS/2, and Macintosh can make use of their own networking software, whereas DOS uses networking software that Microsoft supplies along with NT Server (which can also be obtained from other sources). For a visual aid to these possible software relationships, look at Figure 3-1. You'll notice that software components, called shells or requesters, are needed to communicate over the network. The figure also shows that you'll need a LAN driver to provide the link between software and hardware.

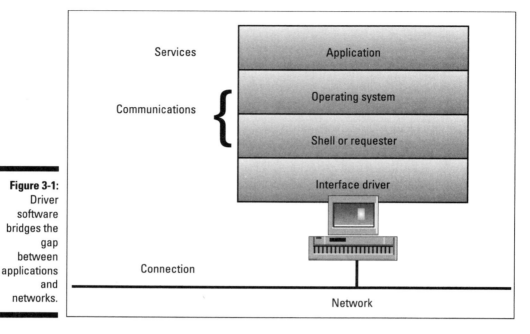

Figure 3-1:
Driver
software
bridges the
gap
between
applications
and
networks.

The Dance of the Seven Layers

Okay, you now know that a protocol suite lets computers share a set of common communications rules. You also know that the protocols handle the movement of information between the hardware on the network interface computer and the applications you run on your machine. The next question is, what's going on between the applications and the hardware while the protocols do their thing?

Much of the interaction between applications and hardware consists of taking messages, breaking them down, and stuffing them into envelopes as you move farther from the application and closer to the hardware. From the other direction — hardware to software — the protocols unpack envelopes and stick individual pieces together to build a complete message. We hope that it is a meaningful message, but remember that the one immutable law of computers is GIGO, or garbage in, garbage out.

It might help to think of a post-office analogy. The post office handles anything that has an address on it and sufficient postage to pay its way. How is a letter delivered? It goes something like this:

1. **You address a letter and drop it in a mailbox.**

2. **The mail carrier who empties the mailbox gets the letter.**

3. The mail carrier delivers the letter to your local post office.

4. The mail sorters check the ZIP code and route the letter.

5. The letter is shipped to the post office that services the destination address.

6. The mail sorters check the street address and route the letter to the appropriate mail carrier.

7. The mail carrier delivers the letter to the address and the recipient gets the letter.

The basic requirements for successful mail delivery are timely pickup, short transit time, and correct delivery. Factors that affect transit time and delivery (barring disgruntled postal workers with firearms) are correct identification of and routing to the mailing address.

The similarity between networking protocols and the postal service lies in the capability to recognize addresses, route messages from senders to receivers, and provide delivery. The major difference is that the postal service, unlike networking protocols, doesn't normally care what's in the envelopes or packages you send as long as they meet size, weight, and materials restrictions. Networking protocols spend most of their time dealing with envelopes of varying sizes and kinds.

For instance, suppose that you want to copy a file from your computer to another computer across the network. The file is sizable, about 1MB. It consists of a spreadsheet covering your sales forecast for the next quarter, so you want it to get there quickly and correctly.

To use the post office (or snail mail), you would copy the file to a floppy and mail it to the recipient, but that's not fast enough. Over the network, it will get there in less than a minute. While the file is moving from your machine to the other machine, there's a lot going on that you aren't privy to.

Size considerations — the biggest chunk of data you're allowed to move across the network — are only one reason why messages are put into envelopes. Handling addresses is another reason. In the post office example, the pickup post office cares only about the destination ZIP code, whereas the delivering mail carrier is concerned with the street address. Along the same lines, one protocol might care about only the name of the computer to which the file is to be shipped; at a lower level, however, the protocol needs to know where to direct the chunks of data moving from sender to receiver as well so that the file can be correctly reassembled upon delivery.

The protocol software spends most of its time taking things apart to deliver them accurately. When you're receiving something, it spends its time stripping off packaging information and putting things back together. The sender and receiver keep talking to each other while all this is going on to monitor the accuracy and effectiveness of their communications and to determine if and when delivery is complete. Protocols also spend a lot of time keeping track of the quality and usability of network links.

We hope this chapter has helped to clear up some of the mysteries that surround protocols. The important thing to remember, though, is that protocols simply allow computers to communicate.

Chapter 4
Rounding Up the Usual Suspects

- -

In This Chapter

▶ Identifying common Windows NT protocols and fellow travelers

▶ Understanding NetBIOS and NetBEUI

▶ Introducing IPX, the NetWare protocol

▶ Toasting TCP/IP: the world's most widely used protocol

▶ Speaking to mainframes with DLC

▶ Applying AppleTalk: bringing Macs into the fold

▶ Mixing protocol stacks

▶ Recognizing and categorizing protocols

- -

*I*n this chapter, you find out still more about how computers communicate over networks, but now you concentrate on the capability to recognize the *kinds* of communications. You also find out which protocols go with which operating systems and applications. After you finish reading this chapter, you should be able to identify what you have been using up until now or what you will be dealing with in the near future.

You've heard this before, but it bears repeating: A *network protocol* is a set of rules governing the way computers communicate over a network; computers must have protocols in common to be capable of communication.

Network protocols are grouped according to their functions, such as sending and receiving messages from the network interface — talking to the hardware — and making it possible for applications to do their thing in a network environment — talking to the software. Protocols are generically referred to as *protocol families* or *protocol suites* because they tend to travel in packs. This pack mentality involves stacking multiple layers of functionality, with software associated with each layer. When the software that supports a particular network protocol is loaded on a computer, it's called a *protocol stack*. All computers on the network load all or part of the stack. They use the same parts of the stack, called *peer protocols,* when they communicate with each other as — you guessed it — *peers.*

Here we introduce you to the most popular protocol stacks in the Windows NT environment. (They are the same for both Workstation and Server versions.) You find out their purpose as well as how to distinguish them. Along the way, you also find out a bit more about how networks work and the kinds of built-in functionality that keep them working.

Just as diplomatic protocols grease the wheels of diplomacy, network protocols keep your network's wheels turning. If you get to know the players, you may be able to help things along.

Warning: Entering the Acronym Zone!

To set up and troubleshoot a Windows NT-based network, it is useful (to put it mildly) to understand what the various protocols do and to be able to make educated guesses as to the kinds of problems that may be associated with each one. In working with these protocols, you are expected to be able to toss off awkward collections of letters (and sometimes numbers) with ease. You are also expected to know which acronyms belong together and, in some cases, how the pieces fit. When things get weird — and you have our word that they will — you have to be knowledgeable about a rogues' gallery of protocols so that you can run down the perpetrators.

Most protocol families are populated by abbreviations and acronyms. Take hope, though: Although familiarity may breed contempt, it will also allow you to discriminate and navigate the alphabet soup!

You Can't Tell the Players without a Program

The Microsoft built-in protocols include four protocol families, plus support for an additional pathway that Macintoshes can use to attach to Windows NT. Here they are, in alphabetical order:

- ✓ DLC (Data Link Control): a printer and host access protocol
- ✓ IPX/SPX (Internetwork Packet Exchange/Sequenced Packet Exchange): the NetWare core protocol, developed by Novell in the early 1980s
- ✓ NetBIOS/NetBEUI (Networked Basic Input-Output System/NetBIOS Extended User Interface): a local-area protocol developed by IBM and refined by Microsoft; originally, the native protocol for LAN Manager and for Windows NT

✔ TCP/IP (Transmission Control Protocol/Internet Protocol): a set of standard protocols and services developed at the behest of the U.S. government in the 1970s and 1980s and now the most widely used networking protocol in the world

Windows NT also includes built-in support for AppleTalk, the networking protocol native to members of the Macintosh family. This allows Mac users to access files, printers, and services on a Windows NT server.

You can use any or all of these protocols on your network, which accounts for both the blessings and the curses of NT networking. In the sections that follow, we tell you a little more about these protocols and provide some guidance as to when and why you might want to use one or more of them.

DLC: golden oldie

The DLC (Data Link Control) protocol is the oldest protocol in this collection. IBM developed DLC to connect token-ring-based workstations to IBM mainframes and minicomputers. Printer manufacturers have adopted the protocol to connect remote printers to network print servers. Unless you use a remote printer (one that attaches directly to your network) or some kind of IBM host connection, you probably won't need DLC.

DLC's primary use is to connect to mainframes and minicomputers through a gateway server. The workstation PC (the one on your desk) uses the DLC protocol to talk to the gateway, and the gateway talks SNA (or some other mainframe protocol) to a host computer.

IPX/SPX: the basic NetWare protocols

IPX (Internetwork Packet Exchange), SPX (Sequenced Packet Exchange), and NCP (NetWare Core Protocol) are the basic Novell NetWare protocols. IPX, SPX, and NCP, with more than 40 million regular users, are the most widely used networking protocols in the world. IPX is used with NetWare on DOS (with or without plain vanilla Windows), Windows for Workgroups, Windows 95, Windows NT Server and Workstation, Macintosh, OS/2, and some versions of UNIX.

You'll need these protocols only if there's a NetWare server somewhere on your network. Although it is one of the default installation selections, if you don't need to connect your users to NetWare resources, there's no compelling reason to install IPX/SPX on your NT Server network.

NetBIOS/NetBEUI

IBM developed NetBIOS as a way to permit small groups of PCs to share files and printers efficiently. We treat NetBIOS and NetBEUI as if they are more or less synonymous. However, NetBIOS is the original edition, and NetBEUI is an enhanced version that performs better on more powerful networks in the increasingly 32-bit world. NetBEUI is built into many applications and older networking products, but it has fallen out of use as the size and scope of networks have increased.

NetBEUI is not routable, which means it does not behave well on a large network interconnected by routers. Because of NetBEUI's large installed base, however, Microsoft still offers NetBEUI as one of its standard NT protocols. Most of the applications that use NetBEUI will gradually migrate to other protocols. For now, Windows NT can talk NetBEUI with the best of them.

Would we recommend NetBEUI for a modern network? Yes and no — with an inclination toward the latter. The simplicity and low overhead of NetBEUI make it the fastest networking protocol around. It also offers the benefits of networking to small workgroups without the inherent complexity and management requirements you find in other protocols (such as TCP/IP). If the scope of your network extends beyond the workgroup, however, NetBEUI is probably not the best choice.

The government protocols: TCP/IP

TCP/IP is the outgrowth of Department of Defense (DoD) funding for networks, which began in the early 1970s in an attempt to tie government computers together. These protocols are commonly referred to as DoD protocols because the DoD requires that all computers they purchase be capable of running them. They are also referred to as Internet protocols because they're required to use the Internet.

TCP/IP is an acronym for two DoD protocols: the Transmission Control Protocol and the Internet Protocol. According to Dr. Vinton Cerf, a founding father of the Internet, 300,000 networks are now part of the Internet, and another 100,000 or more private networks use TCP/IP, making it a major player among protocols. TCP/IP is deeply rooted in the UNIX community. In addition, it is often used to link different kinds of computers, including a plethora of free or inexpensive TCP/IP implementations for PCs and Macintoshes.

Because TCP/IP is the foundation of the Internet, as well the most widely used networking protocol, we consider it a good choice for your network, too. Although it can be a chore to learn and use TCP/IP, it provides more reach and capability than any other protocol.

Connection handling helps classify protocols

IP, IPX, and NetBEUI are *connectionless* protocols, and SPX and TCP are *connection oriented.* What does this mean? Why should you care?

They are all lower-level protocols. Chapter 3 establishes that the most important job of a lower-level protocol is to break up arbitrarily sized application information into digestible chunks when sending, and then to put the chunks back together into their original form when receiving. The chunks, called *packets,* form the basic message unit for information moving across a network. These packets are further divided and stuffed into envelopes by the access method being used. These envelopes are called *frames.* Look at it this way: Packets move up and down the protocol stack; frames dance across the wire.

Connectionless protocols work the same as mailing letters through the postal service. You drop off a letter and expect the post office to deliver it. You may not find out whether the letter doesn't arrive — unless it's a bill. IP, IPX, and NetBIOS provide no guarantee of delivery, and frames can arrive in any order.

Connection-oriented protocols, on the other hand, use a *handshake* to start communications and can be likened to the process of sending a registered letter, in which delivery information is returned to the sender. SPX and TCP packets are sequenced so they arrive in proper order, which makes them more reliable, and they also request redelivery or send error notices when delivery is unsuccessful.

IP and other connectionless protocols are typically fast and require little overhead, but they are considered lightweight. TCP and other connection-oriented protocols run more slowly than connectionless protocols because they keep track of what has been sent and received. More record-keeping information is built into each packet, however, which offers higher reliability.

Other faces in the gallery

A lot of other protocols are on networks all over the world. On Windows NT and NetWare local area networks, however, you are more likely to find the ones discussed in this section:

- ✔ **AppleTalk:** The name of the set of protocols developed by Apple Computer, whose Macintosh computer was one of the first mass-market computers to offer built-in networking capabilities. In most cases, where there's a Mac, there's AppleTalk.

- ✔ **ISO/OSI:** A nifty palindrome that stands for the International Standards Organization's Open Systems Interconnect family of networking protocols. OSI has yet to live up to its promise as the highly touted successor to TCP/IP and the next big thing in networking. The few OSI protocols in common use are in Europe, where OSI protocols have gained a foothold. OSI is out there in industry, government, business, and academia because most governments, including Uncle Sam, require systems to be OSI-compliant. Like TCP/IP, ISO/OSI is available for a broad range of systems, from PCs to supercomputers. Most protocol stacks resemble OSI, and like any good reference model, the OSI Model lets techno-weenies know which protocol stack layer someone is talking about.

✔ **SNA:** Systems Network Architecture, the basic IBM protocol suite. Where there's a mainframe or an AS/400, you'll usually find SNA. Because SNA was one of the pioneering protocols, companies that invested heavily in mainframe technology in the 1960s and 1970s also invested in building large-scale SNA networks. There are more SNA networks than any other kind, but that number is dropping because SNA is old, cumbersome, and expensive. However, there are still enough out there that the newer IBM operating systems, such as OS/2 and AIX, offer links to SNA in addition to other protocols. This is an esoteric networking area, and you won't run into much more of it in this book.

The networking world has hundreds of protocol families, each with its own collection of acronyms and special outlook, but luckily you don't have to know all of them.

AppleTalk: making the Mac connection

AppleTalk is a proprietary protocol stack like IPX/SPX; it is the property of Apple Computer. IPX and TCP/IP implementations for the Mac are available, but AppleTalk is the most frequently used Macintosh networking protocol, simply because it's built into the Macintosh environment and is amazingly easy to use. AppleTalk is a model for plug-and-play networking that other implementations would benefit from following. We wish that more protocols had worked as hard to be as easy as this one.

Although the AppleTalk ease of use has a lot going for it, friendliness and performance have a habit of being at opposite ends of the spectrum. The Windows NT Macintosh capabilities are highly regarded and provide a good way to integrate your right-brained Macintosh users with the PC side of your network.

Keep going — there's more!

We can go on in this vein indefinitely; but by now, you should have the idea that every protocol suite consists of a cast of characters, each with its own special networking job. You have read about most of the common issues, including moving frames across the network (packet delivery), connectionless versus connection-oriented communications, address handling, routing, and service protocols.

Any protocol suite will have some, if not all, of these capabilities. After you understand the importance that frame delivery, routing services, and address handling have to a workable network, things should start making a perverted kind of sense. Don't worry if the acronyms are unfamiliar or the terminology is strange; concentrate on finding out how protocols work to connect programs and services to the network. After you understand these concepts, you know all the really important stuff.

Mixing Protocols: Hybrids

Sometimes, you may need to have more than one kind of network operating from a single computer. This process might require some contortions, depending on the network interface and drivers in use. The key is figuring out whether the machine has to be capable of interacting with both networks at will or whether it's always one *or* the other.

IPX/SPX and TCP/IP run together successfully on PCs every day. Windows 95 and Windows NT Workstation both offer drivers and installation tools to easily mix and match the two environments so that users can use both protocol stacks in a network access.

In the same vein, Macintoshes can run AppleTalk and TCP/IP quite easily, and UNIX is capable of running as many protocol stacks as necessary to provide the range of network services you want. A UNIX machine's protocol collection can include TCP/IP, OSI, and IPX, and more.

The key is getting and installing LAN drivers that can switch between one protocol stack and another as needed. Some drivers are not that flexible. The computer has to be restarted to switch from one stack to another. Or switching might require installing two network interface cards on the same machine to provide simultaneous support for two stacks. This problem is most acute for DOS and Windows because those environments cannot change their configurations on the fly. Most other operating systems and platforms, including Windows NT, OS/2, NetWare, and UNIX, are more flexible and accommodating.

Whatever operating system or machine you're using, there is one consequence of using multiple stacks: The more protocols you use, the more resources they consume. Each stack has a memory requirement, and every stack you add increases system overhead. Again, multiple stacks weigh heaviest on DOS and 16-bit Windows desktops, but it's a fact of networking life that working with multiple network protocols imposes greater overhead than working with only one.

What's What on Your Desktop?

The two ways to figure out what protocols you're using on a network are as follows:

✔ The Sherlock Holmes method: On a desktop machine, you examine the contents of your bootup files (WIN.INI, SYSTEM.INI, CONFIG.SYS, AUTOEXEC.BAT, and so on) and determine which protocol drivers are being loaded. On a Windows NT server, you search the Registry and check under the Network icon in the Control Panel to find out which drivers are loaded.

✔ The Chief Inspector method: Watch what your computer does when it boots up or during network log on, if you have to manually log on. The computer often tells you which protocol stacks it's loading. Unfortunately, this method works better on PCs running DOS, DOS/Windows, or Windows 95 than it does on Windows NT. But there's always the chance that an error message (a mixed blessing, to be sure) may tell you something useful here.

This information is usually enough to identify what's what to the knowledgeable. If neither of the two preceding methods works, go find someone knowledgeable and ask for help!

If you don't know where to look for help, you can always call the people who sold you the machine or the vendor of the operating system. If you learn that what you have is not optimal or could be newer, these people will be able to steer you to a source for the latest and greatest.

The network interface vendor can also be an invaluable source of information, and is usually the owner, if not the author, of the drivers for its gear. Persistence pays off in ensuring that your protocol stacks and drivers are the right vintage for your environment.

Chapter 5

NICs and Knocks: Understanding Network Interface Cards

· ·

In This Chapter

▶ Figuring out what's in a network interface card

▶ Catching the right bus — ISA, EISA, PCI, VLB, or Micro Channel

▶ Plugging in

▶ Avoiding trouble: Do your homework

▶ Reading the manual

▶ Configuring NICs

▶ Troubleshooting your NIC installation

▶ Cabling up to the NIC

▶ Installing drivers

· ·

*H*aving learned the basics of connections and communications, you're finally ready to move on to the joys and sorrows of installing network interfaces. This discussion harks back to the subject of connections, but now you are better prepared to deal with it.

If you have an IBM PC or a PC clone or are using Windows NT on a RISC machine (such as a DEC Alpha), you'll definitely want to read this chapter because we discuss how to install network interfaces for those machines. If you're running a Macintosh or something else that's not a PC or a Windows-capable clone, you can skip this chapter!

Most *NICs* (network interface cards) plug into computers and provide the essential link between the medium of communication and the computer sending and receiving communications.

What's in Your NIC?

A typical NIC is an add-in card configured to fit your computer. Its role is to work both sides of the network connection. The following details how the NIC works:

- ✔ The NIC plugs into the computer's bus so it can talk to the CPU and the CPU can talk to it. This capability makes the connection between the computer and the NIC possible.

- ✔ The NIC's accommodation for a network connection typically involves an external connector that allows the network medium to be hooked up with a cable between the NIC and the network. Some NICs have more than one connector, so if you change your network or your mind, you don't have to throw out the old to put in the new.

- ✔ Your network access method determines the way that the NIC talks on the network. There are NICs for ARCnet, Ethernet, token-ring, FDDI, and ATM networks. Unlike connectors, adapters can't be bought with combinations of two or more access methods.

Figure 5-1 shows the bus connector and media interface of a typical NIC. Bus connectors vary according to the bus on your computer. Media connectors vary according to the network access method and cabling type. Learn how to recognize what you have so that you can select the right kind of NIC for your machine and have it properly connected to your network.

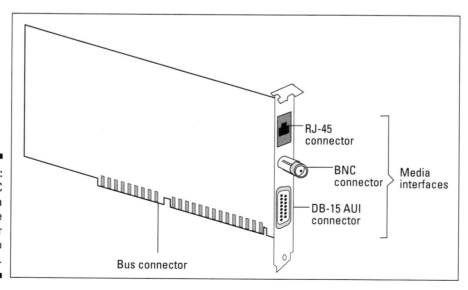

Figure 5-1:
The NIC acts as a bridge to tie your computer to the network.

RJ-45 connector

BNC connector

DB-15 AUI connector

Media interfaces

Bus connector

Not all NICs are cards that live inside your computer. Some laptops, portables, and other machines cannot accommodate standard internal interfaces. For these, you attach an external network interface, called a *parallel-port connector,* which does the same job as conventional NICs. You can also install and uninstall PCMCIA (Personal Computer Memory Card International Association) adapters according to your networking whims. PCMCIA adapters look like fat credit cards. You slide them into and out of your computer's PCMCIA slot. Figure 5-2 shows an external interface that attaches to a computer's parallel port.

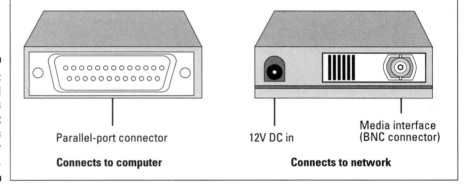

Figure 5-2:
An external interface is the NIC that attaches outside your computer.

Parallel-port connector   12V DC in   Media interface (BNC connector)

Connects to computer   **Connects to network**

Catching the Bus: ISA, EISA, VLB, or Micro Channel

If your computer is a PC, you have to match its NIC to the type of your machine's internal bus. If it's not a PC, you have to decide only whether to go with the NIC or an external interface. Either way, you don't have to grapple with the subtleties that wannabe-networked PCs have to contend with.

The business end of your NIC plugs into the computer and is called an *edge connector.* You should be able to recognize the types of interfaces your computer can handle by looking at the computer's bus. From the other direction, looking at your NIC should tell you which kind of bus it's for. Figure 5-3 shows the three types of buses covered in this section, with their respective edge connectors.

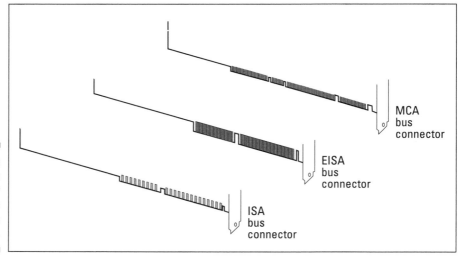

Figure 5-3:
PC buses
and their
connectors
are made to
match up.

MCA
bus
connector

EISA
bus
connector

ISA
bus
connector

ISA and EISA

ISA (Industry Standard Architecture) describes the bus that most PCs have used since IBM introduced the PC AT in 1985. ISA is still the most common PC bus, so it's likely to be the one your NIC plugs into.

EISA, or Extended ISA, is an attempt to extend the capabilities of the ISA bus. EISA is *backward compatible* with ISA. This means you can plug ISA cards into an EISA bus and they work just fine, even though EISA cards use a different edge connector than those on ISA card. Although most EISA adapters give you higher performance than ISA adapters, EISA has never caught on. If your server is an EISA machine, buy EISA NICs to use with it; newer machines will probably feature PCI (Peripheral Component Interconnect) or VLB (Video Local Bus). If these are present on your server, buy interfaces for those bus types instead. (If both are available, choose PCI — its bandwidth is twice that of VLB.)

The difference between ISA and EISA is the result of the two changes made to ISA to create EISA:

✔ ISA uses a 16-bit *data path,* and EISA uses a 32-bit data path. In simple English, this means that an ISA interface can move only half as much data across the bus between the NIC and the CPU compared to an EISA interface.

Widening the bus has two benefits: It enables an EISA interface to move more data in the same amount of time and does a better job of matching modern CPUs built for 32-bit data paths. The PC AT CPU is an Intel 80286 and uses a 16-bit data path; if your processor is an 80386 or higher, it uses a 32-bit data path.

✔ EISA can run much faster than ISA. ISA's bus speed is based on the clock speed of the original IBM PC AT, which was introduced at 4.77 MHz and later upped to 8 MHz. EISA, on the other hand, can run as fast as 33 MHz. EISA not only moves more data than ISA but also moves it four to seven times faster.

Why would anyone use ISA in the first place? Because speed and performance always have a price: EISA computers used to cost at least $200 more than their ISA cousins — and corresponding EISA interfaces cost around twice as much. (It's easy to find $80 ISA Ethernet NICs, for example, but $200 is about as low as you can go for an EISA Ethernet equivalent.) EISA is pretty much passé, so you probably won't be able to buy EISA computers or interface cards, except in the used-equipment market.

The local run: VLB and PCI

Two new buses have been added to the fleet in the past five years. Both are called local bus technologies because they rely on the addition of a special-purpose, high-speed bus to link a PC's CPU to a limited set of peripherals, such as display cards (to drive your video display), disk controllers (to handle your disk drives), and network interface cards. Local bus technologies are built specifically for speed — VLB is a 32-bit bus and PCI is a 64-bit one — and to make the connection of vital computer subsystems fast and efficient.

VESA Local Bus (VLB), the older of the two technologies, is the brainchild of the Video Electronics Standards Association (VESA), San Jose, CA. In 1988, NEC Home Electronics, along with eight leading video board manufacturers, founded VESA. The association's main purpose was the standardization of technical issues surrounding 800 x 600 resolution video displays, commonly known as Super VGA.

VLB is primarily a 32-bit bus and runs at speeds up to 66 MHz. A VLB slot uses one 32-bit Micro Channel slot plus a standard ISA, EISA, or Micro Channel slot. This allows manufacturers to design boards using either the local bus or both buses at the same time. VLB and PCI support bus mastering, which frees the CPU from running the bus. In the process, this frees the CPU to do other things, which speeds up overall system performance.

Intel developed PCI to provide a high-speed data path between the CPU and up to 10 peripherals while coexisting with ISA or EISA (like other expansion buses). With PCI, you plug ISA and EISA boards into their usual slot and plug high-speed PCI controllers into a PCI slot. The PCI bus supports 32-bit and 64-bit data paths and bus mastering and runs at up to 100 MHz. Intel's considerable industry clout means that vendor support for PCI adapters is stronger than for any other kind of expansion bus, including VLB and EISA. Because of this support, we recommend that you consider using PCI NICs if PCI is an available option. (In the past, there was some question about whether PCI was better than VLB, but today it's clear that PCI is the way to go.)

Micro Channel: a better idea?

Like ISA, the Micro Channel Architecture is the brainchild of IBM. Micro Channel is a 32-bit bus, with most of the same advantages as the other buses we have mentioned: higher speed and a broader data path. If you have a Micro Channel computer, you have to buy Micro Channel NICs to go with it because MCA is a replacement bus, not an expansion bus. Micro Channel's main advantage is that you can usually plug in your NIC and it handles its own configuration from there. This convenience does not come cheap, however.

Which bus gets you where you want to go?

We think that high-speed buses such as EISA, PCI, and VLB are great, but they're overkill for many workstations in use today. Even if your machine can accommodate one, don't bother installing an EISA, VLB, or PCI NIC unless the machine will be a high-volume network consumer or will use a fast access method (such as 100-Mbps Ethernet). The following criteria justify the use of such NICs:

- A network server
- A high-speed access method (faster than fast token-ring)
- A dead certainty that your machine will be the focus of a lot of network traffic (using high-volume database applications or a computer-aided design package, for example)

If you're dealing with these situations, spending the extra money will pay off in improved performance or at least more acceptable performance. Otherwise, save your money.

Avoid Trouble: Get Off to a Good Start

Before you start mucking around inside your PC, you should do some preparation. Messing about with the system is one of the few things that can flat-out kill a computer. Taking some preventive steps at the start will ward off trouble and may also get you back to work quicker.

Your NIC installation maneuvers can turn out in one of two ways. With luck, your brand-new NIC will be safely ensconced in your PC, doing exactly what it's supposed to be doing. Otherwise, it will be back in its original packaging, ready to be replaced with what you now have learned that you *really* need!

Unplugged — it's not just for MTV

Electricity is our friend, but there's no reason to get up close and personal with it. *Never, never, never* open a machine that's plugged into a wall socket. This mistake can get you or your machine (or both) fried. This is, technically speaking, not a good thing. So remember to detach the power cord from the case before you open it. While you're into unplugging, it's a good idea to unplug all the other cables from the back of the computer, too.

Getting back to the beginning

What's the worst-case scenario other than something or someone getting fried? You can turn on the computer and get a big, resounding nothing — zero, zip, nada! The really worst case may result in your having to send the computer to a professional for repair. In the not-so-bad (and more common) case, you take out the new stuff (and reverse any software changes you've made) and you're back where you started.

Reverse software changes, you ask? This brings us to a crucial preemptive step you should always take before fiddling with your hardware: *Before* you start fiddling, back up any system that will be affected. Backing up has two vital benefits. First, assuming the worst case with a computer ending up DOA, you can install your backup on another similarly configured machine and keep working until your original machine is back from the shop. Second, if the new installation doesn't work, you can use the backup to quickly restore the machine to the pristine state it enjoyed before you mucked it up. Backups take time and the temptation is always to ignore this safety tip, but ignore it *at your peril*.

Figure out what you're dealing with

A PC can seem like a minefield when you're adding another interface to an already jam-packed machine. If you don't have an inventory of what's installed, as well as the appropriate configuration information, take the time to figure out what's in there before you start changing things. Make a list of what's installed and the settings for each item. This keeps you from trying to occupy settings that are already taken. Doing this makes quick work of an installation and could head off configuration confusion before it happens. Time may be money, but remember that it almost always takes more time to do something over than to do it right in the first place.

Microsoft includes with Windows a peachy utility called the Microsoft Diagnostic Utility (also known as MSD.EXE), which is installed in the root Windows directory. If you run MSD.EXE from DOS, it tells you useful things about your PC's configuration that you'll need to know to install your NIC.

Likewise, if you're installing a NIC in a Windows NT machine, you'll find its built-in diagnostics to be invaluable. The Windows NT Diagnostics are available under Start, Programs, Administrative Tools or from networking commands such as `arp`, `netstat`, `ping`, and `tracert` (covered in Chapter 25).

Be on the lookout for trouble

Things can get weird when you install your NIC, especially with machines that already have lots of stuff in them. For example, you may run into two interface cards (such as the network adapter and the video adapter) that can occupy only overlapping settings — meaning one of them has to go. Or you may not know what changes are needed to get things to fit together.

To prevent potential weirdness, gather all the manuals for your PC and for every interface installed in it. And for good luck, try to find a general-purpose PC book for reference. We recommend *PCs For Dummies,* 4th Edition (Dan Gookin, IDG Books Worldwide, Inc., 1996) or *PC SECRETS,* 2nd Edition (Caroline M. Halliday, IDG Books Worldwide, Inc., 1995).

Room to maneuver

Clear some space for yourself to work. Find some small paper cups or other small containers for holding screws and connectors. If you're really going to take things apart, label what goes where to eliminate guesswork. Also, have the right tools for the job. Go to a computer store and get one of those $50 to $100 general-purpose tool kits that come in nifty little zip-up cases.

Remember that, as you walk across carpets, you build up static electricity. Therefore, always carry a network interface card in the anti-static material it came in, and ground yourself before you put your hands in a machine or handle computer hardware. To dissipate static buildup, use anti-static wristbands or heel-caps. Another solution for static buildup that's nearly as effective is to touch the chassis of the computer before doing anything else.

The lay of your LAN

You will eventually connect to your network any NIC you install. Part of the configuration drill is knowing the names and addresses of the servers, users, and networks around you. Before you start, read the installation requirements and go over any of the network-related details you will need to supply during the installation process. This heads off the necessity of stopping halfway through an installation procedure to dig up information. Invest the ounce of prevention that helps avoid expensive, time-consuming cures.

Beware the Golden Fingers

Reading the manuals from offshore manufacturers gives you an unparalleled opportunity to decipher the bizarre forms that written English can take in the hands of a non-native speaker. For example, one Taiwanese company described an edge connector (the part of the NIC that plugs into a bus slot) as "golden fingers."

Even if the fingers are brass rather than gold, make sure they're firmly seated and fully connected when you plug the NIC into an empty bus slot. That is, make sure the edge connector is hidden from view and that the network interface on the side of the card is well positioned in the cutout on the back of your PC case. Don't jam the edge connector into the computer's bus socket; rock it carefully if you must. Too much force can peel the golden fingers away from the edge of the adapter and then nothing works.

You also should screw the metal tab into place, using the screw that attached the placeholder before you removed it. Figure 5-4 shows the placeholder with the screw notch.

You should remember two things about placeholders:

✔ Be careful with the little screw that holds the placeholder in place. If you drop a screw, you can usually get the screw to show itself more readily by picking up the PC case and rocking it gently back and forth. And *don't ever* use a magnetized screwdriver to pick up a screw you've dropped; otherwise, your computer's data may become screw-ee.

Figure 5-4:
Empty slots
are closed
off by
placeholders,
which keep
dust and dirt
out of your
PC case.

✔ Be sure to put the placeholder in a toolbox or spare-parts drawer so that you can find it again. If you ever have to remove the NIC (or any other interface), you will want to be able to seal the case again. Some cases use odd-size placeholders, so things will be a lot easier if you can find the right one when you need it.

How to Read a Manual

The first rule of reading the NIC installation manual is to skip ahead until you find a picture of the NIC with all the important parts highlighted. In a well-thought-out manual, this step can save you the bother of reading the whole thing. Our suggestion: Go for the pictures — we all know what a good picture is worth!

To successfully install NICs, you have to understand *exactly* what you have to do. If you've peered at the pictures and puzzled through the text but you still aren't sure what something is, call the NIC vendor's technical support hotline and ask them to explain it to you. This step can shortcut the learning process and let you check on your drivers at the same time. The wonderful folks at tech support deal with confused people every day, and they can steer you clear of the pitfalls better than anyone else.

NIC Configuration

Configuring your NIC requires making all the right hardware selections and choosing the right software settings. To have your NIC and PC working in perfect harmony, you must deal with a number of different kinds of settings and make sure that the right information is supplied to the software drivers. To understand what this involves, familiarize yourself with the information in this section.

NICcus interruptus

Activity on the network can take place at any time. To receive incoming data and handle outgoing traffic, the NIC must be capable of signaling the CPU and the CPU has to talk to the NIC.

The most common method for handling this type of activity is to reserve an *interrupt request* (IRQ) line for the NIC's exclusive use. PCs offer 16 IRQs, numbered 0 through 15. Interfaces use them to signal activity. Each NIC must have one of a particular restricted range of IRQs selected for its use; no interfaces are allowed to share the same IRQ.

This should help explain why mapping out your existing configuration is a good idea. Your mission here, whether you wish to accept it or not, is to find an unused IRQ that the NIC can accept. If no IRQ is available, you must reconfigure something to free up an IRQ that the NIC can use. (This is why we told you to get out *all* the manuals!)

Setting IRQs usually means setting *DIP switches* (*DIP* stands for dual in-line package) or moving *jumpers*. Some PCs assist in the configuration process or use software-based configuration tools, especially if you're working with EISA, Micro Channel, or Plug and Play systems.

DIPsy doodles

Most DIP switches, which are really banks of individual switches, indicate which way is On and Off. If you can't tell and the manual doesn't help, call the tech-support department right away. They know the answer and this will save you unnecessary and potentially dangerous guessing and experimentation. Figure 5-5 shows a typical DIP switch.

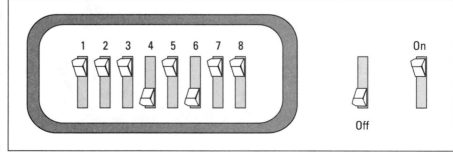

Figure 5-5:
DIP switches and jumper blocks often control the NIC's settings.

Jumping jiminy!

Jumper blocks are made up of two rows of adjacent pins that are connected with teeny-tiny connectors called *jumpers* (see Figure 5-6). The pins are usually numbered. Sliding the jumper over both pins turns the jumper on. To turn a numbered pin set off, remove the jumper from both pins and slide it over one of the two pins so that it sticks out from the pin block. Often, when you are setting IRQs with jumpers, there will be one jumper inserted for an entire block of pins; the pin set you jump with it selects the chosen IRQ. In this case, make sure the jumper covers both pins in the set.

Defaults, dear Brutus . . .

Before worrying about DIP switches or jumpers, check the manual to find out where the factory set the IRQ. If this *default setting* is not in use, you can stick with the default and not do anything. You'll like it when this happens!

Any I/O port in a storm

Each card in a system has a unique I/O port address, with certain addresses reserved for certain interfaces, especially video cards. NICs aren't quite that choosy and normally can get an I/O port address assigned from a reserved range of addresses. This address is generally handled by a DIP switch on most NICs because of the fairly broad range of potential settings available.

Figure 5-6:
A typical
jumper
block.

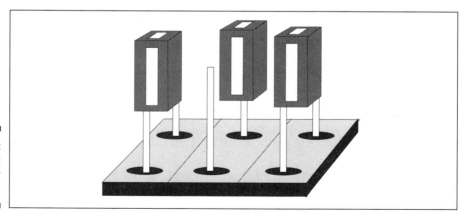

An I/O port is set up to let the computer read from or write to memory that belongs to an interface. When an interrupt is signaled, it tells the computer to read from the I/O port address, indicating incoming data. When the computer wants to send data, it signals the NIC to get ready to receive and writes to that address. The information written to or read from that address is copied across the bus between the NIC and the computer's brain, or CPU.

Computer addresses are often computed in base 16, also called *hexadecimal.* The lowercase *h* after the number tells you that it's hexadecimal, as in the following example:

$$2E0h = 2*16^2 + 14*16 + 0 = 736 \text{ (decimal)}$$

In hexadecimal, the letters *A* through *F* stand for 10 through 15. I/O port addresses for NICs commonly range from 2E0h to 380h; the most common default port I/O address is 300h. However, 300h is a common default for lots of interfaces, so you still have to do your configuration homework before letting your NIC use that address.

Direct access: setting the DMA

Some NICs use a technique called *direct-memory access* (*DMA*) to move information between the NIC and the CPU. The result is fast copying of information from the computer's memory to the NIC, and vice versa. This technique has become less necessary (and less common) as computers and equipment have become faster.

DMA matches up two areas of memory: one on the computer and the other on the NIC. Writing to the memory area on the computer automatically copies data to the NIC, and vice versa. *Setting a DMA address* means finding an unoccupied DMA memory block to assign to your NIC. Again, your earlier research on what settings are already taken will help you avoid conflicts. Just choose an unoccupied block and make the right NIC settings. If you get a conflict, you'll have to figure out a way to resolve it. Remember to check your defaults here, too.

Running the bases: the MemBase setting

NICs contain their own RAM, called *buffer space*, to provide working room to store information coming on and off the network. This buffer space must be assigned an equivalent region in the PC's memory. For DOS and Windows, this area is usually located in the high memory area between 640K and 1024K.

Just as with IRQs and DMA, this setting must be unique. Watch out for potential address conflicts and steer around them. You usually use jumpers to set the base memory address (MemBase) for your NIC. Common settings for network cards include C000h, D000h, and D800h.

If a NIC card is on the Hardware Compatibility List, a possible configuration is probably listed, too, and you won't have to figure everything out. But you'll have to choose basic elements even in the Windows NT environment — including the IRQ and sometimes the base I/O address and the DMA settings. Also, be sure to check your NIC's installation software before you install Windows NT: Even today, many NICs include only DOS installation software. Therefore, you'll need to install the card under DOS, and then install Windows NT (which will probably detect the card's configuration on its own, without requiring any of your help, thank you very much).

In the Driver's Seat

Now that the hardware is in place, it's time to deal with the software. If your NIC is of recent vintage, the drivers on the disk that comes with it may actually be worth something.

In this case — which we rank right up there with your chances of winning the Powerball lottery — you can load the disk, run an installation program, supply a few values here and there, and be ready to roll. If you're not lucky, you'll have to chase down new drivers.

Our advice: Always determine the latest and greatest drivers for your NICs before you begin the installation process. Ask for help in the following order:

1. **From the outfit that sold you the card.**

2. **From the vendor that built the card.**

3. **On CompuServe, GO MSFF and use either NDIS or ODI as keywords in the File Finder. You can also try MSN or the Internet, where Windows NT drivers are also available. For more information about CompuServe, MSN, and the Internet — all good sources for LAN drivers — see Appendix B.**

If the NIC driver installation isn't automated, you may have to manually edit configuration files such as AUTOEXEC.BAT and CONFIG.SYS. If you're running Windows, you may also have to edit SYSTEM.INI to insert the correct .DRV (driver) reference. As always, when in doubt, get some help.

Cabling Up to the NIC

Okay, the software is installed and the hardware is plugged in. All that's left is cabling the NIC to the network. For modular technologies such as twisted-pair ARCnet, Ethernet, or token ring, that means plugging the LAN cable's modular connector into the receptacle on the NIC. For other technologies, it means hooking up a T-connector or a transceiver cable from the LAN to your NIC. Whichever option you have to use, make sure the connection is tight and the NIC is solidly seated in its slot. Then you're ready to fire it up.

Looking for Trouble in All the Right Places

You've navigated through the maze of potential address conflicts and have set your NIC to steer clear of all shoals. The software has been installed, so everything should work, right? Well, sometimes it does (loud cheers and much laughter) and sometimes it doesn't (grinding and gnashing of teeth). You find out that things don't work in one of three ways:

✔ **Your PC doesn't boot.** This one is obvious. When it happens, it's time to start undoing what you just did. First, restore the system to the way it was before you started fiddling around. (You *do* have a backup, right?) If it works, you know that the NIC is the problem. It's time to get some help from one of the recommended sources. If your system still doesn't work when you're back at square one, you have bigger problems. Time to call in a service tech.

✔ **Your PC boots, but it doesn't load the drivers.** The most common reasons for a failure to load drivers follow:

- **Loose connections.** Check to make sure that the wire is tight and properly seated on the NIC, and make sure that it's plugged into something on the other end.

- **Installation problems.** Make sure that the drivers are in the right directory and that the directory is directly referenced in your bootup files or defined in your DOS PATH. If the computer can't see the drivers, it can't use them. Because Windows NT will actively search your hard drives for drivers (as long as your NIC is on the Hardware Compatibility List), this won't normally be a problem for NT machines.

- **Conflict!** You might have missed something and introduced a configuration conflict. Try all your other stuff; it's a dead giveaway if something else has also quit working. Time to go back to square one and recheck all system settings. Something somewhere is squirrely, so be especially careful.

The good news here is that the problem is most likely a loose connection or a configuration boo-boo. If it's not one of those, it's time to get serious.

✔ **You try to use the network, but it doesn't respond.** This is a subtle variant of the second problem and usually has one or more of the same causes. There's an extra layer of mystery here, though, because the conflict could be with another application rather than a driver problem. Or the network might be stymied by an incorrect NIC, an incorrect network configuration, or an invalid login sequence (that is, the software works okay but you're telling it to do the wrong stuff). You have to work your way through a careful process of elimination to find an answer. Good luck and take lots of breaks. Remember, you can always ask for help!

After you've made it over any humps and can talk to the network, you're ready to get to work. Or if you're a fledgling network administrator, you'll have the pleasure of getting someone else to work. Either way, you have pushed the networking wave another workstation ahead.

Chapter 6

This LAN Is Your LAN

....

....

*B*y now, you've been introduced to most of the basic networking principles. You should also have a pretty good idea about how things are supposed to work. As you spend time around networks, however, you'll soon realize that what they *do* isn't nearly as important as what you *know* about what they do. And whether you wrestle with networks regularly or occasionally, you'll quickly discover that there's nothing like a network map to help you find things on the network and keep track of what's on the network.

Time to Make a Map

We recommend that you produce more than just a map that simply indicates where things are located on the network — although that's certainly where you should start. That kind of map should include the following information:

- A list of all computers on your network, with supporting documentation

- A list of all networking equipment — including such things as routers, hubs, and servers — with supporting documentation

- A list of all printers and other specialized equipment on the network, with supporting documentation

- Lines to indicate where network cable runs, and where junctions, taps, and other items are located

Formalizing Your Network Map

Because a network map is so important and such a powerful tool, pause right here and make one immediately. Be prepared to spend time at this; most of the information you need is probably scattered all over the place.

Building a detailed network map is a worthwhile investment, paying for itself many times over. At worst, you will learn more than you ever wanted to know (but not more than you'll ever *need* to know) about your network. At best, you will become so intimately acquainted with your network that it will be unlikely to throw you any curve balls — and you may even find some things to tweak and correct in the process.

Start at the beginning

It will help a great deal if you can get your hands on a set of your building's architectural drawings or engineering plans. If you do, go to an architectural supply house and have copies made that you can mark up and use as your base map. (Most copying technology uses an ammonia-based system called a blueline. You can copy even large-size plans for less than $20 a piece.) If a professional cabling outfit installed your cable, you should be able to get a copy of its cabling plans, which will also work nicely as a master for your network map.

If these plans are not available, you'll have to sketch a room-by-room layout on rectangular grid paper (such as an engineering pad), marking the location of machines, approximate locations for cable runs, and so on.

Put it on the map

Anything that merits attention or costs money is worth recording on your map. You don't need to go into detail about each and every connector or note the exact length of every cable. (Approximate lengths to within a yard or so are useful, however.) Indicate every major cable run, every computer, and every piece of gear attached to the network.

You probably won't have enough room to write all this information on the map itself. Therefore, you should key information to a machine or cable name and record the details in a file on your computer. Or if you prefer a more idiosyncratic scheme, that's fine. Whichever scheme you follow, use it religiously. In addition, include brief notes describing how the scheme works so that someone else can follow it if needed.

Building a Network Inventory

The information you gather in producing your network map will build a detailed inventory. Unfortunately, you will quickly find that this is a *lot* of information. Make things easier on yourself (and your successor) by coming up with a template or form that you can fill out for each item. This ensures that you collect consistent information — and makes it that much easier to delegate the information gathering to someone else. Your inventory should include all the following information for each computer on the network:

✔ The hardware configuration, including a list of all interfaces and their configuration settings, information about installed RAM and drives, and the make and model of the keyboard, display, and so on. If you can find out who sold you the equipment, write that down, too.

Keeping track of equipment is typically the responsibility of the accounting department. Check with them for a copy of your company's capital asset inventory (if any). This should list all the serial numbers and other identification for hardware on the network. If no one in your company has this information already, go ahead and collect it. It's valuable.

✔ The software configuration, which should include listings of configuration files, the operating system (including version number) installed, as well as a list of programs and versions installed on the machine.

✔ The network configuration, including the make and model of the NIC and a list of driver files with names, version numbers, dates, and sizes. (Editing a DOS DIR or similar directory listing should do the trick here.)

For other equipment (such as hubs, routers, and printers), your inventory should include the following:

✔ The manufacturer, model, make, and serial number. If the equipment uses memory modules or disk drives, get the information about them, too. If the equipment uses software, get the software information, too.

✔ A list of all the cable segments on the network. Give each a name or a number, and key information to that identifier. Record the type and make of cable, its length, the locations of its ends, and other significant connections.

✔ A list of all the vendors who have worked on your network or its machines, complete with names and phone numbers. This list can be a valuable resource for technical support. Over time, you will want to add the names and phone numbers of tech-support people who prove to be knowledgeable and helpful.

Essentially, the information you compile while producing a network map will be a database of everything anyone needs to know about your network. The network map is an honest-to-Pete computer database for all this information, although file- or paper-based approaches should be fine. Whatever method you use, be sure your inventory is complete and kept up to date.

Keeping Up with Developments

One thing you can be sure of with networks: They keep changing. Your map is only as good as the information in it. And it's only useful if the information is an accurate reflection of the real world.

Whenever anything changes on the network, make updating the map and its database a priority. It's much less work to sit down and look at a map than it is to walk around and look at actual objects. If the map is current, you can keep on top of things from the comfort of your office. If it's out of date, you better start walking.

Getting Software to Work for You

If your budget allows, you can buy software products to help you maintain your map. Many management consoles include the capability to merge an electronic map of your network that the console finds by a set of scanned-in site plans. Some also include electronic links to the kind of database that can accommodate the information we have recommended that you collect. Although you still have to collect the data that goes into the database, the infrastructure is predefined. Microsoft's System Management, which is part of the Back Office Suite Services (SMS), is worth investigating.

Although third-party alternatives for network inventory are not always network-management products per se, they cost much less — typically, from $300 to $500 per file server. We recommend taking a look at LAN Directory from Frye Computer Systems (a division of Seagate Technology, Inc.), BindView from BindView Technologies, or LAN Auditor from Horizons Technology. All these products offer great database support for network inventories.

After you have built a network map and a database, you have to make a commitment to keep things up to date. This is a real relationship you should be starting. Like any good relationship, it requires maintenance. The lesson here is to stay current. Otherwise, you'll wind up lost following a map that leads to where things *used* to be. Make sure that your map and your database reflect what's out there today.

Chapter 7
Living Off Your LAN

*G*etting a network up and running is — as you have no doubt noticed — a significant accomplishment as well as a genuine milestone. Keeping it running is no less of a challenge, but it doesn't seem to have the same glamour as making something out of nothing. You might think that all the fun has ended when you finally get your network installed and working. In fact, the fun is just beginning, and it will continue for some time as more and more users become familiar with the network and begin to appreciate what it can do for them.

Keeping your network running will become one of the most important jobs you ever do. The trick is to spend time on that task and to anticipate, rather than react to, your users' needs. Proactive is always better than reactive, and in this chapter, you get some tips about how to get proactive with your network. More important, you get the information you need to stay proactive as things change — as you can bet the rent they will.

Paying Now or Praying Later

Look at your network from the perspective of keeping up with its parts and keeping everything working. Although we can't be certain about what you *do* see, we can be confident about what you *should* see:

> ✔ A collection of user machines that belong to the folks who use the network
>
> ✔ A collection of servers and related paraphernalia that provide services to those users
>
> ✔ A conglomeration of cables and, possibly, hubs, routers, or other gear

Each of these is something that somebody uses some of the time, except the servers and the communications media, which are things that everybody uses all the time. Unfortunately, nobody except the person or group responsible for the network is really aware of, let alone wants to manage, all this stuff.

The sad truth is that when a network is doing its job, no one notices, and when it's not working, everyone does. Your job boils down to maintaining the state of cheerful oblivion, which is the hallmark of a well-run network.

Contented users are quiet users

It's a given that you would rather get no attention than have to face the collective ire of your user base. What does it take to achieve such ignorant bliss? In a word, the answer is _maintenance_.

If you keep things running smoothly and shield your users from changes and other sources of discomfort, you may be in the enviable position of being left alone. If you don't, you will be the scapegoat of all and the envy of no one. We know what position we'd choose.

What can you do to make them leave you alone?

When your network is running smoothly and efficiently, you can concentrate on doing your real job without a lot of interruptions from cranky users. Here are a few secrets to keeping them quiet.

Keep the network running at all costs

When network service is interrupted, users become riled. The safest course is to make sure that the network stays up during prime working hours, no matter what contortions you have to go through to make this happen. Even jumping through hoops is a small price to pay for office harmony.

Schedule downtime and spread the word

Every network has to go down occasionally. Such things as backing up the server, as well as most changes to equipment or cabling, can slow things down to the point where the network might as well be out of service.

Schedule these events outside normal working hours, preferably at least a week in advance. Let users know so that the folks who are working late (or early) aren't unpleasantly surprised. You would be amazed at how vicious some people can get when they find that their plans to catch up on last-minute changes or to meet a tight deadline have been eighty-sixed by an unavailable system.

Keep an eye out for trouble

At least half the problems that arise on a network will come as no surprise to anybody who's been paying attention. So pay attention and nip trouble in the bud. If you think that dragons are bad, wait till your users are breathing down your neck.

Educated users are better than ignoramuses

Even when time is tight, it's always easier to answer a question once. Whenever upgrades or additions force changes on your network, let your users know ahead of time what things are going to change and the effect these changes might have on their work. After you make the changes, tell them again, and provide more details about how they will have to deal with the brave new world.

When changes involve upgrading software or changing applications, a little anticipatory training can do wonders in alleviating anxiety.

Keep an eye on growth

It's been said that nothing succeeds like success, and networks are a particularly good instance of this. As your users develop a taste for working with networks, they will almost certainly bang on the network in ways you couldn't possibly imagine. Be ready to grow — and be ready for all that growing entails.

Get your report card regularly

Make the time to check with your users regularly. Don't just ask what they think of the network. Ask them what they want to be able to do and what they want to be able to do easier. The idea is to provide value to your users and to make them better at their jobs. Giving them what they want isn't enough; you also have to prod them to want more than they think they need.

Staying in touch with your users and keeping them informed builds a base of loyal advocates. It also builds you a reputation for getting things accomplished.

Upgrades, Uprevs, and One-upmanship

Living with networks means dealing with a constantly changing landscape. The technology changes as it becomes cheaper and faster. The software changes as it becomes more powerful and adds features. Users change as they discover new and more innovative ways to use network services.

To maintain your network, you have to anticipate and plan for changes. To ensure that all change will be for the better, we strongly recommend scheduling regular network maintenance. Because change is inevitable, why not plan for it and allocate specific times for dealing with it? The worst thing that can happen is that you get to your maintenance period and not have to do anything special to fill the time. If our experience is any indicator, this won't be a problem.

When it comes to software upgrades or new releases, consider taking some extra time to test new releases before inflicting them on your users. At the very least, keep old versions around and available on the network. That way, if the new stuff doesn't work out, your users can easily go back to the previous version.

It's almost always up to you to control the pace of change and take advantage of new releases and new software in a way that best fits your schedule and your users' needs. Random change is the most difficult to tolerate. Train your users and the rest should be easy.

Getting Help When You Need It

Most of the time, networks, like governments, just chug along in a steady state of equilibrium, shifting only with user demand. When things change, however, the network becomes stressed. That's when it is most likely to break down. When you're planning to make changes, plan for the possibility of some unforeseen side effects to the changes. Then, if things do break down, you are ready with Plan B. (For example, suppose that you trash your server during an upgrade. If you have a second machine around, you could turn it into a server temporarily by installing your latest backup from the original machine. That way, you still have a server on Monday morning when everybody shows up at work.)

Before moving on to Plan B, here are some things you can do:

- Schedule major changes over three-day weekends. This practice gives you an extra day to get things working.

- Find out how to contact technical support before you roll up your sleeves and start unplugging things. If this is one of those three-day weekend jobs, make sure that tech support also is planning to work the extra day. Bribery is okay.

> ✔ Find out whether your reseller (the folks who took your money for the original product) or your vendor (the folks who built the system or software and who took your money for the upgrade) can arrange to have someone on tap to help in case things get out of hand. As Hunter S. Thompson says, "When the going gets weird, the weird turn pro," so find out who the pros are at your reseller or vendor.

You should need Plan B only if things become so messed up that you cannot get back to where you started by the time everyone shows up at work on Monday morning. For Plan B, you should arrange to beg, borrow, or steal (metaphorically speaking) a replacement unit for whatever unit is being mucked around with. Then, if worst comes to worst, you can use it to replace your screwed-up system with a reasonable facsimile. Count this ploy as successful if the users never mention it.

Basically, plan for disaster, but hope for a miracle. Be ready to deal with the former. If the latter takes place, you can enjoy a free weekend, just like the rest of the staff.

Building a Routine

The key to successful network maintenance is building a familiar routine. By scheduling regular maintenance, you train all your users — including management — to expect and accommodate change. This also lets you control how and when things change, so that you can plan to deal with potential problems.

The best thing about a routine is that you are prepared for changes. The worst thing that can happen is that you become stuck, unable to go forward or backward. If you're ready for this contingency, you can fire up Plan B and keep right on going.

Maybe consistency really *is* the hobgoblin of little minds. But when it comes to your network, hobgoblins beat gremlins every time.

Noticing the Obvious

Paying attention is a crucial element in maintenance of any kind. When the painters, the air conditioning guys, or the plumbers come calling, keep an eye on them, especially if they're going spelunking in the areas where your network lives. When the electricians come calling, make sure that they know the difference between the conduit for electricity and the one for network cables. Believe us: You'll hate it if they get it wrong. Another concern — and one that is the bane of campus networks — is the guy with the backhoe. More networks have died from a backhoe in the wrong place than you would believe.

Keep your eyes peeled and your ears tuned to your users. And by the way, we recommend keeping up with the latest gossip; the office grapevine can often help you stay ahead of malign influences that could put the hex on your network.

Keeping It Clean

Cleanliness is next to godliness, especially when it comes to resources that everybody shares. Consider the company refrigerator down in the break room. If no one posted a sign saying "Anything left in here over the weekend will be tossed on Monday morning," who knows what life forms would be crawling over the hinges in a month or two?

Your network server is the electronic equivalent of the company refrigerator. Everybody uses it, but nobody wants to keep it clean. And sooner or later, everybody leaves the electronic equivalent of a tuna casserole that's been there since last Christmas.

To keep your network running smoothly, you have to deal with all that unsightly buildup that develops. Fortunately, your network can help you. You can set up the file system on a server so that it limits the amount of disk space users have to play with. If you keep this number low, you can make your users clean up after themselves. For the truly lackadaisical, purge files that haven't been accessed for X days (you choose the number). Or you can use storage migration to copy unused files from the disk drive to a magneto-optical disk or to tape.

From a system perspective, you should keep old versions of software around for a while after adding new ones. But when everything new is old (again) — typically, after one or two months — remember to ditch the even older stuff. If you're truly conservative, you can let the arrival of the next new version seal the fate of the version that's one generation back from the one you're using. That way, you have only two copies of stuff around all the time.

Disk space keeps getting cheaper and the "disk farms" attached to servers keep getting bigger. But it's still worth your while to keep files pruned. After all, you have to make room for all those Windows applications.

Beyond the Network

Our last maintenance tip is to consider the world beyond the network from time to time. The network is usually just one piece of your business, and you should consider the effect of losing other parts of your company's systems. (We know that your network is the most absorbing thing there is, but get a life!)

For example, what happens if the mainframe goes south? What about the phone system? Or even worse, if the whole place goes up in flames, leaving nothing but a charred skeleton?

This stuff falls under the heading of disaster recovery. If any part of your company's business is entrusted to the network, it is essential that you have a plan for recovering from its complete and utter destruction. If all the company business is on the network, that plan becomes imperative.

Consultants can help you devise a disaster recovery plan for a fee, but their advice boils down to a few essentials that we herewith give you free of charge:

- ✔ Always have multiple system backups. (For a thorough discussion of backups, see Chapter 23.)
- ✔ Store at least one backup set off-site (preferably in a fireproof vault or safe).
- ✔ Make arrangements for emergency access to systems similar to yours for fallback use. These arrangements are expensive, but at least you can get back to work without losing everything.

Bear in mind that this kind of planning always seems like overkill until the unthinkable happens.

Part II
The Wonder of Workgroups

The 5th Wave

By Rich Tennant

Wait a minute - since when does our LAN contract include 50 terminals, 6 printers, and 8 "Mr. Bean" espresso machines?

In this part . . .

*H*ere, we introduce you to the Workstation side of the Windows world, which includes some usable networking facilities to let machines share files, printers, and other resources. While Windows NT Workstations are networking, any two machines can take the role of client or server as circumstances dictate, and then change roles at will. This kind of networking is called *peer to peer,* which indicates that all machines have the same capabilities.

If the benefits of networking sound interesting, but you're not ready for a full-blown Windows NT Server network, you might want to think about using Windows NT Workstation's built-in capabilities to tie some of your PCs together. It's usually adequate for groups of up to five or ten users, and pretty economical, too! In the next four chapters, you get an overview of Windows NT Workstation, discover how to install the software, understand how to use its networking capabilities, and explore its relevance to your networking needs. By the time you're finished, you should know whether the networking delivered by Windows NT Workstation can deliver all the networking services you need.

Chapter 8

Taking the "WORK" Out
of NT Workstation

In This Chapter

▶ Groping toward group-think

▶ Perceiving the peer-to-peer schmeer

▶ Understanding that small is beautiful or less is more (more or less)

▶ Teaching users to administer their own workgroups

▶ Introducing crucialware: hardware and software

▶ Choosing a winner: NT Server versus NT Workstation

*W*hen is an NT Workstation network (a workgroup network) appropriate? When is NT Server the right stuff? In this chapter, we answer these questions through more self-analysis than Sigmund Freud at a Tony Robbins seminar. The network ends justify the network means, and the network means can be really mean if you aren't careful. Think about what you need your network to do today — and in the next two years. Every hour you spend planning now will save you many hours later.

A Group-er Isn't Just a Big Fish

NT Workstation uses a concept called a *workgroup* to allow users to share files and printers on a network. If you're familiar with Microsoft Windows for Workgroups, you'll feel right at home with NT Workstation. In a workgroup-style network, usually no one machine is designated as a server. Instead, every machine has the capability to share files and printers with every other user. (You don't have to share your files or printers though.)

This type of networking is called peer-to-peer because each workstation is equal in network stature to every other workstation. They are all peers! Hmmm . . . let's peer deeper into this peer-to-peer peerage. For a graphic look at the peer-to-peer design, check out Figure 8-1.

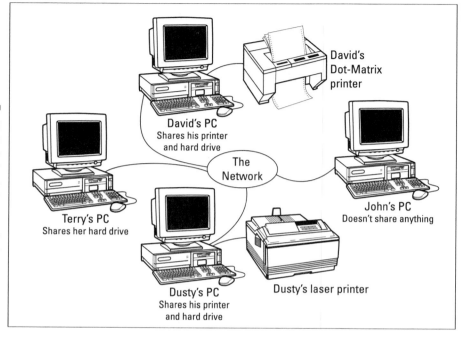

Figure 8-1:
Workgroups
use
peer-to-peer
networking,
where all
users have
the option to
share their
files or
printers with
other users
on the
network.

David's
Dot-Matrix
printer

David's PC
Shares his printer
and hard drive

The
Network

John's PC
Doesn't share anything

Terry's PC
Shares her hard drive

Dusty's laser printer

Dusty's PC
Shares his printer
and hard drive

Blue velvet workgroups

Remember that the physical network — that is, the network's wires, hubs, and such — can host many different groups of individuals, who may be grouped by department, hair color, or dessert preference. When you browse the network, you'll typically see only the resources that are available to your workgroup, plus those that are available universally to everyone, irrespective of workgroup membership.

The workgroup concept, like those big velvet ropes at the movie theater, is simply a way to cordon off your network. Each workstation belongs to a workgroup. Only the users in each workgroup can see the other workstations in that workgroup. For instance, you can create an NT workgroup for each department in your company: the Dweeb workgroup for your MIS department, the BeanCounters workgroup for the accounting department, and so on. When you log on to your machine every morning, you are also logging on to your particular workgroup. You can then access the shared files and printers available on every workstation in your workgroup.

Hey, wait! You mean everyone on my network can see everything on my hard drive and send huge print jobs to my printer? Negatory, good buddy. A user must not only belong to your workgroup, but also have *rights* to access a resource on the network. Suppose you install NT Workstation on your PC and elect to share your printer with other users. NT will create a *share* (which is shorthand for a shared resource) for your printer and initially allow everyone in your workgroup to access your printer. You can then assign access only to those users whom you want to use your printer.

The same access control procedure applies to the directories on your hard drive, too. We discuss how to control access to your directories and printers in more detail in Chapter 9.

Group-ers swim peer-to-peer

The term *peer-to-peer* implies that everyone is on equal terms. A peer-to-peer network is the ideal choice for small networks without a need for a central file and print server. In a peer-to-peer network, each user has the ability to share his or her local files and printers with other users in the workgroup. Each user also has the ability to use the files and printers of others in the workgroup. Sort of an all-for-one and one-for-all mentality.

Peer-to-peer is also the ideal choice when no one has time to administer the network or if it isn't feasible to dedicate one machine to the full-time duties of a file server or print server. Peer-to-peer networks distribute the administration duties to each user. You control access to your stuff, and everyone else controls access to their stuff. This is in keeping with the equality principles of peer-to-peer networking. No one person is responsible for keeping the network "up." You also make the network more resilient by distributing the shared programs, files, and printers across multiple PCs. This can be both a strength and a weakness of peer-to-peer networks, as you find out next.

There are some drawbacks to peer-to-peer networks. The most obvious drawback is that you can't use a resource on a computer that isn't turned on. If Mabel in marketing turns her machine off before going to lunch, anyone using a file or printer that Mabel shares with the network is dead in the water. Peer-to-peer networking requires some education and self-discipline on the part of each user. Even if your machine locks up and you can't get your programs to run, someone else may still be using your printer or one of your files. Hence, always notify the other members of the workgroup before rebooting or turning off your machine. Give them time to save open files or finish their print jobs before you shut down.

Another weakness is performance. Your super-fast Pentium-based PC's screaming performance can be reduced to a crawl when ten users are banging away on your hard drive or when that guy in advertising sends 400-gigabyte print jobs to your little DinkyJet printer. This is one reason why NT Workstation allows you to set the maximum number of simultaneous users for each shared resource.

We touch more on NT workstation performance issues in the next two chapters. For now, realize that you do not get the same speed in a peer-to-peer network as you do in a server-based network if more than a dozen users are trying to access any one resource. Keep this in mind when planning your network. You are working on a network plan, aren't you?

Isn't size what counts?

You bet size is what counts. But more importantly, the right size is what counts. There is no one perfect type of network for everyone, which is why Microsoft sells NT Workstation and NT Server. We believe that NT Workstation and its workgroup concept are the perfect way to implement a network in a small office or where less than fifteen users need to share files or printers. Peer-to-peer computing is the most cost-effective solution for people in this situation. As the number of users begins to grow, you can segment your users into distinct workgroups of ten to fifteen users per workgroup to keep things manageable.

After you have about ten users for a particular resource or more than fifty users on your network, we suggest that you install at least one NT Server and transfer all your workgroup users to members of an NT domain. Domains make it much easier to share many resources among many users. We discuss more about NT domains than you'll ever want to know in Chapter 18.

Who's in charge?

So if everyone is responsible for controlling the access to their own files and printers, who is in charge of the network as a whole? We suggest that someone act as the network coordinator in a peer-to-peer network situation. This person can act as a combination of schoolmarm and network cheerleader, reminding users to police their PCs for unused network files that can quickly fill up local hard drives while serving to keep network resources available to all.

Serve It Up Hot and Fresh!

Now you know all about the workgroup concept and peer-to-peer networks. What about those things called servers? Servers operate in a different type of environment than a workgroup network. On a server-based network, most network resources are centralized on the server (or servers, if you've got more than one). You can store network editions of software on a server, you can hang printers off a server, and you can put backup devices in a server. Check out the look of a server-based network in Figure 8-2.

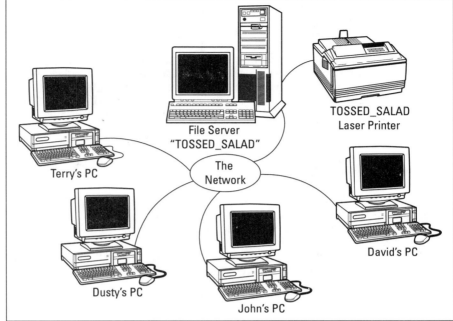

Figure 8-2:
Server-
based
networks
centralize
most
network
resources
on the file
server itself.

Most medium-sized and large companies use server-based networks. Server-based systems are *scalable*, which means that it is easy to increase or shrink the network as needs change. If your users notice that a server's response is slowing, you can analyze your server's resources and see whether the server itself is overloaded. If so, you can easily add another server to your network and split the resources — and, therefore, the load — between the two servers.

Server-based networks are also easily segregated according to departmental or organizational needs. One server could serve print-and-file requests for the marketing department. Another server could provide network resources for the sales department, and so on.

Problems with server-based networks can become more evident when your organization begins to develop needs that cross functional boundaries. When users in the sales department need access to an application on the marketing server, for example, you may begin to see conflicts between departmental servers. NT combats many of these problems with the domain concept, which allows named groups of individuals to cross organizational boundaries with ease and helps to break the identification of specific servers with specific organizational units.

The NT *domain* concept defines resources to the network itself instead of to individual resources. For example, you can create a printer share called Daniels_Printer on the NT server in the shipping department. With NT domains, you don't have to log on to the shipping server to gain access to Daniels_Printer. You simply log on to the domain itself and gain access to all the network resources that the administrator has granted to your user name. As a user, all you need to know is the name of the printer, Daniels_Printer, not to which server and port the printer is physically connected. This key feature of NT makes it much easier for network users to navigate the network.

If you know a shared resource's name, you don't need any other details to access that resource — assuming you have sufficient rights to do so. In the old paradigm, shown in Figure 8-3, you had to physically log on to each server that held a resource to which you needed access. Compare this with the domain concept shown in Figure 8-4.

Back in the old days, when networks were departmental in scope, we had little use or need for domain-based servers. Now, most companies with more than a few hundred users require a method such as the NT domain concept to control access to network resources around a single site or around the world.

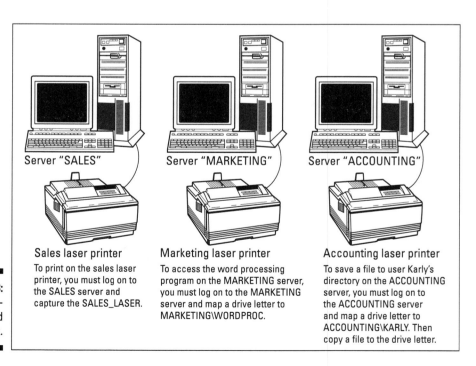

Figure 8-3:
Resource-
based
network.

Server "SALES"   Server "MARKETING"   Server "ACCOUNTING"

Sales laser printer

To print on the sales laser printer, you must log on to the SALES server and capture the SALES_LASER.

Marketing laser printer

To access the word processing program on the MARKETING server, you must log on to the MARKETING server and map a drive letter to MARKETING\WORDPROC.

Accounting laser printer

To save a file to user Karly's directory on the ACCOUNTING server, you must log on to the ACCOUNTING server and map a drive letter to ACCOUNTING\KARLY. Then copy a file to the drive letter.

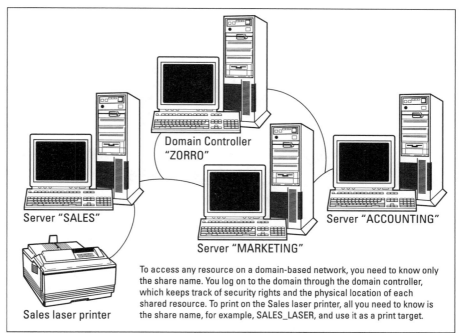

Figure 8-4:
Domain-based network.

Domain Controller "ZORRO"

Server "SALES"

Server "MARKETING"

Server "ACCOUNTING"

Sales laser printer

To access any resource on a domain-based network, you need to know only the share name. You log on to the domain through the domain controller, which keeps track of security rights and the physical location of each shared resource. To print on the Sales laser printer, all you need to know is the share name, for example, SALES_LASER, and use it as a print target.

Hard and Soft: These Are the Wares

Microsoft NT, both in Workstation and Server editions, is a capable but complicated operating system that can tax your existing hardware and software to the max. NT may not run on some of your hardware, and some of your software may not run on NT. If you are buying new hardware, your PC hardware vendor should be able to help ascertain whether the hardware you have or are ordering is NT-compatible.

Software is another matter. NT has been available long enough now that many software publishers are offering native NT versions of their software, in other words, software written and compiled specifically to run under NT. Eventually, most popular software titles will be rewritten to run natively under NT. For now, if you have any doubts about running a particular program under NT, please contact the software publisher to verify that the program runs under NT.

Get Ready to Rumble!

So you're sitting there wondering whether you should go with an NT Workstation-based, workgroup-style network or a traditional, NT Server-based domain network. Here's some good news for those stuck in this quandary: You can use both schemes together because NT Workstation and NT Server can happily coexist. However, we recommend this strategy mostly for migration from a workgroup network to a server-based network.

Departmental workgroups can share all their resources through the peer-to-peer network built into NT Workstation while an NT Server chugs along on the same network, and users can be logged on to both simultaneously.

Let's take a look at the attributes of NT Workstation:

- Uses a peer-to-peer network architecture
- Puts each user in charge of his or her shared resources
- Is appropriate for small networks or departmental workgroups
- PCs sharing resources must be turned on for sharing to occur
- If a user reboots his or her PC while a shared file is in use, other network users can lose their work or get corrupt data
- Decentralizes network resources and administration
- Each workstation must be backed up to ensure that network files are available
- Only NT Workstation, Windows 95, and Windows for Workgroups clients can log on to the workgroup
- Is a less expensive way to network; no dedicated PC required (even cheaper: use Windows 95 machines)
- Does not have the same high level of security found in NT Server

Now let's take a look at the attributes of NT Server:

- Uses a hierarchical network structure
- Allows centralization of network resources and administration
- Provides a very high level of resource security
- Generally requires a network administrator to care for and feed the server(s)
- The server is a single point of failure for the entire network: When the server goes down, no one can access network resources
- Backup of network files and programs is simplified due to the centralized location
- Cost is higher due to the dedicated server PC
- Server resources are available to NT Workstation, Windows 95, Windows for Workgroups, UNIX, OS/2, and Macintosh clients

So, which do you use in what kind of situation? How to choose, how to choose? If you have a small, local network where users simply want to be able to share files and printers among each other, the workgroup network concept works fine. Remember, though, that workgroup networks are not as secure as server-based networks. Dialing into workgroup networks is not as easy as dialing into server-based networks. And once the total number of users is more than about fifty, you will spend a lot more time administering a peer-to-peer, workgroup-based network than you would a similar-sized server-based network.

Distribute the net, distribute the problems

Not only do you succeed in distributing the network responsibilities with a workgroup-based network, you also distribute the potential for problems. This distribution of network resources has both a good side and a bad side.

The good side is that there is no one single point of failure in a workgroup network. Each machine shares its resources with the net. If one user turns his or her machine off, only the resources shared from that one machine will be removed. All other network resources remain unaffected. If Lydia in accounting reboots her PC due to a Windows problem, only her hard drive and printer are removed from the network. The bad side of workgroup networks is that same situation: If Lydia reboots her PC, those users connected to her PC risk losing their work.

Serve you?

With server-based networks, you can put all user data on a single machine, provide nightly backups, and have only one place to administer the security of network resources. This situation also gives you a single point of failure. If the server crashes, everyone on the network loses access to their network drives and printers.

As you can see, pros and cons exist to each approach. In our infinite wisdom, we recommend a server-based network when the network is crucial to the success of your business goals. It's easier and cheaper to make a server machine resilient to network problems than to make every user's PC live up to the same standards as servers. Windows NT gives you the best of both worlds in that you can configure NT Server as a server-based network or NT Workstation as a workgroup-based product.

When choosing a network design, be sure to plan for your network needs in two years. Proper planning will help you choose the smartest solution now and avoid the pitfall of having to redesign everything when user demands overload your network infrastructure.

Chapter 9

Take the Stall Out of the Install

In This Chapter

▶ Taking minimum requirements to the maximum

▶ Doing the boot scootin' bootup

▶ Defining your kingdom: users and their passwords

▶ Learning to share and share alike

▶ Connecting clients to your workstation

▶ Printing 'til you're squinting

▶ Troubleshooting

Min to the Max

What will it take to install this new-fangled NT Workstation software? Well, according to Microsoft, Windows NT Workstation requires a minimum hardware configuration, as shown in Table 9-1, but can also use optional hardware.

Table 9-1	Minimum and Optional Requirements for Intel-Based PCs
System Resources	*Microsoft's Recommendations*
Processor	Any 486 or Pentium
RAM	12MB
Available hard disk space	90MB
Monitor	VGA (any size)
CD-ROM	2x or faster required

The first big requirement is that your PC must sport a 32-bit processor. That's geek-speak for saying you must have a 386, 486, or Pentium processor powering your PC. Here's a hint. Although NT will technically run on a 386 PC, we don't recommend it. You can grow old waiting for NT to boot up on a 386. As for your 486, it works a little better than a 386, but you will still yearn for more power.

We think that the minimum processor requirements listed in the NT Workstation documentation are a bunch of horse pooey. With NT running on anything less than a Pentium, you'll spend more time waiting than working. The faster the Pentium, the better. Of course, if you have the budget for a PowerPC or DEC Alpha chip — both of which also run Windows NT — you'll want it to be as fast as possible, too!

Let's put an end to all the myths in Microsoft's minimum requirements list. Table 9-2 shows you the official *Windows NT Networking For Dummies* minimum equipment list for NT Workstation.

Table 9-2	Minimum Requirements for a Usable NT Workstation
System Resources	*Recommendations*
Processor	Pentium 90 MHz or faster
RAM	16MB for NT Workstation 32MB for NT Server
Available hard disk space	500MB for NT Workstation 1GB for NT Server
Monitor	17" or larger Super VGA
CD-ROM	8x or faster recommended

The Pentium keeps things zipping along at a quick pace. The Super VGA display adapter allows you to open lots of windows and enjoy eye-popping graphics. The 17-inch monitor keeps you from having to squint due to the high-resolution VGA adapter. The 16 megabytes of RAM help you avoid the constant grinding of your hard drive as NT swaps stuff to and from the hard drive. (See the "Swapping your life away" sidebar.) The 500 megabytes of free disk space will provide lots of room to grow without running out of disk space. Sure, NT may only require 120 megabytes or so to install successfully (on a Pentium, that is — it's around 150 megabytes on RISC-based machines), but if you don't have a few hundred megabytes available when you've finished installing, where are you going to put all the cool new programs you buy for your new NT machine?

Microsoft says a mouse is optional. Get real. It's a graphical user interface (GUI). Have you ever tried to navigate a GUI without a mouse? You can do it with keyboard shortcuts, but why bother? Get a good mouse. If you'll be running NT on a network, you'll need an NT-supported network adapter. All reputable network adapter manufacturers, and most ill-reputable manufacturers, include NT drivers with all their products. Check with the retailer or the manufacturer before purchasing if you have any doubts about whether the adapter supports NT.

Swapping your life away

Gather 'round so Gramps can tell you about the old days. Windows 3.0 and programs written to run under Windows are real memory hogs. But way back then, memory chips were frequently the most expensive component of a PC, and few PCs had more than 4 megabytes of RAM. So Microsoft took a page from the UNIX design manual and created virtual memory. (Okay, UNIX took the idea from MULTICS, which took the idea from mainframes, but you get the idea.) When you start a new program in Windows, if the RAM is already full with another program, Windows (and now NT) writes the information currently in RAM out to a file on the PC hard drive called a swap file. This was a really smart way to do things back when few machines had enough RAM to run two or three programs concurrently.

Obviously, the more RAM you have, the less swapping occurs. NT will also swap data and programs to and from the hard drive, as required by RAM availability. If swap files are so cool, why not run NT with just a few megabytes of RAM and let the swap file take up the slack? The reason is that swap files are slooooow. The modern PC uses RAM modules that operate at a speed between 60 and 70 nanoseconds. In other words, it takes 60 to 70 nanoseconds for your PC to move information to or from RAM. The access time of a fast modern hard drive is around 8 to 10 milliseconds. (*Nano* means one billionth and *milli* means one thousandth.)

The moral of the story is: RAM is very cheap these days, so buy all you can afford. The more RAM you have, the less swapping your PC will do, the quicker your NT workstation will operate, and the happier you'll be.

 There is a huge list of NT-compatible hardware on the CompuServe WINNT forum, on the Microsoft World Wide Web home page (http://www.microsoft.com), and with the NT product itself. And last but not least, if you are *not* going to install NT across your network, you'll find life much easier with a SCSI CD-ROM drive. (For just about any kind of drive, NT goes better with SCSI than with IDE.) NT is offered for installation on either a single CD-ROM or twenty-some (!) diskettes. Trust us: the CD-ROM version is well worth it.

Making Preinstallation Decisions

Though we touched on some of the important preinstallation decisions you need to make, there's nothing like beating a subject into the ground. Let's take a closer look at some of the things you should decide before installing NT Workstation.

Stiffy or floppy?

Choosing between CD-ROM or disks is a no-brainer; in fact, Microsoft may make it harder to get Windows NT on diskettes than on CD-ROM. Spend the extra bucks for a SCSI or IDE CD-ROM drive unless you have no other choice. You can install NT in less than twenty minutes from the CD-ROM. You might spend several hours swapping floppies to accomplish the same task with diskettes. On a few rare occasions, we've even had to reinstall NT. If you didn't enjoy installing NT the first time from disks, you'll really not like doing it the second or third time.

Most NT business applications, such as Microsoft Office, and a multitude of modern multimedia software titles ship only on CD-ROM now, so you'll need a CD-ROM drive anyway.

Know your network

During the install process, the NT setup program asks for details about the network adapter you have installed and how it is configured. You'll need to know its I/O port address and RAM address, if one is used, the interrupt number (IRQ), and the network adapter model. You'll also need to know the domain or workgroup name you intend to access on the network, if any. You'll also need a unique name for your computer as part of the network setup. Most companies have a standard naming convention for their computers; if your company does too, follow it at all costs. If you are unsure what to name your computer during setup, contact your network administrator or help desk.

Gotchas and other flotsam

If your NT Workstation will be connected to a local printer, you'll need to know its make and model. If the printer you will use is on the network, you need only know its share name. Your network support folks can help you out if you're unsure.

Be aware that if you have a compression utility such as Stacker or DoubleSpace installed on your hard drive, you will have to reformat your drive as part of the installation process. Make sure you have a current backup of all important data files and programs before starting the installation process.

You'll have the option of keeping a prior installation of Windows for Workgroups intact or installing NT over the existing Windows files. If you choose to keep the existing Windows intact, you don't install NT in the Windows default directory (\WINDOWS). Each time you boot (after completion of the NT installation), you have the option to start DOS, to start the old version of Windows, or to start Windows NT.

Notice that we didn't mention Windows 95 in this list — that's because you can't install Windows NT over that operating system. We didn't mention Windows 3.1x, either, but it's okay to keep it around. It just won't show up in the OS loader menu.

Prepare to Start at the Beginning

We hope we've made it clear that a CD-ROM installation of NT is the way to go. So we'll go that way in describing the installation process. Actually, the floppy and CD-ROM methods and the network install method are nearly identical, except for the source media.

A boot disk and the NT CD-ROM are included in your NT package. If the PC is turned off, all you need to do is turn the machine on and boot from the boot disk. If the PC already has an OS installed and is running, insert the NT boot disk into your A drive (or whichever floppy drive is bootable) and give your PC the old three-fingered salute: Ctrl+Alt+Del.

There are two distinct phases of the NT installation process. Phase one is a text-based boot process that should auto-detect the type of hardware installed in your PC and then copy just enough NT files to your hard drive to allow for a successful reboot. After the reboot, the installation will continue in the wonderful world of the GUI interface.

Phase one: getting started

After the initial boot, you will see the familiar text-based interface used for years for DOS and Windows installations. After NT boots in text mode and runs a hardware-detection routine, you will then begin the GUI phase, where you'll start with a choice between an Express Install or a Custom Install. If you are really leery of or don't fully understand the installation process, use the Express Install. Otherwise, we suggest the Custom Install.

The Express Install makes so many important decisions for you that it may not be in your best interests. The Custom Install gives you control over things such as swap file size and location and whether you bat left- or right-handed.

After you choose the Custom Install, NT will try to find a valid driver for your CD-ROM drive, whether IDE or SCSI. If NT can find and load such a driver, it will access the CD-ROM drive for the remainder of the installation process.

You have the option to verify that the Setup program identified your hardware correctly, and then you enter the dangerous world of hard-drive setup. You can add or delete partitions and format your drive using the NTFS file system. After you choose the file system type and partition assignments, you can select the directory where you'll install NT itself. After making your selections, you are asked to remove the boot disk from the disk drive and reboot your system.

File the system under cool!

You have several options for the file system on which you run NT. You can run NT on the old DOS standard File Allocation Table (FAT) file system or the new, improved, it-slices-it-dices NT File System (NTFS).

We highly recommend NTFS as the file system of choice for NT PCs. One of the best features of NT is the resiliency of the NTFS. NTFS has the capability to correct most common disk and file problems, including some hard drive crashes.

The only bad thing about NTFS is that only NT can read NTFS partitions. You cannot boot a DOS disk and read files on an NTFS partition. (This has an upside — no one can bypass your security with a DOS disk.) You can, however, read FAT partitions with an NT system. The only reason we can see for leaving a FAT partition on an NT machine is to occasionally boot DOS or Windows in place of NT. (But the more we use and enjoy NT, the less we find the need to boot DOS or Windows.)

Phase two: GUI and sticky

After rebooting, your PC will run in a completely graphical mode, which looks a lot like the Windows interface we've grown to love (or hate). After getting information about the devices connected to your computer and their configurations, you get to choose the type of installation (typical, portable, compact, or custom) that you want.

Next, you are prompted for your name and company, and then asked to enter the computer name. Ask your network administrator which name to use. This name must be unique on the network.

If you choose the Custom Install, you'll have more configuration options to select, such as printer and network settings. Next, you can specify swap file settings as well as workgroup choices, or domain choices, or both. Once again, if you have any questions about workgroup or domain names, ask your network administrator.

If you are installing your own network, you can assign your own meaningful names for the workgroup and domain later. We'll cover this in detail in Chapter 18.

The install program then creates the standard NT windows (Main, Accessories, and so on). It also searches the hard drive for existing applications and creates icons in an Applications window for each recognized program on your hard drive, just like the Windows 3.1 setup does.

If you're installing a network for the first time, you'll also want to set up an initial account and password. We'll cover the details involved in this activity fully in Chapters 20 and 21.

Tidying up

After the NT install program creates all the standard icons on the desktop, you have the opportunity to create an emergency startup disk. We *highly* recommend that you create an emergency startup disk at this time. The disk will be personalized for your particular PC and will result in a bootable floppy in case your NT system files become corrupt — or you accidentally delete them — and your system no longer boots from the hard drive.

You should keep this emergency disk in a handy location, although we hope you never have to use it. If you do have to boot from the emergency disk, you can then repair or replace the faulty files on a FAT or an NTFS boot partition. This is a handy feature to have, my friend.

Last but not least, you get to choose your time zone from the list (no peeking at your watch). Remove your emergency disk from the floppy drive, label it so that you'll know what it is, put the emergency disk in a safe location, and reboot your computer. That's all there is to it!

If you're installing a network for the first time, you'll also want to set up an initial account and password. If you didn't set a password for the Administrator account during the installation process, you should do so soon thereafter. We'll cover the details involved in this activity fully in Chapters 20 and 21.

Now, you're ready to begin the big adventure: Log on to Windows NT for the first time. The old three-fingered salute (Ctrl+Alt+Del) takes on a whole new meaning in the NT environment — it's how you tell the system you're ready to log on. After you do this, you are prompted for an account name and a password (and possibly a domain name, if the machine is a domain controller or that's part of your overall setup). At this point, type Administrator. Enter the password if you've already defined one; if you are asked for a domain name, you'd better have that, too. We hope you wrote all this down during the installation process!

If all goes well, you'll be logged on as Administrator (a.k.a. Top Network Banana). If you haven't yet defined a password, go to Start⇨Programs⇨Administrative Tools⇨User Manager. Once launched, double-click on the Administrator icon and enter a password in the dialog box. Write it down and keep it somewhere safe.

Manage the Unmanageable with User Manager

One of the cool things we like about network operating systems is that they give us management experience without having to talk to people. We can manage the users on our network with the NT utility called User Manager.

User Manager is where you create users and groups, assign passwords, and control access rights to files, directories, and printers. You can easily create groups to simplify your administrative duties. For example, rather than giving each individual user access rights to a printer, create a group called Printers, give the group Printers access to a shared resource for the printer, and then add users to the group. See how easy that is? But wait, it gets better — if you get a second printer, you simply add it to the group resource definition, and everyone in the group will automatically gain access to that device. Beats user-at-a-time updates every time!

To add users to domains, you must use a separate utility called the User Manager for Domains. The plain User Manager utility, running on a workstation, can give other users access only to that computer, not to resources across the entire domain. We go into the domain concept in a big way in Chapter 18. But both the User Manager and the User Manager for Domains also give you a great deal of control over what users can do and when users can access the network. The option called User Profile Editor gives you the ability to set several user options, including restricting users from specific areas of the network or allowing users to log on only during specific time periods.

Share and Share Alike

Now that you know how to restrict access to network resources, you need to learn how to create shared network resources. The easiest way to create a share for a particular file or directory is through the Explorer utility in the Main window.

Open Explorer (Start⇨Programs⇨Windows NT Explorer) and click on the file or directory you want to share with other users on the network. Click the Disk menu option and then click Share. You can assign the share name and permissions in the dialog box, as shown in Figure 9-1. You can assign permissions on a user-by-user basis, or you can create and assign group access rights to the new share.

You can share a printer with your network users in the same way you do in the Print Manager utility. Click the printer you want to share, and then click Permissions in the menu bar. Assign rights to users and groups, and your printer can now be accessed across the network, as shown in Figure 9-2.

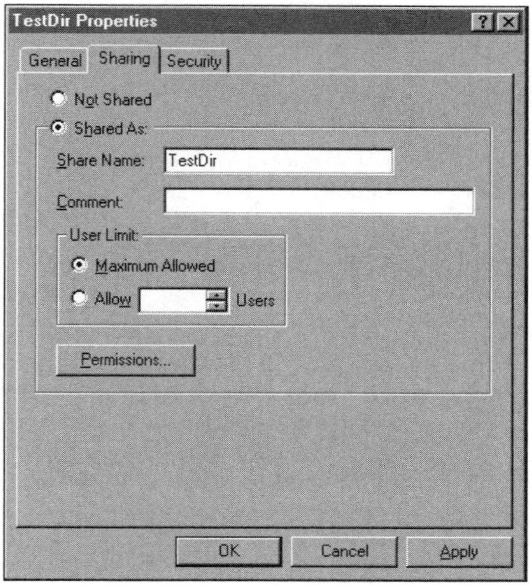

Figure 9-1:
You can easily share files or directories with other network users.

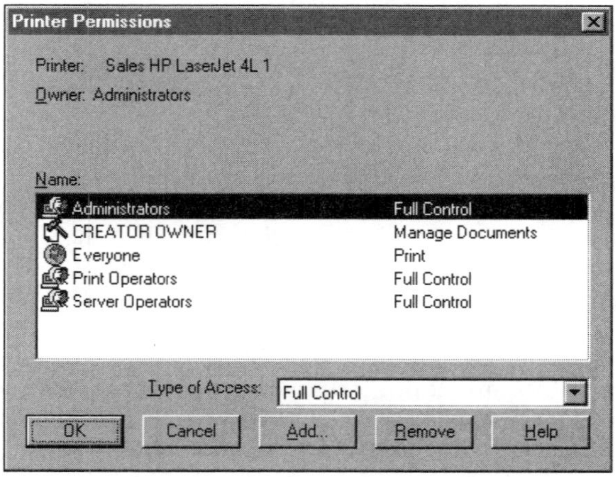

Figure 9-2:
Printers are shared with network users through this dialog box.

Connect the Dots: Clients Akimbo

Now that you've shared your files, directories, and printers with your network users, it's time to set up some other users to access your NT workstation. For the sake of this discussion, we assume that you will use your NT workstation as part of a workgroup-based network.

In a workgroup-based network, all PCs can share their local resources and access other shared resources on the network. The three clients that can participate in a workgroup are Windows for Workgroups (WFW) clients, Windows 95 clients, and Windows NT-based clients.

The NT Server CD-ROM has copies of Windows for Workgroups or Windows 95 for use by clients that cannot or will not run NT Workstation. We remind you that even though Microsoft has been kind enough to include the WFW and Win95 software, you still must purchase a license for every copy of WFW or Win95 that you install from the NT Server CD-ROM.

Whether configuring a WFW client, a Win95 client, or an NT client, the process is identical. For these clients to access shared resources, you must configure the clients for the same workgroup name as the rest of the network resources. You also have to define the users of the machines that are sharing resources with the network. Workgroup-based networks keep track of who can use what resource by user name, but the computer name must be unique so that messages bound for one machine do not end up at another.

Always be sure to use unique computer names on a workgroup-based network or a domain-based network.

Print All Night, Print a Little Longer

Compared to previous versions of Windows, NT has a drastically improved printing function. You no longer need the correct printer driver on each client PC to print to an NT-shared print device. The only place that must have the correct printer driver is the server or the machine to which the printer is attached. In most cases, Windows NT loads the proper driver for the printer automatically (provided, of course, that the printer is on the Hardware Compatibility List).

The client — without the correct printer driver — can map an LPT port to a shared printer on an NT machine and print directly to that print queue. This is fantastic! No more struggling to update the printer drivers on every PC on the network. Only NT PCs that are sharing printers need to be kept up to date with the latest printer drivers. That's a big improvement over the way NetWare handles print devices, and it's easier to manage than the old Windows method of updating every PC on the network.

Roses Are Red, but What If You're Blue?

We've no doubt painted a pretty rosy picture of NT, but that doesn't mean things always go perfectly. And even though we are network legends in our own minds, things occasionally don't work for us. Here are a few common problems and solutions we've come across with NT Workstation:

- ✔ **Installation errors.** Ninety percent of the errors with NT occur at installation, everything from network adapters set to incorrect or conflicting settings to boot failures. Most of these problems have commonsense solutions. If you get a network initialization error, check your network adapter settings. If your SCSI or IDE drive isn't recognized, be sure it is on the compatible hardware list published by Microsoft.

- ✔ **Unknown errors or no error messages.** NT is a major-league operating system that can put quite a strain on marginal hardware. Hardware that operated okay under DOS and Windows may not operate correctly under Windows NT due to the strain that NT puts on it. These days, most PCs come with a hardware diagnostic utility that can test hardware that may be failing under the NT load. (In many cases, however, those utilities won't run under Windows NT. In a worst-case scenario, you might have to install DOS just to run the diagnostics!)

- ✔ **A host of cryptic errors.** There is a database of well-known errors such as NTLDR boot errors and Error 0000001F. These errors are usually hardware-related. You can find a list of possible causes and corrections on the Microsoft Web site (`http://www.microsoft.com`) or on the WINNT forum on CompuServe. Check these areas for hints or, if you're down to your final straw, try contacting Microsoft Technical Support at 206-637-7098. The quality of tech support that we've received from Microsoft has been excellent, but it's hard to get through. So slip into something comfortable and be prepared to be put on hold for a while.

It's a Great Big Ol' World

We've always said that the best way to learn is to do and the best way to do is to dive in. You'll learn a lot more than we could ever cram in a book by installing NT just once. You know the basics of installation and how to find help when you have problems. So strap on your old crash helmet (pun intended) and head out on the highway that we call the NT Expressway.

After you get Windows NT Workstation installed, we bet you fall in love with it the same way we did. We couldn't face our work battles every day without it.

Chapter 10

NT Stands for Network This!

*T*here's no doubt about it: You just can't have a peer-to-peer network without a lot of cooperation. No man is an island, and no woman is an atoll. We must all communicate and cooperate to get our respective jobs accomplished in the modern workplace. And so it goes with Windows NT Workstation.

Peer-to-peer means that every user is a network equal: Each PC on the network can use and share network resources. This concept has a good side and a bad side.

The good news is that it's cheap. Instead of spending thousands of dollars on a mega-PC that will spend the rest of its days toiling away as the network server, everyone gets to be a server for little or no extra cost. Almost any local re- source — a printer, a data file, or a program — can be shared with other users in an NT peer-to-peer network.

Now for the bad news: When the guy with the cool color printer turns his PC off and goes home, no one on the network can print color pictures of their cham- pion pig from the county fair. Squeeeeeeal! The only bad peer, it seems, is the peer who isn't there (or at least the one who's not available).

So the downside of a network made up of all your peers at work is . . . well, all your peers at work. Your network is suddenly at the mercy of every locked-up PC, every crashed hard drive, and everybody who reboots a PC at the drop of a General Protection Fault. (Fortunately, GPFs aren't common with Windows NT.)

Peer-to-peer networks are only as strong as their weakest links, and you wouldn't believe some of the weak links we've seen out there. You must also consider the performance degradation that can affect users who share their local resources. Wouldn't you be irritated if you had to wait for someone's print job to finish just so you could print your own important stuff?

Don't let us dissuade you from going the peer-to-peer route if you think it's an appropriate way to network your office. Just be aware of the pros and cons of the peer-to-peer architecture before you dive in. We've seen some successful and appropriate peer-to-peer networks operating under Windows for Workgroups or Windows NT Workstation. We think the peer-to-peer strategy works best when you and your co-workers have only an occasional need to share data files or to spread out the print resources among several printers.

We don't recommend that you use a peer-to-peer network to share programs (for example, running a copy of Microsoft Word from another person's hard drive). Trying to run large programs — and most modern Windows programs are large — can be time-consuming and frustrating.

This strategy was never the use intended for peer-to-peer networks. Peer-to-peer networks were developed to eliminate the need for sneakernets, that is, copying a file to a disk and then running — in sneakers — to a co-worker's desktop computer and copying the file to that machine's hard drive.

So embrace your peers and don't think about how they might wreck your network. When you begin to feel that the burden of administering and supporting your peer-to-peer network is overwhelming, it's time to start thinking about installing a server. When you realize that no one in your office has backed up a hard drive since the Paleozoic Era, it's time to think about centralizing functions such as backups on a server. And when the guy with the color printer goes on vacation and you can't print the picture of that award-winning pig, order a copy of Windows NT Advanced Server. Now, on to the hows and whys of networking with NT Workstation.

Take Me Away, Protocol: Transports Make It Happen

The backbone of the network consists of the protocols that allow different and disparate devices to talk to each other with the greatest of ease. Well, maybe not the greatest of ease, but it works pretty well most of the time.

Think of network protocols as different dialects of a common language. Like language dialects, protocols have developed over time and have an agreed-upon format and syntax. Various protocols started out being espoused by a small group, sometimes being propelled by an industry alliance or a powerful vendor.

Many protocols have become popular enough to take on a life of their own. Windows NT Workstation comes with four protocols you can choose from: NWLink, the Microsoft flavor of the Novell (NetWare-based) IPX; TCP/IP, fast becoming the most prevalent protocol on earth thanks to the Internet explosion; NetBEUI, a leftover protocol from the Microsoft LAN Manager product; and DLC (Data Link Control), a protocol that lets PCs talk to mainframes on SNA networks. There's also AppleTalk, the native protocol for the Apple Macintosh, which is usually found where more than one Mac congregates in the workplace.

Table 10-1 lists all five of these protocols. The following sections take a closer look at each one.

Table 10-1	The Five Protocols Included with Windows NT
Protocol	*Uses*
NWLink	Provides NT-to-Novell compatibility. NWLink is a clone of IPX/SPX.
TCP/IP	Provides connection to the Internet and any other TCP/IP-based device (mainframes, minicomputers, UNIX-based computers, and so on).
NetBEUI	Provides connectivity to all other Microsoft Windows operating systems (Win 3.*x*, LAN Manager, Win95, DOS-based MS clients). NetBEUI is the Microsoft version of NetBIOS.
DLC	Provides connectivity between NT and gateways. Also provides connectivity to direct-connect network-capable printers.
AppleTalk	Provides connectivity to Macintosh computers and laser printers. Because modern Macs can also use TCP/IP, AppleTalk is mandatory only for older models.

NWLink: your link to NetWare servers

The biggest obstacle to the Microsoft plan to dominate the network operating system market was the small problem of the huge installed base of the Novell NetWare 3.*x* and 4.*x*. If Microsoft hadn't been able to find some way to seamlessly interact and cooperate with existing NetWare servers, they would have had no chance of toppling NetWare from the network throne.

Obviously, Novell didn't want to tell Microsoft how to interact with its servers, so Microsoft reverse-engineered the Internetwork Packet Exchange (IPX) protocol. Reverse-engineering is the process of trying to copy another company's process — or in this case, protocol — without all of the technical details. In other words, you try to decipher how software acts and reacts based on trial and error programming. Microsoft was quite successful in its efforts, and they copied the IPX protocol almost perfectly.

Microsoft quickly dispensed with the few bugs in its version of the IPX protocol, called NWLink, with the release of NT version 3.51. NWLink allows existing IPX clients to attach to an NT server as if it were a NetWare server.

In other words, an IPX client, whether DOS-, Windows-, or Windows NT-based, can log on to a NetWare server and run programs, access files, print to NetWare print queues, and generally not tell the difference between a NetWare server and an NT server. This is a vitally important detail for Microsoft because it removes the last remaining impediment to widespread adoption of NT as the new server platform of choice: the huge installed base of IPX clients.

Another reason that NWLink is important is that it allows companies to adopt NT Workstation as their client operating system without requiring any changes to the existing NetWare server environment.

One other distinct advantage to the NWLink protocol is that you can connect from an NT server to a NetWare server, create a share for that connection, and allow non-IPX clients to "pass-through" the NT server to the NetWare server. This feature of the NT server software is an invaluable aid to migrating from a pure NetWare environment to a mixed NetWare and NT environment to a pure NT server environment. Good job, Microsoft!

TCP/IP: from Internet to intranet to everynet

The Transmission Control Protocol/Internet Protocol (TCP/IP) was the granddaddy protocol of the Internet from day one. As the Internet has grown in prominence and popularity among commercial companies, many of those companies have come to embrace TCP/IP as their internal protocol of choice. Because TCP/IP was developed to be used across WAN links, it's particularly well suited to that environment.

As more and more companies expanded their LANs into WANs, they discovered just how inefficient IPX is as a WAN protocol. IPX wants to see an acknowledgment of each packet sent before it will send the next packet. This is an inefficient method of transmitting data across long distances because the latent delays in WAN links cause concomitant delays in the IPX protocol in general. TCP/IP does not have such limitations.

TCP/IP can send a number of packets serially before waiting for an acknowledgment for the entire string of packets. If one or two packets don't arrive successfully, TCP/IP will automatically request a retransmission of the lost or damaged packets. The entire process is transparent to users. This fact, combined with the overall explosion of the Internet among the world's corporations, boosted the acceptance of TCP/IP in both LAN and WAN environments.

NT Workstation supports TCP/IP as a native protocol and, in some ways, is becoming the NT protocol of choice. This is especially true for the release of additional Internet-focused products designed to run on NT Advanced Server, such as the new Microsoft Web Server product. You can also set up an NT server as an Internet *firewall* (a network node set up as a boundary to prevent traffic on one segment from crossing over into another), a proxy server, or an FTP server. All these functions are predicated on the smooth operation of the NT version of TCP/IP in the network environment.

NetBEUI: blast from the past

NetBIOS Extended User Interface (NetBEUI) is the protocol that Microsoft chose to include from the old days of Microsoft's LAN Manager product. LAN Manager, also known as LAN Man, was a competitor of NetWare before Microsoft got serious about competing with Novell for the server OS market. Naturally, Microsoft has included NetBEUI with the NT Advanced Server product, primarily to provide compatibility with existing LAN Man servers in the few companies that purchased the various versions of LAN Man throughout the years.

We don't recommend that you use NetBEUI as your primary networking protocol. Although NetBEUI is technically feasible as a departmental or small office network protocol, NetBEUI is not routable and is, therefore, an inefficient protocol for wide-area links in much the same way that IPX is unsuitable for such links. We recommend NetBEUI only when connection to an existing LAN Man server is a requirement.

AppleTalk: do the Mac thing

AppleTalk is the only protocol in this collection that antedates the ISO/OSI Reference Model, so it's the only one that implements that model fully and completely. Although it's self-configuring, manages its own addresses, and is easy to use, AppleTalk has never caught on outside the Macintosh community. That's partly because, like the OSI Model itself, it's more complicated and full-featured than it needs to be. It's also because Apple kept its protocol under wraps too long in its developmental stages, and, therefore, the development community moved on to adopt more open protocols.

You'll probably use AppleTalk protocols to support only older Macintoshes, whose capabilities to support more standard protocols such as TCP/IP may be hampered by a lack of system resources. Or you might be inclined to use it if yours is an Apple-oriented network and most of your clients use Macintoshes. Either way, it's an easy add-on to your Windows NT machine.

DLC: mainly for mainframes

DLC is the last of the protocols that Microsoft includes with the NT product line. DLC is used primarily for access to SNA-based devices, usually through some type of gateway software. If you have an SNA-based gateway installed on your network, you are already aware of the requirement for DLC protocol support on your client PCs, and this is exactly the situation for which the DLC protocol support of NT is suited. If you do not need to connect your NT clients to an SNA-based minicomputer or mainframe, you can ignore the DLC selection in your network setup.

Mix and match: stir it up!

So NT supports all these different protocols. But what if you need more than one of the protocols? What if your NT server needs to connect to a NetWare server via NWLink and to the Internet via TCP/IP? No sweat! NT Workstation allows you to configure any and all supported protocols on multiple network adapter cards in an NT Workstation and NT Server computer. You can bind multiple protocols to a single network adapter if your network doesn't require multiple network interfaces in your NT machine. The next section describes at length how to configure multiple network adapters and multiple protocols using Windows NT.

The Control Panel's Network Utility: Get a Grip!

You install and configure the network support of Windows NT using the Network utility, which is in the Control Panel group. Figure 10-1 shows the Network utility's main menu screen.

After you start the Network utility, you have the option of adding software (protocols) and hardware (network adapters) to your NT configuration. If you preinstall your hardware using DOS, NT should automatically detect the addition of network hardware and start the Network utility after your next reboot so that you can configure that new hardware and add new protocols.

The first two lines on the screen tell you the network name and the workgroup or domain name of the PC on which you are working. The only requirement for the computer name is that it be unique to the network. However, the computer name must have an account in an existing NT domain or you must know the correct domain name so you can enter the information in the Domain/ Workgroup Settings.

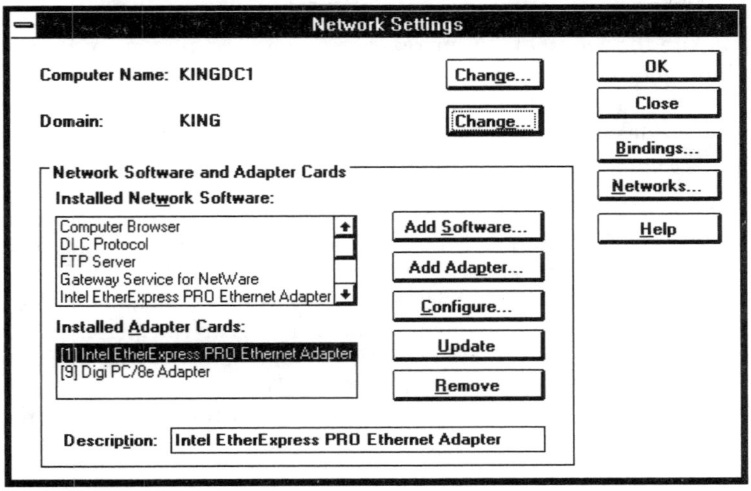

Figure 10-1:
The main
menu for the
Network
utility in
Windows
NT.

For our discussion of Windows NT Workstation, you will find it easier to define
your new users' computer names on the NT domain before configuring the
network adapters on their individual PCs. But even if you do not define the
users first, you can create new domain user accounts directly from the Network
Utility Domain/Workgroup Settings screen.

Before configuring your network adapters, you should do the following:

1. **Select the Adapters tab, click the Add button, and select the card from
   the list, or click the Have Disk button (which means you need a diskette
   with the drivers as well).**

   This may require that you adjust such settings as the I/O address, the RAM
   memory address, and the interrupt number of the adapter being installed.
   Typically, no two devices in your PC can be set to the same settings. See
   your PC and adapter card manuals for more details on resource conflicts
   and how to resolve them.

2. **Document the settings you chose for your network adapters.**

   NT needs to know not only which network adapters you install, but also
   the resource settings you selected. Have this information handy when you
   go into the Network utility to set up your network adapters.

When you complete these two steps, start the Network utility and select Add
Hardware. Enter the correct resource settings for the adapters you are installing
in the PC. Carefully enter the values requested; a mistake in the adapter settings
can cause your PC to lock up. Luckily, NT is usually smart enough to detect
resource conflicts between two adapters in the same PC, but caution is advised
nonetheless.

After you install and configure the network adapters, you can install and configure the protocols to run on each adapter. Remember, you can configure, or bind, more than one protocol to each network adapter. To add a protocol, select the Protocols tab and click the Add button. Select the desired protocols one at a time. If you select a protocol that has configuration options, such as TCP/IP, you will have to enter the required configuration information in the Network utility.

After adding all desired protocols and configuring each protocol, you'll be asked to reboot the PC for the changes to take effect. If you have made a mistake or if there are any errors in your network setup, you will get a network error message as the PC reboots. If you need more details on the meaning of the message, use the Event Viewer (Start➪Programs➪Administrative Tools➪Event Viewer) to look at the Event Log. You can also run the Windows diagnostic tool, Windows NT Diagnostics (a.k.a. WINMSD.EXE) from either the File Run command or a command-line prompt. See Figure 10-2 for a look at the WINMSD main screen.

Figure 10-2:
WINMSD can help you uncover adapter and resource conflicts in your NT Workstation installation.

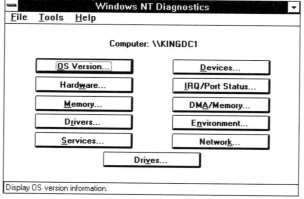

WINMSD is the NT equivalent of the Microsoft Diagnostics program you may have used with Windows 3.*x*. WINMSD can help you resolve adapter and resource conflicts in your NT Workstation setup.

An additional feature of the Control Panel Network Utility is its capability to configure modems as virtual network adapters. In other words, you can configure your modem as a network adapter and bind TCP/IP to the adapter. You can then connect to your Internet Service Provider as if you were a node on the network. You can also configure a modem for dial-in use through the Network Utility. Both these functions are part of the Remote Access Service (RAS) in Windows NT. The next section tells you everything you need to know about RAS on an NT Workstation PC.

Keep RASing Me: Dial-in and Dial-out

The Windows NT Remote Access Service (RAS) is your key to remote connectivity. You use it to seamlessly dial in to your NT network or dial out to other networks. You can install RAS either as part of the initial NT installation process or after Windows NT is already installed. To install RAS, you must already have a communications device installed in your NT PC or be connected to a router with an ISDN or higher speed connection. The communications device can be a modem or an ISDN adapter. For outgoing communications through a router (which must be MPPP compliant, with a fixed IP address and the NT machine), the NT PC will require a working network connection to that router.

When installing RAS, you will generally use the Modem applet in the Control Panel to install the modem or internal ISDN adapter. Otherwise, you must change the default gateway address in Start⇨Control Panel⇨Network⇨ Protocols on the IP Address tab. To add the RAS protocol to a modem or ISDN adapter, click the Add button in the Services tab. Enter the complete path to the source files — probably the NT CD-ROM from which you installed the base operating system — and then click Continue.

When the RAS files are successfully copied to your hard drive, a dialog box pops up asking you which Remote Access Compatible device to use. The communications device should appear in the list. Select your modem or whatever device you want to configure for RAS, and click the OK button. If your communications device is not in the list, NT will offer to automatically detect it for you.

After your hardware is installed, click the Configure Port button. This is where you have the choice of configuring NT RAS for dial-in, dial-out, or both types of remote access. Dial-in is when users will call in to the network from another location. Dial-out is when users want to connect to external networks.

You can configure RAS to automatically reconnect to a remote network when you log on to Windows NT. If you are using RAS to connect to a remote network through long-distance phone lines or if you are connecting to a remote network that charges connect time for access, you will probably want to de-select this choice so that you can control when NT dials out to your remote network connections. When you have completed the RAS setup process, reboot your PC so that the changes can take effect.

You also have the option of using your NT Workstation as a dial-in server. You can dial in to your office PC from home or from the road, or you can share your remote PC's resources with other users in your office. To set up RAS in server mode, select the proper protocols you want to support for users connecting to your PC.

Use the Permissions button to assign security rights for any users who want to dial in to your machine. Be sure that you select the dial-in option under the Remote Access Service options (in the Network utility's Installed Network Software window). Without the dial-in option selected, no one will be able to dial in to your NT Workstation "server." That's all there is to the RAS dial-in server setup for Windows NT Workstation. Not too hard, is it?

And Now for Something Similar

We would be remiss if we didn't spend a few paragraphs warning you about the vagaries and frustrations of dealing with network hardware. At times, your network will cause you to pull out your hair and will turn any remaining hair gray. At other times, your network will purr like a kitten.

The problem with complex networks is that they are, well, complex. So many things can go wrong. Unfortunately, the symptoms rarely give an accurate indication of the underlying problem. A flaky network adapter in a client PC can cause errors in servers. Poorly written software can cause errors that look like cabling problems. Don't even get us started on cabling!

Every tool you can get your hands on will help you narrow down the source of a problem. Here is a partial list of some hardware and software products that help diagnose and troubleshoot network problems:

- **Cable scanners.** These devices send an electrical signal through the cable and can diagnose cabling shorts and opens with some degree of accuracy. A cable scanner can also crash your network if you use it on a cable that is currently plugged in to the network.

- **Network management tools.** Network management software, such as HP's OpenView, can monitor your network components and notify you when certain hardware and software errors occur.

- **Protocol analyzers.** These devices, like the Network General Sniffer, can actually capture packets as they fly across your network. Protocol analyzers usually offer some degree of diagnosis about the source of network problems based on the packet errors they see.

- **Documentation.** One of your best tools in troubleshooting is a complete set of documentation, so you'll at least know how the network looked when you started. Document everything and keep it current.

Remember, the best defense is a good offense. You'll need some of these tools to keep your network humming along, so plan ahead.

Chapter 11

NT for Life?

*W*ith the release of Windows NT Version 4.0, Microsoft not only has a contender for king of the network heap, but also has shown us the future of the client operating system. Users and PC administrators alike have been complaining for years about the various bugs and limitations of DOS and Windows version 3.*x*.

The root of these limitations goes back to Microsoft's decision not to fully exploit the capabilities of the 32-bit processor architecture introduced with the advent of the 80386 CPU chip. Although we can understand Microsoft's reluctance to offer an operating system that was somewhat incompatible with previous versions of existing software, the PC-user community has been paying the price ever since. No matter how much RAM you stuff into your PC, the inherent limitations of 640K of DOS memory have hampered development efforts since the PC was first introduced.

Clearly, somebody had to do something. OS/2 represented the first effort to overturn the limitations of DOS while providing some level of compatibility with existing DOS and Windows applications. Unfortunately, OS/2 was a casualty of the fierce rivalry between IBM and Microsoft and was ultimately too little, too late. Table 11-1 shows the strengths and weaknesses of NT Workstation as compared to OS/2 and other client operating systems currently available.

Table 11-1	NT Workstation and Other Client Operating Systems			
	Windows NT Workstation	*OS/2*	*Windows 95*	*UNIX*
Supports DOS-based programs	Yes, but limited	Yes	Yes	Only in a compatibility mode
Supports Windows-based programs	Yes	Yes, but limited	Yes	Limited to compatibility mode
Supports 32-bit Windows-based programs	Yes	No	Yes	No
Includes a high-performance file system	Yes: NTFS	Yes: HPFS	No	Yes: NFS
Multithreaded, multitasking	Yes	Yes	No	Yes
Supports multiple processors	Yes	Only OS/2 server currently offers MP support	No	Yes

NT Workstation to the Rescue!

One positive result of the rivalry between IBM and Microsoft has been the development of NT Advanced Server and NT Workstation. Although both products are based on the same code, Workstation excludes all the necessary files for participating as a server PC in a domain atmosphere.

Instead, NT Workstation takes all the security, robustness, and memory protection of NT Advanced Server and delivers it to the desktop for power users everywhere. What price do we pay for the marvels of NT Workstation? We do have to forfeit a few things in exchange for preemptive multitasking.

Whoa, pardner! You might be wondering what in the world *preemptive multitasking* means and how it can help you do your job better. Well, if you've ever used Windows version 3.1 and had your machine reboot itself or freeze, you'll be able to appreciate preemptive multitasking. Preemptive multitasking protects the memory space and processor power used by applications so that one ill-behaved or poorly written program cannot — at least, theoretically — crash or lock up the entire system.

In reality, NT Workstation is not completely immune to such applications, but it is much better at protecting you and your programs from rogue or poorly written applications. Likewise, it's better at keeping on even when combinations of applications make your machine get weird.

If your machine experiences an application lockup, goes into an eternal loop, or otherwise starts acting goofy, you can press Ctrl+Alt+Del to display an active task list (just as in Windows 95). Then click on the offending program and click on the End Task button. This usually removes the bad program from memory and restores your system to a normal state. We say *usually,* because not even Microsoft can cover all the possible permutations of bad programming, although segmenting the memory so no two programs access the same area in memory at the same time goes a long way in this regard. Table 11-2 compares the memory and processor protections of Windows NT Workstation, Windows 3.1, and Windows 95.

Table 11-2 Protection in NT Workstation and Other Operating Systems

	Windows NT Workstation	Windows 95	Windows 3.1
Flat memory model	Yes	Yes	No
Application memory protected from operating system	Yes	No	No
Auto detection of hardware during installation	Yes	Yes	No
Auto detection of new hardware after installation	No	Yes	No
Runs 16-bit Windows applications	Some	Yes	Yes
Runs 32-bit Windows applications	Yes	Yes	Some
Built-in network support	Yes	Yes	Yes
Preemptive multitasking	Yes	No	No
Runs DOS-based applications	Some	Most	Yes

NT Workstation offers the highest degree of application protection from misbehaving programs. NT also provides crash-worthiness by generally not letting any program talk directly to the hardware in your PC. Under DOS or Windows 3.1, a communications program could physically attach to a communications (COM) port or a printer port on your machine, thereby shutting out all other programs from accessing that hardware.

If a program that handles communications locks up and your computer reboots because of that one bad program, that's not playing well with others, is it? NT avoids this situation by not allowing programs to take direct control of most of the hardware. Instead, NT intercepts hardware requests and acts as though it were the hardware in question.

By buffering the hardware from the software in this manner, NT can allow you to terminate the application without rebooting your PC if an application breaks one of the rules and locks up or otherwise behaves badly. In this strategy, NT can also act as a traffic cop, allowing multiple programs to execute commands and access "hardware" at the same time.

Under DOS, you can generally run only one application at a time. Under Windows 3.1, you can generally run more than one application at a time, but Windows 3.1 does not have NT's built-in safeguards that protect programs from each other and from locking up your PC hardware.

NT solves these problems with preemptive multitasking. *Multitasking* means that multiple programs can be running simultaneously, each in its own memory space. *Preemptive* means that the NT operating system can interrupt a program any time it begins to hog the processor or other resources and allow other programs to get a word in edgewise.

NT Workstation represents the client operating system of the future and should finally overcome the limitations of DOS and Windows 3.1 for good. NT doesn't merely run on top of DOS as Windows does; NT replaces DOS as the local operating system. By replacing DOS, NT offers all the benefits we have just discussed while maintaining the highest possible level of compatibility. Most DOS and Windows 3.*x* applications should run fine under NT, but you will encounter the occasional exception.

Which programs won't run? You can bet that most programs that have been designed to directly access hardware in the PC will not run correctly under Windows NT. This includes a lot of communications software, video-intensive programs, and older DOS-based programs.

The good news is that most major software developers are already releasing 32-bit versions of their software. These programs are generally written specifically for the Windows NT and Windows 95 operating systems and most will not run under Windows 3.1. This should remove any lingering doubts about converting your system to Windows NT.

Originally, Microsoft thought that the move from 16-bit software to 32-bit software would bring a commensurate increase in speed. After all, instead of working with 16 bits of data at a time, you could now work with 32 bits of data. Theoretically, this should double the speed of every application ported from 16-bit Windows to 32-bit Windows NT or Windows 95.

In reality, applications have not become significantly faster, and many 32-bit applications are slower than their 16-bit counterparts. There are several reasons for this phenomenon:

✔ Relative inexperience with coding efficient 32-bit applications. Many software developers have become expert at writing efficient 16-bit code. Unfortunately, 32-bit development is quite different in terms of how you make programs do things. Although the data itself moves around faster, programmers may sometimes take more steps to perform the same task in a 32-bit application than in a 16-bit application because they're unfamiliar with the interfaces involved.

✔ More overhead built into the operating system itself. You don't get something for nothing; all the cool protection and multitasking features of Windows NT come at a price. The operating system itself is larger and slower, so if you upgraded your existing PC from Windows 3.1 to Windows NT and from Microsoft Office to the new 32-bit version of Microsoft Office, you might think you've taken a big step backward in terms of performance. And you probably have. But when it comes to running lots of programs, Windows NT will keep working long after Windows 3.x has curled up and died!

If you plan to upgrade from Windows 3.1 to Windows NT, you might want to upgrade your PC to a faster processor and more RAM at the same time.

Peer, Peer, Pumpkin Eater

We've already discussed the process of building and administering a peer-to-peer network using Windows NT Workstation. But just when is that the appropriate way to go, and what are some of the inherent problems with the peer-to-peer concept? As we mentioned earlier, peer-to-peer networks, known as workgroup networks in Microsoft-speak, are best suited for small workgroup environments.

If you can't afford the time or expense involved in administering a standalone server, a workgroup network may be your best choice. Just remember that the workgroup concept requires a great deal of consideration and cooperation among your network users.

You can think of your entire workgroup network as a giant file and print server with multiple administrators. Just like a real file server, if some part of the server crashes — or a user turns his or her machine off or reboots — the whole network can suffer. Be aware of the pitfalls of the workgroup network before you dive in.

Movin' on Up

Suppose that you've had your workgroup network running for a while and you're beginning to wonder whether the whole thing is becoming a bear to maintain. When you realize that someone is spending more than 50 percent of his or her time just working on the network, resolving users' problems, and performing backups, you need to reevaluate your commitment to the workgroup concept and start thinking about a server-based network.

Migrating from a workgroup-based network to a server-based network is simple, except for the hard parts. Okay, there aren't that many hard parts.

Microsoft has a well-thought-out strategy to take users from standalone Windows 3.1 to Windows NT or Windows 95 to networking by means of the workgroup process to blossoming into a full-blown server-based network. Each step is fairly painless and provides a logical stepping stone to the next level of network computing. Figure 11-1 shows a natural progression from DOS through the various versions of Windows to a server-based network. Notice how the computer becomes bigger and faster, and DOS programs are supported less and less.

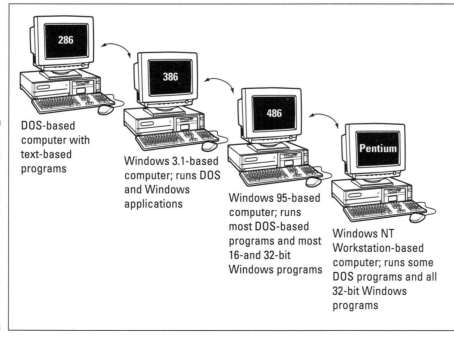

Figure 11-1: Microsoft has a simple, coherent strategy to take users from a standalone DOS PC up to a fully networked NT client.

DOS-based computer with text-based programs

Windows 3.1-based computer; runs DOS and Windows applications

Windows 95-based computer; runs most DOS-based programs and most 16-and 32-bit Windows programs

Windows NT Workstation-based computer; runs some DOS programs and all 32-bit Windows programs

---

Bonus city

One of the nicest features of Windows NT for a small network is the Remote Access Service. With NetWare-based networks, you must install and support a third-party solution just to dial in and dial out of your network. Windows NT supports dial-in and dial-out right out of the box. As long as you have a modem connected to your PC, you can dial in and dial out for no extra charge and just a little extra setup time.

Another big plus of Windows NT is its built-in TCP/IP support. With Windows 3.1, you had to purchase a usually very expensive add-on software package to get TCP/IP support. With Windows NT, that support is included for no extra charge. Best of all, TCP/IP works seamlessly and great because it was designed into the product from the ground up. Some third-party TCP/IP stacks sold for Windows 3.1 cause as many problems as they solve.

Microsoft has sent many third-party software developers scrambling for market share as more and more of their old product features turn up in Windows NT, but the third-party software market is unlikely to dry up. Not even Microsoft can cover all the bases, and users will always want more features than even NT can provide. Third-party development will always be there to fill in the gaps of Windows NT.

Considering the ease of migrating from one platform to another, you shouldn't be afraid to say "uncle" when your network Frankenstein has outgrown its current confines. Purchase a server PC with a Pentium processor, at least 64MB of RAM, a tape backup unit, and at least a 2GB hard drive. Purchase a copy of Windows NT Advanced Server, install it on the new PC, and go to town!

Windows NT gives you the option of supporting a simultaneous workgroup and domain logon. This allows you to move network applications to the server gradually, rather than trying to replace a workgroup network with a server-based network in one fell swoop.

Living in a Diverse Network World

We've talked about the migration path from Windows 3.1 to Windows NT Server, but what if you don't want to migrate? What if you like things just the way they are, but the way they are is a real mish-mash of operating systems and devices?

Fortunately, this is an environment where Windows NT really shines. Windows 3.1, Windows for Workgroups, Windows NT Workstation, Windows NT Server, and even the Macintosh can happily coexist and share resources on your network without any ill effects. NT Server is usually the center of such integration efforts because it's the one operating system that can talk directly to every other client device on the network. In this kind of situation, you'll want to bring Windows NT Server into the heart of your network.

Attack of the killer apple

Network administrators have always moaned and complained about integrating Macintosh computers with a predominantly PC network. Although NetWare has long offered Mac support on its server operating system, this support has been plagued by bugs and implementation problems. We've had to rebuild many a hard drive scrambled by NetWare's support for Mac long filenames.

Good news: NT Advanced Server directly supports the Mac by means of the native AppleTalk protocol. NT Server also supports the Mac's long filenames. The Windows NT Server appears as another AppleTalk server in the Mac's Chooser under Network Connections.

The following shows the many types of clients that can coexist and share resources on an NT Server-based network. It's enough to make us networking old-timers teary-eyed just thinking about how much easier this makes our jobs:

DOS-based Microsoft clients	Basic redirector can only use network resources; Enhanced redirector can share and use network resources
Windows 3.*x*	Share and use resources
Windows 95	Share and use resources
Windows NT Workstations	Share and use resources
Apple Macintosh computers	Macs can share with any other Apple-based network client (NT and Macs); Macs can use NT resources directly while also using other Mac-based network resources.

After you have established the NT Server as the center of your network universe, you no longer have to restrict users to certain client operating systems due to compatibility problems with network protocols or the server operating system. You will have other support issues surrounding a diverse mix of client operating systems, but there is no longer a technical reason restricting a user's choice of client software. Allow your users to choose the best solution for their job duties and existing hardware platform — with the confidence that you'll be able to hook up that user with the rest of your network.

Make Up Your Mind

So now you have enough gory details about NT Workstation and the other choices out there to make an informed decision as to whether NT Workstation is the client operating system for you. Remember that Microsoft does a good job of giving you and your users a path to migrate from one platform to another as your PC and network needs change. Remember, too, the increasing hardware requirements as you go up the migration path from DOS to Windows NT Advanced Server. And remember the increased capabilities as you follow that migration path up to the NT operating system.

Due to Microsoft's excellent planning of the migration process, most of the various flavors of Windows can happily coexist and share resources along the way. Use Remote Access Server to provide dial-in and dial-out services for NT Workstation users. And don't forget that the NT Advanced Server will allow a single point for network dial-ins and dial-outs. Last, evaluate your current needs and hardware budget.

If you do upgrade to an NT Workstation, you will probably find significant value in also upgrading your applications to 32-bit versions as they appear. The 32-bit versions should take advantage of the NT architecture to provide more features and better protection from system crashes and lockups.

On the other hand, some peripheral devices are not supported under Windows NT. Apparently, some manufacturers still believe that the majority of their customers will use Windows 3.*x* or Windows 95, and therefore haven't built drivers that work with NT. Also, Windows NT 4.0 does not support plug-and-play. This currently makes Windows 95 a better alternative for laptops, which typically use the most exotic adapters (for example, PC cards for modems, network adapters, and external drives). Because configuring these by hand can be a pain, plug-and-play gives Windows 95 the upper hand.

Part III
Networking with Windows NT Server

The 5th Wave · By Rich Tennant

"BETTER CALL MIS AND TELL THEM ONE OF OUR NETWORKS HAS GONE BAD."

In this part . . .

Microsoft's Windows NT Server is emerging as the new networking operating system of choice. Many leaders in today's marketplace have already selected Windows NT Server as their networking system, including companies such as CompuServe, Aetna, and Chevron. Because selecting a network is more than just a popularity contest, there must be some good reasons why these industry heavyweights are using Windows NT.

Windows NT lets all kinds of computers — including PCs, Macintoshes, and UNIX machines — work together and share files, printers, and services. Windows NT also includes significant built-in networking services, and combines with the other elements in the Microsoft BackOffice to create a powerful and comprehensive set of capabilities.

Part III lifts the hood on Windows NT Server to show you what this system can do. You are exposed to the full range of Windows NT Server's capabilities, beginning with basic installation and configuration, through networking, communications, naming services, remote access, and the file system. You're also properly introduced to Windows NT Server's security, printing, backup, and configuration. After you comprehend what this baby can do on the information superhighway (so to speak), we'll teach you some racing tricks and lead you to some tools so you can get the most out of this system.

It will take some time and a fair amount of your attention to fully appreciate what Windows NT Server can do for you and your network. But if you put in the time, you'll be well on your way to understanding Windows NT Server, and you'll be prepared to make it a part of your network. We hope you find the task interesting, challenging, and enjoyable!

Chapter 12

A Road Map to Windows NT Server

*M*S-Net, introduced in the mid-1980s, was the first network developed by Microsoft. MS-NET was a DOS-based, peer-to-peer network that provided print- and file-sharing capabilities among PCs. If that basic concept sounds suspiciously similar to Windows for Workgroups, it should, because it is a similar product. Although the network user interface has changed a lot over the years (going from the DOS command line to the NET interface to the Windows 3.1 interface), the underpinnings are remarkably similar. In fact, the DOS-based NET menu system remains nearly unchanged in Windows for Workgroups.

What's the First Thing Adam and Eve Wanted to Do? Network!

So what's the big deal with networks, anyway? Why spend all this time and money just so we can talk to each other? We now don our philosophical hat to answer this question.

Human beings are by nature animals of communication and cooperation. Just as our ancestors gathered together to harvest and hunt, modern networks allow us to communicate, cooperate, compete, and complement each other.

Did you ever wonder why most companies have a separate accounting department and sales department? Because we are not all equally skilled at or interested in the tasks of modern business. Networks allow us to specialize in the area where our skills and interests can best be utilized.

Computer networks allow us to communicate with each other in a way not seen since the telephone network was invented. A computer network is even better than the telephone network in some ways: We can easily share information and ideas; we have a common repository for our collective work; and we can pass electronic items from one area of specialty to another without losing things in a giant paper shuffle. So don't fight the network — embrace it. It is both your destiny and your density. Wow! That was way deep, junior. Let's take that darn hat off before we get a headache.

The Network Speaks: NetBIOS, then NetBEUI, then IPX and IP

Before we dig any deeper into the pedigree of Windows NT, let's take a few minutes to talk about the glue that binds your network together: (trumpet fanfare) the network protocols. Chapter 17 provides a thorough discussion of protocols, but let's take a few paragraphs now to look at the network protocols supported by NT.

The networking world has lots of protocols; some were designed specifically for the LAN environment and some were adapted to the LAN environment. Each protocol has quirks and eccentricities, like my weird Uncle Howard, who always brings a huge bowl of tapioca pudding to our family reunions. The following is a quick recap of each of the prevalent LAN protocols supported by Microsoft NT.

NetBIOS and NetBEUI

NetBIOS was originally designed by IBM as a (somewhat) logical extension of the BIOS (Basic Input/Output System) built into each PC. NetBEUI is the Microsoft extension to the basic NetBIOS protocol and is the default protocol of the Microsoft LAN Manager product. For the sake of this discussion, unless otherwise specifically noted, we use the term NetBEUI to mean both NetBIOS and NetBEUI. NetBEUI is a nonroutable, connection-oriented protocol that works best on small networks.

Nonroutable connection-oriented protocol — what in the world does that mean? *Nonroutable* means that NetBEUI network traffic cannot be routed. In other words, the only way to pass NetBEUI traffic from one physical segment to another is by means of a bridge. A bridge simply takes everything from LAN A and puts it on LAN B. You can see from Figure 12-1 that this puts all network traffic on both sides of the bridge, which can bog down the whole network.

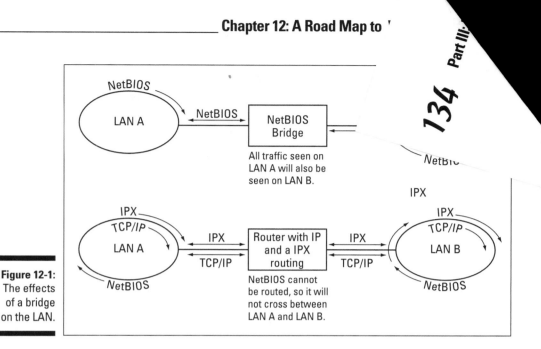

Figure 12-1:
The effects
of a bridge
on the LAN.

Connection-oriented means that there is a virtual connection from one device to another — like when you dial the telephone and someone else answers. Connection-oriented protocols make a connection between two network devices behave just like a phone conversation. These two devices talk back and forth in such a way that one always expects the other to be there until they agree to sever the connection. It also means that when one device sends a chunk of information, known as a packet, across the network, the other device will know whether the packet arrived safely.

IPX and the packets that BURST!

While IBM and Microsoft were busy debating the merits of their flavors of NetBIOS, IPX (Internetwork Packet Exchange) was quietly conquering the West — and every other part of the world.

IPX is the local area network (LAN) protocol developed by Novell in the early 1980s. It is important to note that IPX was developed as a LAN protocol. As such, IPX does not travel very well across long distances, such as wide area networks (WANs). This fact has become painfully obvious as more and more companies have converted their LANs into WANs and noticed that IPX offers slow response across wide area links. Slow response is the result of a high overhead-to-data ratio, as well as the necessary acknowledgment for each chunk of data sent across the network, as you can see from the protocol comparison in Table 12-1.

Table 12-1	A Comparison of Protocols			
	NW Link (IPX/SPX)	**TCP/IP**	**NetBEUI**	**DLC**
Suitable for LAN transport	Yes	Yes	Yes	Yes
Suitable for WAN transport	Yes	Yes	No	No
Overhead/Speed	Medium/ Faster on LAN, slower on WAN	Medium/ Slower on LAN, faster on WAN	Low/Fast on LAN	Low/Fast on LAN
Routable	Yes	Yes	No	Yes

Overhead is the amount of control or system bits it takes for a given packet to safely traverse the network. IPX expects an acknowledgment, or ACK, for each packet sent before it will release the next packet. Consequently, in a large network or across slow WAN links, IPX can be excruciatingly slow.

Novell finally attempted to remedy the situation by issuing a revision to the IPX protocol called packet burst. Packet burst technology requires that each server and client support packet burst mode drivers. In contrast to a standard IPX transmission, packet burst packets can be sent without individual acknowledgments. A single ACK is generally sent for a group of packet burst packets. If one or more of the group didn't arrive at the destination intact, the receiving device says, "Hey, I didn't receive all the packets you sent — please resend." This multiple transmission, followed by a single ACK, makes packet burst IPX much more efficient across long or slow links.

Wow. Packet burst IPX is a great idea. I wonder how Novell came up with it?

The Internet protocol: TCP/IP

TCP/IP (Transmission Control Protocol/Internet Protocol) is where Novell got the idea. TCP/IP was developed by a collection of companies, the government, and academic institutions worldwide. They needed a protocol that would be highly efficient and effective across the burgeoning Internet in the late 1970s. (Note, though, that the Internet didn't take on that name until the 1980s.)

The TCP part of the TCP/IP protocol suite provides a mechanism for sequencing packets and guarantees the delivery of those packets. If TCP detects that packets were not received correctly, it automatically requests a retransmission of the error packets. IP is the format of packets sent across the Internet or any

IP network. The IP portion of the TCP/IP protocol specifies the format of each packet — the header, the address, error correction information, and the data itself. The two pieces combine into the most popular protocol in the world.

TCP/IP is a robust, low-overhead protocol that guarantees error-free delivery while maintaining an efficient delivery mechanism. Try it — you'll like it!

LAN Man's the Man!

Microsoft LAN Manager, or LAN Man as it is affectionately known, was Microsoft's first foray into the network file and print server market. At the time of LAN Man's introduction, Novell's NetWare virtually owned the file and print server market. LAN Man did little to slow Novell's market momentum. LAN Manager was too slow and did not boast the security, print, or administration features found in NetWare. LAN Man also lacked key third-party support for everything from remote print services to network backup devices.

We suspect that LAN Man was merely an attempt by Microsoft to quiet the critics who said Microsoft could not offer a complete product line without a file and print server product. LAN Man also gave Microsoft the time needed to develop their much-rumored new server product called New Technology, a.k.a. Windows NT.

NT Rises from the DEC Ashes

Although Microsoft learned a lot about network operating system software and the network marketplace with its earlier forays into networking, Windows NT came from a different place and time: Digital Equipment Corporation (DEC) and the mid-1980s. DEC had tried to develop a next-generation operating system to replace its successful MVS operating system.

The development project eventually failed at DEC, but Microsoft knew a good opportunity when it saw one. Microsoft promptly recruited a lot of the designers and programmers from the Digital project to staff Microsoft's new NT operating system project. Despite the fact that Microsoft continued to market the LAN Manager product well into the early 1990s, Microsoft Windows NT was the network operating system on which Microsoft was betting the future of the company.

All this background is to show you how thoroughly Microsoft thought out and researched the NT operating system. From MS-NET to LAN Man to OS/2 to Windows, and even to Novell's NetWare, the success or failure of each of these network technologies played an important role in what was and was not included in Microsoft Windows NT Server and NT Workstation.

Taking NT to the nth degree

In 1993, Microsoft finally released its much-ballyhooed network operating system, Windows NT Advanced Server version 3.1. Microsoft cleverly avoided the appearance that NT was a new, unknown product by using version number 3.1, a continuation of the last release of LAN Manager. As we've already discussed, LAN Man and NT Advanced Server have little in common, but the version number was still a stroke of marketing genius by Microsoft.

The first release of NT was nothing to write home about, unless you were Microsoft. NT version 3.1 suffered from an insatiable appetite for memory and had no provision for interconnecting with the vast installed base of NetWare servers. Still, you could see the shape of things to come.

NT 3.5 is almost there

While NT Advanced Server version 3.1 was turning heads around the network world, Microsoft was quietly going about the business of making NT a real contender for the network throne.

The memory requirements in NT version 3.5 were brought more into line with those of NetWare. Optimization of the operating system code led to significant speed increases. Microsoft, recognizing that its Windows product was installed on an ever-increasing number of desktop PCs, developed and included a set of server administration tools that ran under Windows for Workgroups, thereby giving most network administrators tools to administer the new NT servers from their desktop PCs.

Beginning with NT Advanced Server version 3.5, NetWare support and TCP/IP support were included in the box at no extra charge. The support for NetWare was a particularly important point for NT's success in the network marketplace. Without a slick and easy way for an existing client PC to connect to a NetWare file server and an NT server at the same time, NT would be facing an uphill battle in those shops where NetWare was already the chosen server operating system.

Back in 1993, when NT version 3.1 was released, hundreds of thousands of companies around the world had NetWare servers installed and running. There had to be a clear and simple path for migration. Large companies couldn't switch server operating systems overnight; changes of this magnitude must be phased in to be successful. No matter how impressive NT's performance, real-world situations dictated that NetWare interoperability be an important feature of NT. So Microsoft spent a lot of time and money making sure that NT Server 3.5 could peacefully coexist with NetWare clients and servers when it was released in late 1993. And it does a magnificent job in this respect. While they were at it, the NT team at Microsoft also included connectivity for Macintosh clients in the finished product.

The next to the last in the relatively short line of released NT products is NT version 3.51. Although basically a "compatibility fix" for the mature version 3.5 product, version 3.51 added a few unique and important features (including support for Office 95) to permit this new 32-bit application to function seamlessly with Windows NT, as well as Windows 95.

Let's run through a list of all the major features included in NT Server version 3.51:

- ✔ **Based on the domain concept**: Allows for a single log on to all network resources, regardless of the NT server on which the resource resides.

- ✔ **Multithreaded, multitasking operating system:** Allows the operating system to execute multiple instructions and tasks concurrently (that is, NT can do more than one thing at a time).

- ✔ **Supports multiple processors:** Customized versions of NT Server can support up to 16 processors per server. The stock NT Server supports up to four processors per server. NT Workstation supports up to two processors per workstation.

- ✔ **Supports lots of RAM:** NT Server supports up to an astounding 4 gigabytes of RAM in each server.

- ✔ **Available on multiple hardware processor platforms:** Native versions of NT are available for MIPS-based machines, RISC-based machines, and Intel-based personal computers. Ports to other hardware platforms are fairly easy due to the use of the C programming language for the majority of the NT program. The small amount of NT that is processor-specific is in a well-defined area, known as the hardware abstraction layer, or HAL. Rewriting just the HAL is all that is required to port NT to different processor platforms.

- ✔ **Server logs account activity:** NT has the capability to log almost every action a user makes on the server, such as file accesses, log ons, and log outs.

- ✔ **Server logs system events:** NT can also log system events, such as tape backup messages, service errors, and disk anomalies.

- ✔ **Interconnects easily with NetWare clients and servers:** NT supports IPX as a native protocol through the NWLink stack, Microsoft's IPX-compatible protocol. This allows NetWare clients to log on and map drives directly to an NT server much like a NetWare server. Alternatively, you can log the NT server on to the NetWare server and then share NetWare directories and files through the NT server to Windows or NT client workstations. A cool feature when coexistence or migration from NetWare to NT is required!

✔ **Built-in Macintosh connectivity:** NT Server talks AppleTalk, the language of the Mac, with little effort on your part. After you enable the AppleTalk service, the NT server appears to the Mac on your network like a regular Mac would. You can then share files, directories, and printers on the NT server (or servers) with the Mac.

✔ **Server fault-tolerance, such as multiple NICs, mirroring, and RAID:** With NT Server, you can enable fault-tolerance, which is a fancy way of saying that if something breaks on the server, a backup system automatically takes over. So, in a way, fault-tolerance also means that the network stays up even when hardware in the server goes down. RAID (redundant array of inexpensive drives) means you can use ubiquitous, cheap hard drives without losing the security that expensive dedicated drives provide. NT Server supports RAID levels 0,1, and 5. We'll talk a lot more about RAID later in the book.

✔ **Remote Access Service (RAS) built-in:** With RAS (pronounced "razz") built into NT Server, remote users, either on the road or calling in from home, can call directly to the NT Server and access server-based applications and printers, just like a local user. In addition, RAS has many built-in security features that you can enable to prevent unauthorized access from network ne'er-do-wells. See Chapter 15 for an exhaustive discussion of RAS.

✔ **Extensive protocol support (IPX, NetBEUI, TCP/IP, DLC):** NT supports a wide variety of standard network protocols. The only one we haven't mentioned before is DLC (Data Link Control). DLC is used primarily to talk to mainframe gateways and remote print servers. We discuss protocols in greater detail in Chapter 17.

Look into the crystal ball: the future of NT

As we write this book, the latest versions of Windows NT, both Workstation and Server, have just been released by Microsoft. These new versions build on Windows NT 3.51's considerable strengths, remedy most of Windows NT 3.51's deficiencies, and offer users some new features as well. Here's a rundown of the features and fixes in the current NT Workstation version 4.0 software:

✔ **New Win95 Shell:** The latest version of NT sports a new shell that is a replica of the user interface found in Windows 95. Its best features are its increased flexibility and ease of customization. The new GUI provides built-in capabilities for shortcuts, menu definition, and other interface changes that the earlier interface couldn't support without additional software.

✔ **Expanded NetWare support:** Microsoft has continued to enhance NT's capability to coexist and cooperate with NetWare servers and clients.

✔ **Enhanced hardware support:** Microsoft has expanded the number of hardware drivers included with the NT software to include more video boards, printer drivers, tape backup devices, and hard drive controllers than ever before. This expansion of drivers will help those who have complained that their particular type of hardware did not have NT drivers.

✔ **Improved TCP/IP support:** Microsoft continues to make TCP/IP more central to its networking capabilities. Enhancements to the default network installation and numerous improvements to NT's IP capabilities are included in this latest release.

✔ **Bundled Internet/intranet services** (NT Server only): NT Server 4.0 includes Microsoft's Internet Information Server, a fully functional Web server, plus the Front Page Web site authoring and management product. This means organizations will be able to set up and run Web servers "right out of the box" when they purchase this version of NT Server. The product also includes a Gopher server, plus a management utility that provides a single interface to manage Web, FTP, and Gopher servers from within a single utility.

✔ **Improved administration:** NT 4.0 has streamlined access to the system's administrative functions and utilities, making it easier to navigate and manage than ever before. You'll also find helpful wizards that can steer you through all the administrative utilities, one item at a time.

✔ **Microsoft License Manager:** NT 4.0 includes a License Manager utility to help administrators manage software licenses for NT components (including both Server and Workstation) as well as BackOffice components. It's a first toward providing uniform, built-in software license management right in the OS.

We think Windows NT 4.0 will be the version that helps this outstanding operating system invade networks everywhere. Its combination of features and functions makes it hard to beat for organizations of all sizes!

NT on Parade: a Retrospective

You should now have a good idea of where Microsoft Windows NT came from and where it's going. Each design and marketing decision Microsoft makes seems to ensure that NT will continue to be a popular and widely used operating system. From the beginnings of MS-NET through the trying years of LAN Man to the current incarnations of NT Server and Workstation, Microsoft has used a keen eye to focus on the competition and the needs of the network user community. This focus continues to worry Novell as NT grabs much-valued marketshare from NetWare operating systems.

As both NT and NetWare mature, they are slowly converging on a common set of features and capabilities. The winner of this contest will be the company that can best support its existing customers while offering the biggest bang for the buck. Although Novell has held a commanding lead of network operating system marketshare for the last ten years, you cannot overlook the considerable marketing might of Microsoft. The sheer number of PCs in the world that run a Microsoft operating system indicate that Microsoft will always be an important player in the network world. We have seen the future and it is NT. Our magic eight ball told us so.

Chapter 13

SCSI-Wuzzy Wasn't Fuzzy, Was (S)he?

*T*he Small Computer System Interface, or SCSI (pronounced "scuzzy"), is a language and hardware interface designed to connect computer peripherals, such as hard disks, CD-ROM drives, tape drives, and scanners. It's an input/output (I/O) parallel bus specification adopted by the American National Standards Institute (ANSI) in 1986. Although there are other types of interfaces in wide use, such as Integrated Disk Electronics (IDE), SCSI is faster, supports more types of devices, and is the standard interface of choice for business use — especially on network servers. Therefore, it's the focus of this chapter.

As of mid-1996, Windows NT supports more than

- ✔ 60 SCSI host adapters
- ✔ 30 SCSI CD-ROM drives
- ✔ 40 SCSI tape drives
- ✔ 10 SCSI removable media systems
- ✔ Some SCSI scanners

That's a lot to choose from, and should cover nearly everybody's peripheral attachment needs for the Windows NT Server environment.

Plumbing the Hardware Interface

A hardware interface allows computer devices to communicate with one another. For example, a SCSI host adapter (interface card) plugs in to a slot in your PC and connects a peripheral device to the computer. Just how fast communications take place depends on the level of SCSI technology (SCSI-1, SCSI-2, Fast SCSI-2, FAST/WIDE SCSI-2, and so on) you purchase. As you might guess, the more words in the SCSI title (FAST/WIDE SCSI versus SCSI), and the higher the number (SCSI-2 versus SCSI-1), the faster your peripheral device should be able to communicate with your computer's CPU.

At one time, SCSI was the only way to connect disk drives to computers that contained more than 528MB. Today, that limitation can be overcome, but most old-time NetWare servers probably contain SCSI drives for that very reason. Even though Windows NT supports more options than SCSI, we think SCSI is still your best choice for attaching peripherals to your computer, be it for Windows NT Workstation or Server flavors.

For SCSI to work properly, you must buy a peripheral device that supports SCSI technology, and you must have the proper SCSI cable (which is thick and not very pliable because it typically has 50-68 pins in it). On a single host adapter card, you can supposedly daisy-chain up to seven SCSI devices (or more on some advanced models such as the Adaptec 2940 UltraWide). Theoretically, you can have seven SCSI cards in a computer — if you have that many slots! (You'd also need a heck of a lot of electrical sockets, too — we've seldom seen more than four or five SCSI devices on any single computer, whether it be a server or workstation.)

After you install a SCSI adapter card in your computer, you can connect any SCSI device to that card using the special cable mentioned previously. Each SCSI device (or peripheral) is identified by a unique ID number, so it won't be mixed up with any other devices you connect to that card.

When you have all the hardware in place, you need to install some software, known as drivers, to initiate and control the communications between peripheral devices and the computer. Software drivers are small computer programs written specifically to enable such communications. Typically, manufacturers provide these drivers on a disk that ships with the device or permit you to download them from some on-line source. Figuring out which driver to use can sometimes be the most challenging part of the whole exercise!

TECHNICAL STUFF

More about SCSI

If you're not scared by details and want to know more specifics about SCSI, continue reading. If you've obtained enough technical jargon for now, skip this sidebar.

Work on SCSI standards began early in the 1980s. Upon its conception, it was known simply as SCSI. Back then, SCSI emerged from a need to increase disk transfer rates as newer applications demanded faster speeds. Seagate's ST506 transfer rate of 300 Kbps lost its position as "king of the road" when SCSI stepped in at a whopping 1 Mbps. Pretty funny now, eh? But then, SCSI was three times faster than existing technology, and it started getting some serious attention.

The only pitfall was that the technology included only two devices: the disk drive and the host adapter. There weren't any devices like CD-ROMs available for PCs. The original SCSI technology was unsophisticated: it didn't even support daisy-chaining multiple devices into a single adapter card. Unfortunately, many vendors interpreted their SCSI implementations loosely, creating a nightmare for anyone who tried to interconnect SCSI products from more than one vendor. When these problems surfaced, it became apparent that a SCSI revision was required, which led to the birth of SCSI-2.

SCSI-2

In 1986, a proposal to enforce a stricter interpretation of the SCSI-1 standard initiated the birth of the SCSI-2 standard. Its intent was to eliminate the multivendor SCSI interconnectivity problem. Four years in the making, it was submitted to ANSI, where it spent another three years before being finalized. That's a long time! But where SCSI-1 boasted 1 Mbps, SCSI-2 supported a 10 Mbps transfer rate and also widened the bus. Later additions to SCSI-2 to incorporate FAST and WIDE technology brought it up to 20 Mbps. This was fast!

SCSI-3

As Bill Gates and other software giants began to pound the industry with more and more graphics and data-intensive applications, SCSI had to evolve to yet another level to keep pace with the demand. ANSI was brought back to the drawing table to finalize SCSI-3 specifications of speeds up to 40 Mbps. SCSI-3 was finalized in 1995.

Table 13-1				The levels of SCSI	
Standard	**Width (bytes)**	**Cable name**	**Pin count**	**Max transfer rate (Mbps)**	**Description**
SCSI-1	1	A	50	5	Asynchronous
SCSI-2	1	A	50	10	Fast
SCSI-2	2	A+B	50+68	20	Fast+Wide*
SCSI-2	4	A+B	50+68	40	Fast+Wide*
SCSI-3	1	A	50	10	Fast
SCSI-3	2	P	68	20	Fast+Wide
SCSI-3	4	P+Q	68+68	40	Fast+Wide*

* Uses 2 cables

Configuring NT for SCSI Devices

You can't install a SCSI device on NT without an NT SCSI device driver. In other words, you can't use an old SCSI device on NT unless you've obtained the proper NT driver. If the device is listed in NT's Hardware Compatibility List (HCL), you're in luck because the NT network operating system ships with that driver included. If you opt to go with a device that's not on that list, you have to get the driver from the manufacturer.

Be aware that not all manufacturers offer NT drivers for their devices. This is particularly true for old or obsolete hardware, so you should never purchase used equipment that contains components that don't appear on the HCL. Before you make your purchase, ask the seller about NT compatibility or go on-line to the manufacturer's Web site and do a little poking around. Whenever possible, stick with well-known SCSI manufacturers, such as Adaptec, BusLogic, and DTP. It might cost a little more, but your life will be simpler.

If your device is supported by NT and is on the Hardware Compatibility List, it should be easy to install and configure. In fact, NT should automatically recognize your SCSI device at installation. You need to make sure that the ID of the SCSI CD-ROM drive from which you install NT is set to anything other than zero or one because some SCSI BIOS setups reserve these ID numbers exclusively for disk drives. It's also a good idea to stay away from SCSI ID 7 because this is usually reserved for the SCSI card itself.

When you install NT from the CD, you still have to load three disks first. As you might have guessed, drivers for popular SCSI devices are contained on these disks. That's why we suggest that you stick with popular devices.

As NT's Setup program starts up, it takes the SCSI drivers from the floppies and loads them into memory. The NTDETECT program tries to recognize your CD-ROM drive, and then loads the appropriate drivers.

Don't panic if your device isn't automatically recognized during installation. You can always copy the device drivers to the setup disk and proceed. (Note: This is an extra step you wouldn't have to mess with if you purchased one of the popular brands.)

SCSI devices require termination — plugs on both ends of the SCSI chain. SCSI adapters require that termination power be provided on the SCSI bus, either by the device or the adapter, and may or may not require configuration options. Check your card and device manuals for specific information about termination. Whatever you read there, please remember this: Most SCSI problems can be traced back to improper termination or no termination. So it's especially important that you learn about the devices you've purchased and read the famous manual (RTFM).

Adding a SCSI device after you've already installed NT is straightforward. In most cases, NT will automatically install the proper drivers. But you can do it yourself, if you must. Here's how: In the Control Panel, use the Devices option to configure the device's startup type. If you're adding a CD-ROM device, set the Startup value for that device to System. Most likely, you'll want these devices to start up as either System or Automatic, depending on how critical they are to your system's operation. For more information on these Startup options, highlight one of the SCSI devices, click on the Startup button, and then click on the Help button.

The information you change here will be reflected in NT's Registry under the HKEY_LOCAL_MACHINE\SYSTEM\CurrentControlSet subtree. We cover the NT Registry, and when and how to make changes to it directly, in Chapter 24.

You can also tinker with the order in which your devices load, but we don't recommend this if you're a newbie. Here's why: If you make an incorrect entry in the Registry, you could render your machine inoperable. In other words, you'd be shooting yourself in the foot! We suggest you reserve manual Registry edits for when you're feeling especially knowledgeable about NT. (We do it only in cases of the most dire necessity.)

SCSI Configuration Tools and Techniques

Unless properly configured, any SCSI adapter can create memory conflicts with other cards — such as network interface cards (NICs). This is particularly apt to occur when an interface card uses jumpers that must be set manually. But with the right configuration tools at your disposal, you can avoid most of these problems. That's probably why both Adaptec and Corel offer SCSI configuration toolkits.

Adaptec

Adaptec, Inc., is probably the most popular SCSI host adapter company; visit their Web site at http://www.adaptec.com. If you purchase one of their cards, you'll lessen the odds of encountering installation woes.

Certain Adaptec cards and revisions have known sensitivities, incompatibilities, or anomalies. For example, Adaptec's AHA154xC card is sensitive to termination and cabling, so you should use a SCSI-2 cable and terminator to avoid problems.

Adaptec provides its EZ-SCSI software with its SCSI controller to ensure easy configuration and to provide diagnostic utilities for Adaptec SCSI devices. They also license this software to other vendors who use Adaptec's SCSI controller chipsets. EZ-SCSI is tailored for Windows 95 or NT, so make sure you get the NT version. It includes a helpful tutorial called SCSI*Tutor* that will help you learn about and use SCSI features. If you have an Adaptec board or one that's built around an Adaptec chipset that didn't ship with EZ-SCSI software, contact Adaptec at 800-959-7274 (inside the U.S.) or 408-945-8600 (outside the U.S.) for information on how to obtain this useful utility. Even if you have to pay for it, you'll still find it worthwhile!

Corel

Corel's SCSI tool set, unlike Adaptec's, is not hardware-specific. It's called Corel SCSI and is shipping at version 2.5 as we write this chapter. Corel SCSI includes some useful CD-ROM applications, drivers, and utilities. Currently, their Network Manager product supports only Novell's NetWare, so NT users can't take advantage of the Corel product that permits CD-ROMs to be shared across a network. If you want to keep up with where Corel is headed, visit their Web site at http://www.corel.com.

Other sources of information and inspiration

Adaptec and Corel aren't the only names you'll encounter in the SCSI world. Vendors such as BusLogic, Future Domain, Maynard, and UltraStor manufacture SCSI adapters. PC manufacturers, including Compaq, Dell, and IBM, also ship PCs with built-in SCSI devices. Some motherboards feature built-in SCSI adapters.

When SCSI gets strange, the pros turn weird!

If you have a SCSI device that's listed on the HCL but seems to be acting strange, even though you think it's configured properly, consult the Microsoft TechNet CD-ROM to see whether there are any known incompatibilities. Just because it's a supported device and on the Hardware Compatibility List doesn't mean that it's compatible when used in combination with other supported devices. (It would be impossible for Microsoft to test every combination of devices.) Therefore, before you spend hours banging your head against the wall when beset by strange installation or behavior problems, use tools such as the TechNet CD-ROM or Microsoft's on-line Knowledge Base to look for known gotchas.

If you plan your installation on paper, you can go on-line and easily find out whether there are any known incompatibilities in the configuration. If you've already bought the hardware, it could be too late. But if you check these resources before you break the shrinkwrap, you can often return any potential troublemakers for equipment that doesn't show up in the discussions of installation gotchas and problem children.

An unusually good source of NT information

If we haven't yet promoted Microsoft's own TechNet CD adequately, we'd like to re-emphasize it here. It's worth its weight in gold. With two CD-ROMs packed with scads of technical information on everything from how the technology works to why it might not work, it's a very useful compendium of NT-related information (not to mention the rest of Microsoft's products). Each time a particular technology manifests compatibility problems, the findings are posted there for all to learn. If there's a workaround to such problems, it's also posted.

You can probably find on the TechNet CDs most of the help you need in configuring SCSI devices. True, the CDs do cost $395 a year for a subscription. If you can't afford that, talk to your local reseller or the company that sold you your copy of Windows NT: Chances are good they'll have one you can use, or perhaps you can persuade them to use it on your behalf.

One of the best ways to obtain information about SCSI is to go directly to the vendors. Often, they have faxback services if you can't interact with them directly on-line. It's not uncommon to find Frequently Asked Questions (FAQs), white papers, and a host of other technical information available from these companies; sometimes, they even offer useful tutorial information on SCSI, as well.

 If you're leery about downloading information that you think might be biased, visit one of the popular search engines on the Internet (that is, `http://www.search.com`) and type *SCSI* as the search keyword. You might be surprised at the number of resources and the technical depth of much of the material you'll find.

If you're still scratching your head, one of the following publications can help your quest for SCSI knowledge:

- Lohmeyer, John B. *SCSI: Understanding the Small Computer System Interface*, Prentice Hall
- Stai, Jeffrey D. *The SCSI Bench Reference*, ENDL Publications, Saratoga, CA, 1989 (408-867-6642)

SCSI Devices Unveiled

The beauty of installing a network operating system that's been designed recently and is SCSI-aware is that you shouldn't have too many headaches during the installation and configuration of such devices. Most of your troubles will come from mixing vendors' products, from conflicting configurations or termination woes, or from trying to use nonsupported devices (that is, stuff that's not on the HCL).

The following characteristics should help you understand when you'll need to use SCSI. Most of the deciding factors depend on your organization's networking needs. However, here are four salient reasons why you might want to consider using SCSI devices on your Windows NT server:

✔ **NT's multithreading capabilities:** NT was designed as a multithreaded, multitasking operating system. It can take advantage of the multitasking nature of SCSI technology to provide better performance than other technologies.

✔ **Intelligence and independence:** Each SCSI device houses a built-in controller that frees up the CPU to perform other tasks, making the server more efficient.

✔ **I/O that is independent of the system bus:** You can attach SCSI devices to different types of computers, which comes in handy if your organization uses different kinds of platforms (for example, PCs and Macs).

✔ **Similar characteristics:** Classes of SCSI devices (such as CD-ROM drives) are easy to upgrade because of their similarities, especially at the interface level. That's why you can unplug an older 2X SCSI CD-ROM and replace it with a 6X or 8X equivalent without going through too many contortions.

There's just one more thing we'll mention before we go on: If you need to buy SCSI for one reason or another, it's prudent to standardize all your devices so that they're all SCSI. Smaller organizations may think that we're hitting them square in the wallet with this recommendation. But can you really save money by using several technologies and being forced to learn how to configure them all? Or do you perhaps save some money by standardizing and then ironing out as many kinks as you can all at once? We can only recommend standardization — after all, it's your money!

SCSI is for hard disks, too

Remember, lots of I/O action happens on your server's disk drives. The more users that access the server, the more action these drives will see. Don't soup up your servers and then use slow disk drives — you'll just create a huge bottleneck. And if that happens, your users will be sure to notice!

Using SCSI technology for hard disks is a brilliant way to go. Some will argue that it's the only way to go. SCSI technology does for disk drives what Speedo bathing suits did for swimmers! If you're not convinced, visit your local computer store and ask them for a demonstration. You should see a noticeable difference between SCSI and non-SCSI drives.

In today's world, faster is better, particularly if these drives will house an application server that's bound to pound its hard drives. If the drives will be used for mere file and print services, you might be able to squeak by with another kind of controller. But here again, you need to consider the number of users and the size of the files to be accessed. Why not save yourself some potential grief and use SCSI from the get-go?

CD-ROM players

Whether you use SCSI technology for these CD-ROM players is strictly a judgment call on your part, depending on the intended usage of the drive. For example, if you intend to use the drive merely to install NT, you don't need a particularly fast drive (unless you're in a hurry to get NT installed). If you intend to share the CD player across the network, however, plan to use SCSI drives — you'll need the speed!

While you're pondering this point, check the HCL and compare the number of non-SCSI CD-ROM devices supported by Windows NT versus the number of SCSI options available. Frightening, isn't it?

It's easier to install NT with SCSI-attached drives than with IDE drives. Microsoft is working feverishly to offset SCSI's substantial advantage.

Tape drives

When backing up data to tape drives, you'll want to get the data on the drives as fast as possible. This means you'll want nothing but SCSI. Even if your backup strategy requires you to perform a full backup only once a week, you can significantly reduce the time it takes by using SCSI drives. And if you ever have to restore a tape, you're not going to want to fumble around with a slow drive. This is particularly true when you have 300 users looking over your shoulder, waiting for their data to be restored!

Scanners

Scanners are graphics-intensive devices and, therefore, transfer a lot of data. Just how fast you want that data to transfer depends on the device's level of usage. If it's in heavy demand, SCSI would be the smart choice. If an occasional user wanders by and that user's time isn't billable at $350 an hour, you might be okay with a slower interface. But you can plug a scanner into an existing SCSI controller (all part of one big, happy daisy-chain), so why not make it SCSI? You should be glad to know that most quality scanners are SCSI-based.

Avoiding Preinstallation Jitters

When it comes time to install a SCSI device, recall that SCSI technology boils down to three basic components: a host adapter card, a cable, and a peripheral. These three components form a communications channel called a bus. Each end of the bus must be terminated. You can expand one end of the bus by daisy-chaining additional SCSI devices to the end where peripherals are attached. If you remember these simple facts, you'll be well equipped to detect difficulties as they occur and to conquer them with grace and panache.

Don't be scared by the terminology or the big, fat cables. Your best defense against problems is to gather knowledge before you attempt to configure and install SCSI devices. The technology itself is simple.

When Trouble Comes, Ask Questions First, Shoot Second

We found oodles of troubleshooting information in Microsoft's TechNet CD. Some of the information was incredibly specific, down to the device level, the driver level, and more. For example, one of the notes in the database referred to troubleshooting a particular HP scanner. The solution suggested that you turn on the scanner before booting the PC so that NT could recognize the device. It also mentioned certain revision numbers of the driver that weren't supported by NT.

So if you're experiencing trouble, there's no need to employ brute force. There's plenty of information on these CDs to assist you. Use as many of the resources we provide in this chapter as you can to assist your installation. Call your friends and neighbors because NT is gaining popularity quite quickly and they're probably installing it, too!

Doing the Update-Upgrade Shuffle: Dealing with Devices

The last piece of advice we want to leave you with is this: Don't upgrade just for the sake of upgrading. If your setup works and a newer version of a driver comes out, don't install it unless it specifically addresses a problem you want to solve. If that driver provides newer capabilities that you need and don't have, install it with caution. Some new drivers, when loaded, have been known to wreak havoc in an otherwise perfectly stable environment. When possible, install a new driver on a test system first and see how it behaves (or at least survey the on-line complaints about the driver before jumping into unknown waters).

Chapter 14

Connecting Your NT Network

● ●

In This Chapter

▶ Preparing for installation

▶ Dealing with client-side differences

▶ Logging on to NT

▶ Logging off of NT

▶ Bringing the server down gracefully

▶ Getting a charge out of lightning

▶ Making a system backup

▶ Documenting the network

▶ Using a UPS

▶ Ensuring network integrity with spare parts

● ●

*I*f you're installing NT for the first time, and don't have other network operating systems to contend with, consider yourself lucky. The NT installation takes about one hour if all your equipment is listed on the Hardware Compatibility List. (Okay, even if you have all the right equipment, you could experience some configuration issues.)

For a plain old install (we don't recommend that you try a complicated install your first time out), you'll need a server, monitor, CD-ROM drive, 3 ¹/₂-inch floppy drive, hard disk, and RAM. You'll also need NT's installation software, which ships a few different ways. The most commonly used method is a CD-ROM, with three floppy disks on the side.

Gather all your manuals together (both hardware and software) so they're handy in case you need them. Assemble all the different vendors' phone numbers and keep them handy, too. Then take the plunge! Practice if you can at first, and install on a machine where it doesn't matter if you have to start over (or leave yourself enough time to try a few approaches, in case your first try doesn't work out).

You'll also need to understand the ins and outs of NT domains, but we cover those separately in Chapter 18.

Examining Client-Side Differences

There are many different client operating systems to worry about if you — like most people — live in a mixed network environment. If your organization uses standardized client setups, take a bow because your organization is a rare exception. If not, be prepared for a few extra gyrations along the way.

Before you go live and install your network, you may find it handy to set up a small test network. This can be as simple as a server and a workstation connected by a single cable. With this setup, you can test how different client operating systems will behave with the applications you're proposing to use.

Windows 3.1, a 16-bit application, behaves differently than Windows 95, a 32-bit application. Even though all Microsoft client types are supported in the NT networking environment, each one requires a different network installation. In general, clients designed to be network-aware are much easier to connect to a network. That's why Windows 3.1 and DOS require the most work to get connected — they don't have as many built-in networking features as do later versions of Windows. The older the operating system, the more work it is to hook it up to a network.

Microsoft has stated that NT Workstation is their workstation platform of choice for the future. This doesn't mean that if you've recently purchased 30 copies of Windows 95 you're in trouble; it just means that, eventually, most applications will be written specifically for NT. It also means that Microsoft will soon encourage everyone to migrate to NT Workstation. However, there are still plenty of DOS users in this world, and there will always be different client types, such as Macintoshes and UNIX machines, no matter what Microsoft wants everybody to do. Dealing with multiple clients will remain a fact of networking life well into the next century.

Log ons

Logging on to the network is an essential part of maintaining a secure environment. And we don't mean setting up your network so everyone logs on as Guest either! The logon process involves entering a valid logon ID and then a valid password. If they're authenticated (that is, if the user name and password combination match what's in the logon database), the user can gain access to the network resources that he or she is permitted to use.

You probably lock your house when you leave for work, lock your car door when you park it, and keep your checkbook in a safe place. You do this because those things are valuable to you. And although most of the world contains honest citizens, a small percentage insists on relieving people of their worldly goods. Data on the network is your organization's worldly goods, so treat it as reverently as you treat any of your other valuables.

By requiring users to log on using their own account names, you can limit where they can go on the network. If you allow them to log on to the network using the same account name, everyone can access the network with that same account. In this setting, everyone obtains the same access to the network, which can be dangerous. You and your users will be better off if you can identify them (by using unique account names). That way, you'll also be able to grant rights to resources based on a person's duties (accounting people need to be able to use the accounting database, but someone in the mail room probably doesn't) and a person's stature in your organization (maybe the mail room manager does need access to his budget from the accounting database, but the mail clerks don't).

Log offs

Logging off the network is another essential piece of the security process. Leaving your workstation unattended while remaining logged on to the network opens the door to potential security breaches. Now let's magnify that situation: What if the network administrator logged on with full rights to the system and walked away without logging off?

There's no way to force users to log off, but you can make it a network policy. Then remind them if you pass by their desk and find them gone but still logged on to the network. We once worked for an organization that periodically had the local police department come through and perform a security audit. The police would place little cards on folks' desktops whenever they found purses or other valuables out in the open in vulnerable areas. You could use this same concept on your network, and leave little cards to remind your users. Make the cards nonthreatening — you want to inform your users, not alienate them.

Lower than a Snake's Belly: Bringing the Server Down

If you've ever installed an NT server and then made a change, you're painfully aware of how often NT requires that the server be brought down after such changes. You can't add enhancements to your NT server during business hours.

Okay, you can, but then your users will lose their connections to that server when it shuts down, as well as any information that hasn't been saved. If you've ever seen this happen, you know that it's not a pretty sight!

A better way to handle this is to schedule your maintenance work for non-peak hours, and then notify your users when you plan to do the work. The more notice you give them, the better. I prefer a two-week notification process. Your users are contributing to the sales (and other measures of success) of your organization. When you take their network resources away, they can't earn money for the company or do whatever it is that they do. If you take their resources away without giving them a chance to work around your changes, they'll get angry.

Case in point: Mr. Network Administrator, Jim Nasium, decides he needs to add some software on the network. It's Tuesday, so he figures that he'll wait a few days until Saturday, because very few employees work on Saturday. But Ms. Sales Manager, Ima Salesrep, has to give a sales presentation to the President (Mr. Luke Warm) on Monday, and decides to wait until Saturday when it's quiet around the office to get her presentation together. When Ima arrives at the office on Saturday and finds the network down, she's mad, and can't seem to find those darned IT folks. How could this have been handled better? The network administrator might have sent a general email message to all network users with the following information:

- Header information (To, From, and Date Posted).
- Downtime date and time.
- Expected uptime.
- Reason for downtime (upgrade, maintenance, and so on).
- The person who's taking the system down.
- Exactly what systems and resources will be down. (Some users don't know the difference between your NT server and the IBM mainframe. If one system will be up but the other will be down, specify which functions they will and won't be able to perform.)
- Who to call if the downtime conflicts with a business unit's planned work.
- A way for users to know exactly when the system is back up (for example, leave an outgoing voicemail message on someone's extension).
- Who to call if users experience problems.
- Thank the users for their cooperation. (It never hurts to end a memo or message with a thank you.)

Here's a sample email to users:

```
TO:    Network Users in Building A
FROM: Network Administrator, Jim Nasium
DATE POSTED: May 1, 2001
In two weeks, on Saturday, May 14, 2001, at 10:00 AM, I
plan to take down the network for maintenance and
upgrade work. I anticipate that the system will be down
until Sunday morning at 8 AM.
When I bring the system back up and test it, I will
place an outgoing message on my voice mailbox, x6210.
Therefore, if you intend to work on Sunday, please call
x6210 and listen to my outgoing message before traveling to
the office to make sure that it indicates the network is up.
I will be available by pager (512-555-6451) on Sunday
should you experience any problems after the system
is up.
On Monday, please contact the Help Desk if you
experience any difficulties. They will be standing by
to take your call and page and dispatch an IT person
to assist you.
This downtime will affect any users accessing Microsoft
Office on the network and any printers. It will not
affect access to the data on your local drives, nor any
mainframe access.
If this downtime will impact your business unit, please
contact Jim immediately at x6210 to reschedule this
procedure.
Thanks in advance for your cooperation!
```

Make the email message only one screen in length. Any more, and your users will be too busy to read it. The idea is to make it easy for users to read the message and then continue on with their work, but to make sure that they do read it.

If you educate your users properly, they'll become accustomed to the idea that you respect their time on the weekends, and they'll become confident that your network will be up unless you specifically send a note informing them that it won't.

For network broadcast messages to work, don't blast unnecessary messages like "Today is so-and-so's birthday." Instead, use broadcasts sparingly, only when you have something important to say about the system.

Some users have been known to go an entire week or two without logging on, so make sure you have a way to reach those employees as well. For example, you might have remote salespeople who dial in to the network only once a month to upload sales reports. In this case, you could try to send an email or voicemail message in addition to the network broadcast message.

Finally, it's important to take down your NT servers gracefully. Don't simply hit the power button; rather, select Start⇨Shut Down from the server's desktop. Shutting down gracefully gives the system an opportunity to close all its system files so that they don't become corrupted. It also gives the system a chance to perform any assigned cleanup tasks that otherwise might be left in limbo.

Lightning Can Be a Real Charge!

Although some of Mother Nature's forces (rain, for example) are helpful and serve a purpose in our lives, others can be destructive. Lightning and other natural phenomena, such as tornadoes and hurricanes, can play hob with your supply of electricity, which can, in turn, wreak havoc on your network, servers, and workstations.

The best ammunition against these destructive forces is preparedness. Here are a few steps you can take to reduce their risks at your organization:

- ✔ **Regular backups:** If you back up your system on a regular basis, chances are good that, if disaster hits, you'll have a recent tape from which you can restore data. That is, you will if you don't store the backup tapes in the same room as the system equipment.

- ✔ **Off-site storage of tapes:** Rotating your tapes off-site once a week to a location at least 20 miles away is considered good business practice. The farther away you can store the tapes, the better.

- ✔ **Placement of equipment:** This might seem obvious, but if your organization sits in the middle of a hurricane- and tornado-prone location, place your critical equipment away from windows. It's preferable to have an interior computer room. Don't place system equipment in the basement, either, because this increases the odds of loss in the event of a flood.

Look, Ma — It Eats Out of My Hand!

Just as you clip your nails and trim your hair from time to time, so must you groom your network and give it the care it needs. Regular preening helps your network keep its healthy glow. Ignoring your network leads you down the path of eventual disaster.

Make an appointment with yourself every week (for example, Friday mornings at 9:00) to perform maintenance checks on the network. For example, knowing how much disk space is consumed on a weekly basis gives you a head start on ordering additional disk space when needed. If you don't monitor disk usage, and wait until it's at zero bytes, you could disrupt your entire organization until the immediate problem is corrected.

Visit the event logs in your NT server on a daily basis if possible or once a week at a minimum. Look at what types of events occur on your network and with what frequency. An event that happens repeatedly could be the symptom of a larger problem. Know the peak usage times on your network and the load that's placed on it at those times. Typically, peak usage occurs first thing in the morning when users log on, and also around 1:00 or 2:00 in the afternoon.

Also, make an appointment with yourself once a week to walk the floors of your organization and make yourself visible and inquisitive. Users are probably your best gauge as to how the system is running, so ask them. Encourage them to call you when it's running slowly. You'd be surprised how many users experience a slow system, but never pick up the phone to report it. Call back every user who calls to report a problem and let them know you appreciate their feedback. Keep a log of all calls of this type so you can analyze this information at the end of the week.

Hold brown-bag seminars for users every month or two and give them your undivided attention. Tell them about the direction of things to come in your group, and ask for their input and suggestions. You'd be surprised at the power that a bunch of brains gathered together can generate. Send out an inquiry before the seminar, asking your users what topics they'd like to cover. The key is to show them you are interested in what they're thinking and share their concerns. Free pizza never hurts, either!

Backups, Backups, and More Backups

Step onto the soapbox. *DON'T RUN A NETWORK WITHOUT A BACKUP SYSTEM.* Step off the soapbox.

You cannot prevent data corruption. It happens to everyone, everywhere. Regardless of how much planning you do, you won't be able to prevent it.

The only way to survive this eventuality is to make sure you budget for a backup system for your network before you install the system. Don't put a system in place without one. Think of how sheepish you'll look when one of your users has corrupted data and comes to you to restore the file from tape, only to find that you didn't purchase a backup system yet.

It's a waste of users' time to redo lost work. And the cost of re-creating work just a few times will probably pay for a modest tape backup system.

We recommend that you make a full backup of your system once a week, and then perform incremental backups throughout the remainder of the week. You'll also want to take the full backup off-site somewhere safe.

Chapter 23 is devoted to LAN backups and restores. If you're not convinced here, flip to that chapter and read it. We're sure we'll convince you there!

Documentation, Documentation, Documentation

Look up the word *documentation* in any network administrator's dictionary, and you'll find a hole in that page where the word appeared at one time. None of them like the word. If you ask network administrators for their network documentation, some will look like they don't know what you're talking about. They've rehearsed that look just to fool you into thinking it's an odd request.

At least that was in the old days, before the task was somewhat automated. It was also before people started taking networks seriously. Now that some mission-critical data is on networks, vendors have designed software to assist in documenting a network.

Good documentation for a network starts at the physical layer of the OSI model and works its way up to the application layer. Most of the software available today is for Novell-based networks because they've been around for a while. However, inventory software and reporting tools are beginning to sprout for NT networks, as well. BindView Development Corp., based in Houston, Texas, provides software that analyzes your servers and workstations right down to the IRQs in use. Check Appendix C for information on contacting that company for more information. Peter Norton Software, a subsidiary of Symantec Corporation, is working to extend its Norton Administrator for Networks, which is built around a terrific inventory database, to encompass NT servers and networks. Many other vendors supply software that hooks into HP OpenView's Network Management Console. Software to aid the documentation task is available, if you want to spend the time, money, and effort required to find something you can live with.

Even if you can't afford to purchase software to automate this task, get yourself a huge three-ring binder and add some tabs. Here's a list of some labels for the tabs and information you'll absolutely want to include in your network documentation:

- ✓ **Servers:** Include serial numbers, brand names, amount of RAM, NICs, hard disks and capacity, applications, NOS version and patches loaded, IRQs, other configuration information, slot usage, and licensing, warranty, and maintenance information.

- ✓ **Workstations**: Include serial numbers, brand names, amount of RAM, NICs, hard disks and capacity, operating system and level, IRQs, configuration information, software, and licensing information.

- ✓ **Bridges/Routers:** Include serial numbers, brand names, connection points, filters used, protocols used, IP address information (if applicable), and usage reports.

- ✓ **Cabling:** This might require a separate notebook, but you'll want to record cable runs, types of cables (such as UTP, STP, Cat 5), numerical numbering schemes, blueprints, cable drawings, and more. Everything you think might be important probably is and should be noted.

- ✓ **Protocols:** Include names of protocols in use, special information about any of the protocols (such as "TCP/IP uses DHCP to assign IP addresses"), dial-up protocols, and so on.

- ✓ **User, group, and domain information:** It's also important to document how your network is structured. Make a list of all user names and the real names of the individuals with whom they're associated. Do the same for computer names: Compile a list of names, with a brief description of the location and person associated with each one. Provide a one-sentence description for each named group and domain. Provide a list of all your domain controllers, both primary and backup. Draw a diagram that relates users to groups, and both to domains. This will provide an excellent symbolic overview of your network.

- ✓ **Communications links:** Document all links with the account number of the link and the company charged with maintaining the link. Also note on a diagram any modems and links to places outside your building. This helps to quickly pinpoint danger zones on your network, because these links are most prone to security problems.

- ✓ **Downtime reports:** Keep a daily log of all device downtime and the amount of downtime (that is, minutes, hours, days), as well as the cause and resolution of downtime.

- ✓ **Maintenance logs:** Each device should have a separate maintenance log where you record every change made to that device. In addition, you should have a master log that covers all devices and all changes to the network (for example, changing a cable, changing a NIC, or updating a Service Pack). The master log will have less detailed information. Each time you make a change on the network, record a general entry in your master log and then go to the device log and record a detailed account of the work you've performed. If the network experiences downtime, your associates will check the master log first to see what has happened recently on the network and then go to the specific device log to pinpoint or narrow down the problem.

✔ **Diagrams:** You should have an up-to-date diagram of your entire network, complete with connecting lines. (A hand-drawn diagram is better than nothing.) Software programs such as Visio ship with preconfigured network templates that you can use to drag and drop predrawn network symbols onto a drawing board. Visio also permits layered drawings; for example, layer one could represent the physical layer, layer two could contain the servers and workstations, and so on. You can print each separate layer onto transparencies. Then, to look at your entire network, place all the transparencies on top of one another. If you want to look at a specific layer, you pull out that transparency.

Did We Mention Backups, Backups, and More Backups?

In case you skipped our section on backups, we wanted to remind you here that you're in charge of your entire organization's data safety. Losing it could prove disastrous for your organization (and for your employment status). Make frequent backups of your system!

Meet a Different UPS

An uninterruptible power supply, or *UPS*, is an essential part of a healthy network. It's basically a battery backup system. It says, "We know the power will fail at some point, and we don't care if it does because we're protected."

Servers can crash if there's a glitch in the power or a complete power failure. If you don't protect your servers against such electrical problems, you might find yourself restoring your server from a backup tape. This is because when a server crashes, you never know whether the data and hard disk will withstand the crash. However, if you place a UPS onto that server and the power fluctuates or stops flowing, the UPS will supply power to the server until you can shut it down gracefully. (Some UPS devices are smart enough to instruct the server to shut itself down without requiring operator intervention; just the thing for a 4 A.M. power outage.)

If you feel lucky and your organization doesn't care whether it loses data, you can do without a UPS. If you haven't won the lottery in the five years that you've been buying tickets, however, you should consider yourself unable to beat the odds, and shell out the dough to get one.

NT has a built-in utility for UPS tie-ins, but it's not too fancy. However, you still have to buy the actual UPS unit. Perhaps the most popular vendor that supplies UPSs today is American Power Conversion (APC). They have a variety of models that will fit just about any budget. See Appendix C for their address and phone number. They have software designed for NT that provides some pretty sophisticated graphical interfaces and monitoring capabilities. APC even offers cards that monitor UPS status and send alerts to your network management console when anomalies occur (if SNMP is enabled on your network).

Spare Parts

Wouldn't it be nice if your car came with a spare battery so that when one fails, the other kicks in? Will you need to maintain spare parts for your network? It's advisable, but not required. You could get by with just purchasing the equipment you need to make the network run.

The key to determining whether you should buy spare parts is figuring out how long your network can stand to be down while you're out getting a replacement part. Only you and your organization can answer this question. Once you determine the number of hours your network can be down, you can then perform a cost/benefit analysis on each component of your network to see whether it's worth buying spare parts.

For example, if your organization stands to lose $350,000 for every hour the network is inoperable, it might be prudent to purchase spare parts for your entire network to prevent even one hour of downtime. However, if your organization determines that it can be down for an entire day without too much impact on the business, it might be wiser to purchase a maintenance agreement that will cover same-day replacement.

If your network contains mission-critical data, you can look at "hot-swappable" spare parts. These parts replace bad components while the system is live. It's not uncommon to find hot-swappable disk drives, power supplies, and more. These parts are typically more expensive, but if they keep your network up and running, they might not be that expensive after all.

The best way to determine the amount of network downtime your organization can afford is to look at the nature of the business and the data on the network. Next, you'll want to survey the department heads for their ideas. Often, IT technical folks don't see the network the way the business folks do.

Anything that has movable parts is likely to wear down. As long as you plan how you're going to replace the parts, and as long as you have your organization's backing, you shouldn't have any problem. Just don't get caught with a broken network and no plan of action.

In this chapter, we covered some basic network security practices, from logging on to the network on the users' end to backing up the data on the administrator's end. We also covered a few ways to notify and work with the user, in hopes that you can maintain a healthy dialogue. We even described the process of documenting your network, in hopes that you can build a working profile of what's in, on, and around your networked world. In the next chapter, we cover the ins and outs of Microsoft's Remote Access Server (RAS).

Chapter 15

Making NT Server Communicate

● ●

In This Chapter

▶ Handling the NT Remote Access Service

▶ Dialing in to and out of the network

▶ Explaining "RAS-aware"

▶ Examining RAS hardware

▶ Installing RAS

● ●

As more employees travel and telecommute, they need a way to communicate with the office network. Microsoft includes Remote Access Service (RAS) in NT to accomplish this. If you want to go beyond the documentation and on-line help provided with Windows NT Server, you can download a RAS white paper from Microsoft's Web site at

```
http://www.microsoft.com/NTServer/ras.htm
```

The following list shows a few of the ways to use RAS:

✔ Give remote users the ability to dial in to your NT Server network.

✔ Dial up and connect to on-line resources.

✔ Dial up to on-line bulletin board systems.

✔ Dial up and connect to other networks.

✔ Operate applications and share files and devices over long distance communications links. (A communications link is the type of connection you use. It's usually a plain telephone line. But RAS allows you to connect over ISDN, ATM, and other sophisticated communications media.)

✔ Set up your NT Server to act as a router to the Internet for your local area network (LAN).

The question isn't, "Will I need RAS?" It's "When will I need RAS?" And because it's free when you buy NT, read on!

Individuals, as well as organizations of different sizes, have been dialing in to on-line services, such as America Online, CompuServe, and the Internet, over regular telephone lines for many years. These services offer masses of information, advice, and freebies on just about any topic.

The Internet, and some interesting and useful items, can also be accessed over a simple dial-up link to an Internet Service Provider (ISP). Although most ISPs provide a suite of TCP/IP tools for cruising the World Wide Web, transferring files, searching the Internet, and so on, Windows 95 and Windows NT include the same kind of software built in. Whether the software comes from your ISP or your OS, simply dial up the ISP and connect to the Internet through their equipment. This is a simple and cost-effective way to learn about and have access to the Internet.

Your organization probably has more than one individual who has a computer at home. These co-workers may want to access your network from home. NT's RAS gives your users the ability to dial up to your Windows NT Server from home and connect to and access all or part of your Windows NT network. This is especially handy for those whippersnappers who absolutely must continue working even when they go home! RAS provides them with all the network resources at home, just as if they were sitting in the office doing the work. This is also very handy for telecommuters and salespeople who are on the road often.

Understanding Network Dial-Out and Dial-In

RAS is a communication service that comes as part of NT's Server and Workstation operating systems. So when you buy NT, your users can dial in to the network with little effort and some low-cost equipment like modems. In addition, RAS allows you to dial out of the network from your server.

This might sound a little confusing at first if you're new to network communications. Let's look at the pieces of RAS so that we can break it down into understandable chunks.

The server side of RAS

You can configure an NT Server several ways:

- ✔ As a RAS server
- ✔ As a RAS client
- ✔ As both a RAS client and server

When you install RAS to act as a server, your remote users can connect to the network and function as if they were physically connected to the network. This means they can access the network resources for which they have permission.

The easiest way to think of RAS is to imagine that the serial cards in your server are actually NICs and the phone lines are network cables that extend to your users' homes. This means your users communicate with your network using the NetBEUI transport protocol over the phone lines to your network.

RAS permits up to 256 simultaneous connections. If you wanted to stretch RAS to that limit and you're using modems to connect users, you'd have to have 256 modems and some multiport serial equipment attached to your server.

If you want to use your NT server to dial out to another host (such as another RAS server) or an on-line service (such as CompuServe or your ISP), you would configure RAS as a client. The last sentence may sound funny when you read it out loud because you're not used to thinking of your NT server as a client. Although it's acting as a server to your LAN and dial-up clients, it's acting as a client to the hosts it dials in to.

While your server is acting as a client, you can also configure it to act as a router to the Internet. That's right — the clients on your network can access the Internet through your NT server. This is in lieu of adding a router to your network, and we don't advise it unless you have ten or fewer users on your network with small network activity, such as checking email.

If you want the flexibility to dial in to or out of your network, you can configure RAS as both a server and a client.

Later in this chapter, we guide you through setting up RAS as a server so that your users can dial in to your network.

The workstation side of RAS

You need to configure your users' PCs before they can connect to a RAS server. Doing this isn't tricky, but it is a different setup depending on what client software they're using. For example, NT Workstation comes RAS-enabled, and you just need to install it. DOS, on the other hand, was written before RAS was developed, so you have to load software on those PCs and configure them differently.

So how does all this work? A remote PC dials into a RAS server, establishes a valid connection, and becomes a node on the network. Once connected, the user can run applications from the network or locally on the dial-up PC. This type of dial-up communication is often referred to as a remote node connection.

It's more efficient to load software, such as word processors and spreadsheets, on the user's PC at home so that the applications are executed locally. If that arrangement isn't suitable, users can execute software from the network. For example, if you have a laptop with only RAS installed on it, you can dial in to the network and execute word processing software from the network. This is a much slower method because the software executables must download from the server across the telephone wires to PCs at home.

An example of remote access use is an off-site salesperson who has Microsoft Office loaded on a laptop and has just finished a sales report and wants to transmit it to the office. The salesperson could email the report, fax it, or (better yet) dial in to a Windows NT server running RAS and use the local File Manager utility to copy the file from the laptop to the office NT server's hard disk. We cover RAS client installation in-depth in Chapter 16.

What Does RAS-Aware Mean?

Some Microsoft desktop software, such as Windows for Workgroups (WFW), Windows 95, and Windows NT Workstation, is RAS-aware. This means that RAS capabilities are built in to the operating system; you simply activate and configure those capabilities to use RAS.

As mentioned, DOS and Windows 3.*x* were designed before the birth of RAS and therefore require you to load additional software on the PC to access a RAS server. When you installed your NT server, it loaded this additional software for you, so you only need to create some RAS client disks for DOS and Windows workstations from the server.

Making Good Connections: Handling RAS Hardware

Repeat this sentence over and over: "I will install only hardware that's listed on Microsoft's Hardware Compatibility List." Using equipment on this list helps to ensure that the hardware is approved to work with NT.

If you buy equipment that's not on the list but is very low in price, you might find yourself tinkering with it to get it working. We call this back-end cost. Try not to save a little money on the front end of your equipment (the purchase price) only to spend hours on the back end (the hours-of-tinkering price).

RAS provides a file called MODEMS.INF that you can use to modify modem settings to the umpteenth degree if you want to waste some valuable time. If you buy a modem on the Hardware Compatibility List, however, you'll never have to look at the file.

If you don't have a copy of the Hardware Compatibility List, you can go to the Internet to get it:

```
http://www.microsoft.com/NTServer/hcl/hclintro.htm
```

Installing RAS with Class

In this section, you learn how to install RAS on your NT server. Then you learn how to install it on your client PCs. Obtain the items in the following checklist before you attempt to install RAS. Otherwise, you might find yourself running around in the middle of the installation gathering the necessary items — a waste of time.

Items to have now:

❑ **Software:** Windows NT Server 4.0 installation CD-ROM, along with its manuals.

❑ **CD-ROM:** You need a CD-ROM drive attached to your NT Server during the installation. Setup copies the distribution files necessary for DOS/Windows and Windows for Workgroups clients from the installation CD-ROM to the server. Also, make sure you have the CD-ROM drive's manual(s) on hand.

❑ **Modem:** You need at least one modem from the Hardware Compatibility List (internal or external) for the NT 3.51 Server.

❑ **Serial cable:** If you're using an external modem, you need a serial cable. The type of cable you need (9-pin to 25-pin or 25-pin to 25-pin) depends on your server's COM port pinout.

❑ **Analog line:** You need an analog (not digital) line for testing. If you don't intend to test at this time, you can skip this item.

If you're using ISDN, ATM, or some other communications link that doesn't rely on an old-fashioned telephone, the last three elements will vary. But the basics will remain the same: You need an interface device, a cable to connect between the device and a communications link, and a working communications link for the device to talk to over that cable.

It's a good idea to document any kind of installation, whatever it might be. Write everything down, even if it seems tedious at the time. You'll be glad when you need to refer to your notes a month later!

Obtain the following configuration information:

❑ Phone number of office NT RAS Server (analog line number)

❑ Available COM port assignments in workstations and server

❑ Available IRQ numbers in workstations and server

Installing RAS on your NT 4.0 server

Before you can perform any type of RAS activity (dial in to or out of the server), you must first install and configure the RAS service.

The following is a step-by-step guide to setting up RAS service on the server:

1. **Load the NT Server Installation CD-ROM into the drive.**

2. **Log on to the server as Administrator. Press Ctrl+Alt+Del at the server's console, and type** Administrator **when prompted for the user name. Type the case-sensitive Administrator's password. Click OK.**

3. **Access NT's software installation setup (the location where you install RAS). Double-click My Computer from the desktop, and then double-click the Control Panel icon. Double-click the Network icon.**

4. **Install and activate Remote Access Services. Click the Services tab, and then click Add. Scroll down through the list and highlight Remote Access Service, and then click OK. When Setup prompts for the location of the Windows NT distribution files, type:**

```
D:\PROCESSOR\
```

In this example, *D* represents the drive letter of the CD-ROM drive that's attached to your NT server and *PROCESSOR* represents the processor subdirectory (for example, I386 for Intel). Setup will copy files from the Server's Installation CD-ROM to C:\WINNT\system32, where C represents the drive containing your system files.

If your modem is already installed, skip the rest of this step and go to Step 5. Otherwise, you'll be asked whether you want to run the Add New Modem wizard. Respond "yes" and let the wizard guide you through its steps. (We won't tell you how, because it will!) After running the Add New Modem wizard, RAS displays a dialog box showing the installed modem.

5. **To configure the port, click configure in the Remote Access Setup dialog box. This gives you the choices shown in Figure 15-1. Choose Dial out and Receive calls. Click OK. (If you want to only dial out or you want to only receive calls, choose the appropriate option instead.)**

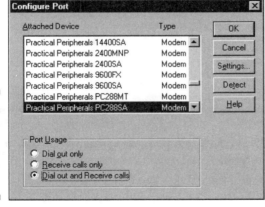

Figure 15-1:
Choices
for the
Configure
Port dialog
box.

6. **If you click OK without configuring all the networks selected, each one of those networks will display its configuration dialog box.**

Mark the proper Encryption Settings radio button for each network. Mark and unmark the protocols you want to use (and not use) on your network.

Be sure to select TCP/IP if you plan to interconnect this server with the Internet now or later. Click the Configure button next to TCP/IP. Mark the radio button for the Entire Network option under Allow remote TCP/IP clients to access. If you're using DHCP to assign IP addresses, click the Use DHCP to assign remote TCP/IP client addresses option.

When you are finished with the configuration, click OK to exit the Network Configuration Box.

7. **Click Continue to exit the Remote Access Setup box.**

8. **What you see next depends on your network configuration. In the simplest case, a dialog box will pop up saying that the service is currently disabled and asking whether you want to enable it. If that happens, click Yes and you're finished.**

   Otherwise, you may have to run Setup to bind Remote Access Service to the protocols and NICs you installed on your server. If you installed other protocols, for example IPX/SPX, it stops at the IPX/SPX protocol and prompts you for the frame type. Accept Setup's default of auto-frame detect and then click OK. Setup presents the MS TCP/IP Properties dialog box. Look over the information, make any changes, and click OK.

9. **Setup prompts you to restart your server now to make these new settings take effect. Click Yes.**

10. **Log back on to the server as Administrator when your server boots up. Grant permission to your users' accounts to dial in to the network.**

    (*Note:* Steps 11-15 must be completed for each user who needs access to dial in to the network, and these steps assume that you already set up user accounts on your system.)

11. **Using the Start button, highlight Administrative Tools (Common), Remote Access Admin.**

12. **Choose USERS from the pull-down menu, and then select Permissions from the Users menu.**

13. **Select a user, and then click X in the box next to Grant Dial In Permission To User.**

14. **Repeat Step 13 for all users who require dial-in access to the network.**

15. **Click OK.**

Installing RAS on your client PCs

Your NT server is capable of dialing out to other hosts. This is when the NT server acts as a RAS client. Many administrators are confused at first when they try to think of their server as a client. It's easier to understand if you remember that the server can function as both the client and the server. Although it provides server functions to the clients on your network, it can also dial out to other hosts and act as a RAS client to them.

Your NT server can also be configured to act as a router between your LAN and the Internet. By doing this, you allow the users on your LAN to communicate with the Internet without having an individual analog line and modem. Your users would use the LAN cabling to access your NT server, and share the modem(s) on the server to get to the Internet. We cover this more in Chapter 16.

The next phase in your RAS setup includes adding phone book entries of the hosts to which your server will dial out. After you create your entire phone book (whether it's one entry or a list of entries), you can call other hosts by simply invoking the phone book and choosing the entry.

1. **In My Computer, select Dial-Up Networking.**

2. **A dialog box is displayed, stating "The phone book is empty. Press OK to add an entry."**

3. **Click OK to display the New Phonebook Entry dialog box.**
   Here you'll add entries for the services you want to dial in to.

4. **Set up your entries.**
   See Figure 15-2 for an example phone book entry that you can use as a guideline when setting up your own. *Note:* Add 9 and a comma at the beginning of phone numbers (for example, 9,555-1212) if you must dial 9 for an outside line. If your location uses call-waiting, be sure to turn it off by adding *70 and a comma (for example, *70,555-1212).

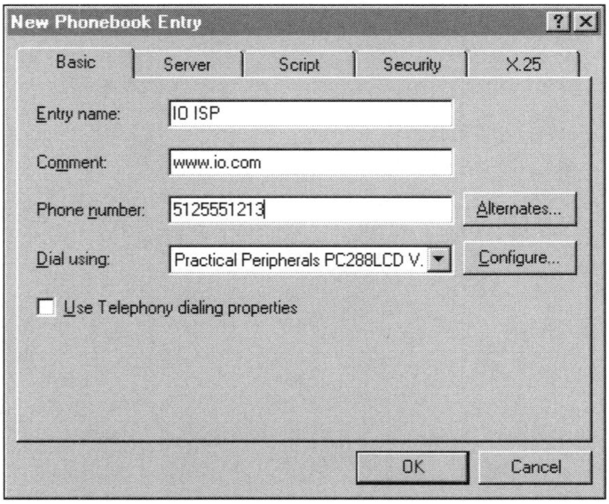

Figure 15-2:
An example phone book entry.

5. Click OK.

6. Test your new phone book entry by highlighting the host entry you want to access and clicking Dial.

Chapter 16

Communicating with NTS

· ·

· ·

*T*his section guides you step-by-step through configuring workstations so they can dial in to the network and function as if they were physically connected to the network.

Lots of operating systems are available for workstations. In this section, we focus on the following operating system combinations for clients:

✔ DOS/Windows 3.*x*

✔ Windows for Workgroups

✔ Windows NT Workstation

✔ Windows 95

If only DOS/Windows 3.*x* clients will dial in to your network, skip to that section in this chapter. If you have different client types, you'll need to visit many of the sections in this chapter.

You want to test in the environment that matches that of your remote clients. Therefore, if you're setting up and testing PCs at the office for your users to take home, re-create the user's home environment at the office. Have an analog line and modem handy, and remove the NIC from the workstation. If you test on a workstation with a NIC installed and connected to the network, you will get erroneous results because a workstation cannot be connected to an NT 3.51 Server using both a NIC and a serial connection. If you test with a NIC in the workstation, disconnect the network cable from the NIC.

Preinstallation Checklist

In this section, you learn how to install RAS on your clients. Obtain the items in the following modem connection checklist before you attempt to install RAS. Otherwise, you might find yourself running around in the middle of the installation gathering the necessary items — a waste of your valuable time. If you're using ISDN or another kind of digital connection, you'll need to obtain similar items, but not exactly what we specify here.

Items to have on hand:

❑ **Software**: If you're connecting Windows NT workstations and you used Express Setup on the workstations, you'll need the Windows NT Workstation 4.0 installation CD-ROM along with its manuals.

> Windows for Workgroups may ask for the original WFW installation Disks 7 and 8.

❑ **CD-ROM:** For the client — if you're installing Windows NT Workstation RAS clients and you originally installed using a CD-ROM, you also need to attach a CD-ROM drive to the workstation.

❑ **Modem:** You'll need at least one modem from the Hardware Compatibility List (internal or external) to test your workstation. If desired, you can move the modem to each client you install for testing.

❑ **Serial cable**: If you're using an external modem, you need a serial cable. The type of cable (9-pin to 25-pin or 25-pin to 25-pin) depends on the workstation's COM port pinout.

❑ **Analog line:** You need an analog (not digital) line for testing. If you don't intend to test at this time, you can skip this checklist item.

❑ **Blank, formatted floppy:** If you plan to install DOS/Windows RAS clients, you need either one or three floppies. (If the floppies contain information, it will be overwritten.)

If the workstation already has the networking client installed, you need only one formatted floppy. Label it

> RAS Client V1.1a — Disk 1 of 1

If the workstation has no networking client installed, you need three floppies. Label them

> Network Client V3.0 for MS-DOS & Windows — Disk 1 of 2
>
> Network Client V3.0 for MS-DOS & Windows — Disk 2 of 2
>
> RAS Client V1.1a — Disk 1 of 1

It's a good idea to document any kind of installation. Write everything down, even if it seems tedious. You'll be glad when you need to refer to your notes a month later!

Obtain the following configuration information:

❏ Phone number of office NT RAS Server (analog line number)

❏ Available COM port assignments in workstations

❏ Available IRQ numbers in workstations

Installing DOS/Windows RAS Clients

This section provides step-by-step instructions for installing and configuring a DOS/Windows RAS client.

DOS/Windows clients aren't RAS-aware, so they don't have a handy icon that you can click on to install RAS. Instead, you have to manually install RAS from client diskettes you create off the NT server.

1. **Log on to the Server as Administrator.**

   Press Ctrl+Alt+Del to log on, and then type Administrator when prompted for the user name. Type the case-sensitive Administrator's password. Click OK.

2. **Using the Start button, highlight Programs⇨Administrative Tools (Common), then click the Network Client Administrator menu item.**

3. **Choose Make Installation Disk Set. Click Continue.**

4. **Click Share Files to share files off the CD-ROM. In the Share Name box, you'll see Clients, which is fine (but you can change this if you want). Click OK.**

5. **Choose Network Client v3.0 for MS DOS & Windows on the Make Installation Disk Set screen.**

6. **Get the disks you formatted and labeled in the "Preinstallation Check-list" section (Network Client V3.0 for MS-DOS & Windows — Disk 1 of 2 and 2 of 2, plus the RAS Client disk). Setup creates RAS installation disks for your DOS and Windows workstations by copying files from the server's hard disk onto floppies. Place the correct floppy in the drive. Click OK in the dialog box that says "2 directories were created and 75 files were successfully copied. Press OK to continue." When Setup completes this task, take the floppy out of drive A.**

7. Setup creates one more disk. In the Make Installation Disk Set screen, highlight the Remote Access v1.1a for MS-DOS option. Place the third floppy in the drive and follow the on-screen directions. Click OK in the dialog box that says "9 directories were created and 35 files were successfully copied. Press OK to continue." When Setup completes this task, remove the floppy from drive A.

8. Setup has finished creating RAS client disks for your DOS and Windows workstations. Click Exit when you see the Network Client Administrator screen.

9. Proceed to a DOS/Windows workstation on which you want to install the RAS client software.

10. Connect and install a modem on the workstation.

11. Boot the workstation.

12. Insert the disk labeled "MS-DOS & Windows Client-Disk 1 of 2" into the workstation's drive A and type:

```
A:\SETUP
```

13. When you see the welcome screen, choose "To set up Network Client now, press Enter" by pressing Enter.

14. Setup proposes to install RAS in the workstation subdirectory C:\NET. Press Enter if this is okay. Or type in a new subdirectory and press Enter.

15. When Setup asks you to select a network adapter card, choose asynchronous driver instead of NIC. Highlight "MS-DOS Remote Access MAC Driver" (at the bottom of the list) and press Enter.

16. When Setup asks you to type in a user name for this workstation, choose one that is unique for your entire network and press Enter. You should have already set up this name on the NT Server and given it permission to dial in to the network. (We'll use the user name Jack.)

17. Setup provides a screen of the following configuration options: Names, Setup Options, Use the full redirector, Run network client, and Network Configuration. Modify your adapter and protocols with this option.

18. The defaults on the screen should be okay, but look them over for accuracy. Then choose the "The listed options are correct" option and press Enter.

19. Setup tells you that it has changed your AUTOEXEC.BAT and CONFIG.SYS files and made backup files of them (*.001). You'll see a message that reads "Press enter to restart the computer OR Press F3 to quit setup without restarting the computer." Press F3.

20. Insert the "Remote Access v1.1a for MS-DOS" disk into drive A. Change the directory to C:\NET. Type `RASCOPY` to execute a batch file, which copies RAS files from the floppy to a new RAS subdirectory in your C:\NET directory. When prompted for diskette #2, just press Enter. There is a bug in the batch file and it thinks it's looking for disk #2, but it's not! All the files are on the first diskette.

21. When the process is finished, reboot your workstation.

22. You'll see the user name you set up. Press Enter.

23. Next, you'll see a prompt that says "There is no password list for [your username here]. Do you want to create one (Y/N)?" Enter the password you assigned to this user.

24. Setup next asks you whether you want to create the password list. Answer Yes. Setup asks you to type the same password again for verification. Do so. When you see "The command completed successfully," you're finished!

Installing Windows for Workgroups RAS Clients

This section provides step-by-step instructions for installing and configuring a Windows for Workgroups (WFW) RAS client.

WFW has a RAS-aware component that you'll need to install and configure. You'll also modify a few settings from your original WFW installation. Setup may ask you for your Windows for Workgroups installation disks 7 and 8.

1. Boot the WFW workstation.

2. Double-click the Network icon.

3. Double-click the Remote Access icon. If this is your first time installing Remote Access on this workstation, you'll get a message from Setup. Click Install.

4. You might see the following message on your screen: "The component that you want to install requires Microsoft Windows Network. Do you want to install Microsoft Workgroup Network now?" Click Yes if you get this message.

5. If you don't see Step 4's message, Setup asks whether you want to copy over other file versions. Click No when you see these messages.

6. Setup asks you to insert the WFW installation disks. It prompts you for Disk 7, or Disk 8, or both. Setup is looking for the following files: NDIS.386 (WFW Installation Disk 7) or MODEM.INF (WFW Installation Disk 8). Insert the necessary disk and continue.

7. Setup displays the Remote Access Configuration dialog box so you can enter the COM port and modem information. Choose the COM port (COM1 or COM2) to which your modem is attached on this workstation. Then select your modem from the list. Note: If your modem isn't on the list, select Hayes-Compatible *XXXX* (where *XXXX* represents the baud rate of your modem: 1200, 2400, 9600). If your modem is not on the list and you choose Hayes, it does not guarantee that your modem will function properly. Click OK.

8. If Setup presents you with a Microsoft Windows Network Names dialog box, fill in the requested information, and then click OK.

9. If Setup prompts you for Disk 7 or 8 of the WFW installation disk set, insert the necessary disk and continue.

10. Setup displays a Remote Access dialog box with a message about your system.ini and protocol.ini files. Record the filenames of the old versions.

11. Setup prompts you to restart WFW and your workstation. Click Restart Computer. Press Ctrl+Alt+Del to reboot.

12. When your workstation reboots, you'll modify some components that you configured when WFW was originally installed on this workstation. Double-click the Control Panel icon, and then double-click the Network icon.

13. Click Startup. Click to select the option called Log On To Windows NT Or LAN Manager Domain.

14. Type the name of the domain that this user will dial in to. Click OK.

15. If you're connected to a network, click Restart when Setup prompts you to reboot the workstation. Otherwise, you can proceed without restarting.

Phone Book Setup

This section provides step-by-step instructions for setting up a RAS phone book. You'll create a phone book entry that contains the phone number of the NT server that the workstation will dial in to. You'll find the Remote Access Service icon in the Network group.

1. Click the Remote Access Service icon.

2. Click the Remote Access icon.

3. You'll see a pop-up message that says "The phone book is empty. Press OK to add an entry." Click OK. Then you'll add an entry, and click OK again. (Adding entries is covered next.)

You may want to add a few entries for the user that cover different types of dial-in scenarios. For example:

- Dial to office network from hotel (for example, 8,1-512-555-1212)

- Dial to office network from another office (for example, 9,1-512-555-1212)

- Dial to office network from home, no call waiting (for example, 1-512-555-1212)

- Dial to office network from home, call waiting (for example, *70,1-512-555-1212)

4. **Setup displays your phone book screen. If you'd like to test this workstation's capability to connect to your NT RAS server now, do the following:**

   a. Highlight the appropriate phone book entry, and click the Dial button.

   b. You'll see an Authentication dialog box on your screen from RAS asking you to fill in some information. The user should type his or her regular network account ID and password here.

   c. Click OK.

   d. Your WFW RAS client dials the NT RAS server you selected, establishes a connection, and verifies the authentication information you filled in.

   e. If successful, you'll see the following text on your screen: "Connection Complete! You have successfully connected to the Remote Access server. You may now use the usual Windows programs and utilities as if you were directly connected to the network." Mark the Minimize On Dial box and click OK.

   Ta dah! You're finished!

Installing Windows NT Workstation RAS Clients

This section provides step-by-step instructions to set up an NT Workstation RAS client.

1. **Insert the Windows NT Workstation Installation CD-ROM into the workstation's CD-ROM drive.**

2. **Log on to the NT workstation as Administrator.**

   Press Ctrl+Alt+Del to log on. Then type `Administrator` when prompted for the user name. Type in the Administrator's password. Click OK.

3. **Access NT's software installation setup (the location where you install RAS). Double-click My Computer from the desktop, and then double-click the Control Panel icon. Double-click the Network icon.**

4. **Install and activate Remote Access Services software. Click Add on the Services tab. Scroll through the list and highlight Remote Access Service and click OK. When Setup prompts for the location of the Windows NT distribution files, type:**

```
D:\PROCESSOR\
```

In this example, *D* represents the drive letter of the CD-ROM drive that's attached to your NT workstation and *PROCESSOR* represents the processor subdirectory (for example, I386 for Intel). Setup copies files from the workstation's Installation CD-ROM to \Winnt\system32 on the hard drive.

5. **At this point, NT displays the Add New Modem wizard. It guides you through the process of adding the modem to your configuration, so we'll let the wizard take over from here.**

6. **When the wizard displays the Remote Access Setup dialog box, choose Dial Out, and click OK.**

7. **Configure the protocols. Click Network to display the Network Configuration dialog box. If you're running NT Server, mark the proper Encryption Settings radio button for your workstation. Note: If Setup prompts you to choose protocols, select the TCP/IP protocol.**

   When you are finished with the configuration, click OK to exit the Network Configuration dialog box.

8. **Click Continue to exit the Remote Access Setup dialog box.**

9. **Next, you'll see the Network dialog box. Click Close. Setup will bind RAS to the boards and protocols you have installed. If you installed other protocols such as IPX/SPX, Setup stops at the IPX/SPX protocol and prompts you for the frame type. Accept Setup's default frame-type (auto-frame detect) and click OK. Setup presents the MS TCP/IP Properties dialog box (if you selected that protocol). Look over the information, make any changes, and click OK.**

10. **Restart your workstation so the new settings can take effect. Click Yes.**

11. **Log back on to the workstation as the user (not Administrator). To configure a phone book entry to the NT Server that this workstation will dial in to, follow the steps in the "Phone Book Setup" section.**

Installing Windows 95 RAS Clients

This section provides step-by-step instructions to set up a Windows 95 RAS client. Windows 95 comes RAS-aware out of the box, through its built-in Dial-Up Networking option. Therefore, you need to simply activate it on your Windows 95 clients. You're gonna love how simple this is!

1. **Install a modem on the Windows 95 PC. Connect the serial cable to the workstation and the modem. Connect the phone line to the jack on the modem.**

   If you're at an office, ensure that the phone line is an analog line, not a digital line!

2. **Check to see that RAS is enabled on Windows 95. Double-click My Computer and see if Dial-up Networking is there.**

3. **Configure RAS on this PC. Click Start at the bottom of your screen. Choose Programs⇨Accessories⇨Dial-Up Networking.**

4. **Windows 95 displays a wizard screen. Click Next.**

5. **You should see the Install A New Modem dialog box on your screen. Make sure your modem is connected and turned on, and then click Next.**

6. **Setup tries to detect your modem. If Setup finds your modem, it inputs the modem information for you. Click Next and skip to Step 8.**

   If Setup doesn't see your modem, it prompts you to click Next, and then it presents a list of modems. Find and click on your modem manufacturer listed on the left. This displays a modem model list on the right. Find your modem's model. If you don't find your modem's manufacturer or model listed, choose a Hayes-Compatible *XXXX* modem (where *XXXX* represents the baud rate: 1200, 2400, 9600). Click Next.

7. **Choose the COM port the modem is attached to (COM1, COM2, and so on). Click Next.**

8. **Setup presents a Location Information dialog box. Type the requested information and click Next.**

9. **Click Finish.**

10. **Type a name for the NT Server (or other host) this workstation will dial in to.**

11. **Click Next.**

12. **Type the phone number for the host computer that this workstation will dial in to. For now, type the phone number of the analog line to your NT Server running RAS. Later, you can make changes to this phone book. Click Next.**

13. **Setup displays a message that you successfully created a new Dial-Up Networking connection. Click Finish.**

14. **Setup displays a Dial-Up Networking folder. To test your configuration, double-click your NT Server icon. Your Windows 95 PC should dial the NT Server at this time. Once connected, choose Start⇨Windows Explorer⇨Tools⇨Map Network Drive. If it works, you just "did something" through your connection.**

The RAS Protocols

RAS supports the Point-to-Point Protocol (PPP) and the Serial Line Interface Protocol (SLIP). These are industry standard framing protocols designed to permit PCs to dial up and communicate with other devices (that conform to the PPP/SLIP spec) over telephone links. Some will argue that PPP is the more efficient protocol; others will point to benchmark tests that reveal SLIP to be the better choice.

If you intend to connect your NT server to the Internet through an ISP, most Internet Service Providers offer support for both protocols. Before you set up your RAS connection, however, check to see which protocol(s) your provider supports. SLIP requires you to input more configuration information than PPP, giving you more opportunities to make mistakes.

Windows NT includes remote access support for TCP/IP, IPX, and NetBEUI protocols. So, for example, a Windows NT remote workstation running PPP over IPX can dial in to your RAS server and communicate with a Novell server running the IPX protocol on your network.

Troubleshooting RAS

This section provides possible solutions to technical problems associated with RAS. Most of the recommendations seem basic, but we've found that most of the problems we encounter are simple!

✔ Are you using an external modem on either the server or workstation? Is it turned on? Did you connect the proper serial modem cables? Are the cables plugged in tightly to the modem?

✔ Are you using an internal modem? If so, are there any IRQ or COM port conflicts on either the workstation or server? Possible symptoms would include loss of another adapter (in addition to the modem in your PC) or its complete failure (if, for instance, a conflict between the modem and your disk controller is introduced).

✔ Check for a dial tone to see whether the lines are working. You can test the line with an analog phone.

✔ Check each telephone cable that connects the modem to the phone line plug in the wall to see whether it has been damaged. Take a telephone cable from a setup that you know works and test again.

✔ Did you use the proper phone number in the phone book setup? If you're testing from the office, check to see whether you need to dial 9 to get an outside line.

✔ Try to disable call waiting (dial *70 before dialing the number on a handset). If that works, disable it with the modem dial string and try again.

✔ Is the RAS service running on the server? To receive incoming calls, it needs to be active. You can check this in Control Panel➪Services.

✔ Did you set up a valid account for the user with dial-up permission?

✔ Do your modems support the speed at which you're trying to connect? Try a slower modem rate and test again.

✔ Does the workstation you're testing from have a NIC installed and connected? This could give you erroneous results. Disconnect the network cable from the NIC and try again.

Administrator utility

The Remote Access Administration utility provides real-time information about active connections and is a good place to start when troubleshooting RAS. For example, you can look in the Administration utility to see whether ports are functioning. If you have four available ports, but only two users can dial in at one time, two of your ports may be malfunctioning, or cables could be bad, and so on.

Try to use this utility as users attempt to connect so you can view what's going on at the RAS server.

Event Viewer

Event Viewer allows you to look at a log of audit and error messages that Remote Access generates, in addition to the events the serial driver records.

MODEM.INF file

If your modem isn't listed on the Hardware Compatibility List and the modem wizard can't set you straight, you could be in for a rough ride. You'll need to do some fancy footwork to get a modem to work if you're still having trouble with it:

1. **Make a backup copy of the MODEM.INF file located on the server's \WINNT35\SYSTEM32\RAS subdirectory.**

2. **Open the MODEM.INF file and copy one of the sections in the file to the end of the file. This will give you a guideline from which to place your modem information.**

3. **Modify the section name you added to reflect your modem's name.**

4. **Make changes to that section based on information from your modem manufacturer's documentation.**

5. **Save and close the file.**

6. **Stop and restart the RAS service.**

Internetworking with RAS

At some point, you'll probably want to connect your network to the Internet. Until recently, Microsoft's position was that this was not possible. However, in January 1996, Microsoft RAS engineer Tom Ollerenshaw coauthored an article explicitly explaining how to connect your NT server to an ISP so that your network could communicate with the Internet via RAS. (See "Top 10 RAS Problems Solved," written by Thomas Ollerenshaw and Roy Scabourne, published in the January 1996 issue of *Windows NT Magazine*.)

If that article doesn't give you all the information you need, you can look at a great article in the June 1996 issue of *Windows NT Magazine* that goes into more depth on the topic. (We know it's a great article, because we wrote it!)

NT 4.0 has an extensive on-line guide in RAS about Internet connectivity. You'll find it most helpful to look extensively in this guide before attempting to perform any internetworking connectivity.

Chapter 17
The Properties of Protocols

In This Chapter

▶ Understanding NetBEUI and NetBIOS

▶ Pushing IPX/SPX to the max

▶ Introducing TCP/IP

▶ Doing the DLC dance

▶ Choosing the right protocol

▶ Using multiple protocols

*W*hat is a protocol? An electronic conversation in an agreed-upon dialect would smell as sweet. With apologies to William Shakespeare, that's exactly how we like to define a protocol. That is to say: "A protocol is a common language agreed upon by both parties in an electronic conversation."

Protocols include such information as how we know when it's okay to talk, how long we can talk, how often we can expect an acknowledgment, and how to correct errors that might creep into a conversation. After a network client PC adapter has been configured with a particular protocol, it will ignore all other protocols that it sees zooming across the wire.

As we mentioned in Chapter 4, Windows NT protocols come in five standard flavors:

Protocols included with Windows NT	Suitable for
NW-Link (IPX/SPX)	LANs; WANs if running Packet Burst
TCP/IP	LANs and WANs
NetBEUI	Small LANs
DLC	Mainframe/minicomputer gateways; direct-connect printers
AppleTalk	Connecting to older Macintoshes or AppleTalk-only printers (for example, Apple LaserWriter I and II)

Alphabet soup defined

NetBIOS stands for Network Basic Input/Output System. IBM eventually extended the functions of NetBIOS into a new protocol called NetBEUI (pronounced net-boo-ee), which stands for NetBIOS Extended User Interface. IPX/SPX stands for Internetwork Packet Exchange/Sequenced Packet Exchange. TCP/IP stands for Transmission Control Protocol/Internet Protocol. Last and certainly least, DLC stands for Data Link Control.

How can you communicate with other computers if you don't talk their language? You can't. NT supports IPX so NT users can access NetWare servers. NT supports TCP/IP so its users can talk to the Internet or on private intranets. NT supports DLC so users can talk to printer-based print servers and to mid-range and mainframe computers. So you see, Virginia, Microsoft has (finally) lifted many of the previous roadblocks from the path to widespread acceptance of Windows NT in the corporate world. Windows NT-based computers can talk to almost every other kind of computer in the electronic world right out of the box. No coupons to clip, no add-on protocol packages to buy!

But why so many protocols? If Microsoft likes NetBEUI and has used it before as the protocol of choice for many different network programs, why not sell Windows NT with NetBEUI as the only protocol? Because, Virginia, no NT server or workstation is an island. The whole point of this network thing is to communicate with other computers.

NetBIOS/NetBEUI

For this discussion, we treat NetBIOS and NetBEUI synonymously and refer to them collectively as NetBEUI. NetBEUI was developed by IBM as a way to allow small groups of PCs to share files and printers efficiently way back in the early 1980s. Though NetBEUI has fallen from grace as the size and scope of networks have increased, it is still used by many applications and older network products for communicating across a local area network.

NetBEUI is not routable, which means that it does not behave well on a large network interconnected by routers. However, Microsoft still offers NetBEUI as one of the standard supported protocols in NT because of NetBEUI's large installed base of applications and servers. Granted, most of the applications that use NetBEUI will gradually migrate to other protocols over the next few years; but for now, Windows NT still talks NetBEUI with the best of them.

So, we would never recommend NetBEUI for a modern network, would we? Actually, because of its relative simplicity, NetBEUI is the fastest protocol around. NetBEUI offers a small workgroup network the many benefits of networking without the inherent overhead of protocols designed to connect hundreds or thousands of people over large distances.

Our rule of thumb is: small rooms, NetBEUI zooms. Once you begin to network more than 25 users on a single network segment — and remember that NetBEUI isn't routable, so the entire network is considered to be one large segment, regardless of the number of routers — you should consider installing a more robust network protocol.

When you install Windows NT for the first time, NetBEUI and the IPX/SPX-compatible protocols are automatically configured and enabled by default. If you have no desire to run NetBEUI and no applications that require NetBEUI support to operate, you can safely disable NetBEUI in the Network Application selection under the Control Panel. One caveat: NetBEUI is required if you have DOS-based PCs that connect to your NT Server using the Microsoft DOS client. The same is true for IPX/SPX; if you don't have NetWare somewhere in your network picture, you can disable it, too.

IPX/SPX Spells Success

When Novell developed the NetWare network operating system in the early 1980s, it decided to develop a new network protocol to go along with its zippy little server software. It based the new protocol, called IPX/SPX, on the Xerox Networking Services protocol (XNS). IPX has become the protocol of choice for many networks around the world simply because it was the only protocol that Novell offered for many years.

The huge popularity of NetWare guaranteed similar popularity for the IPX/SPX protocol. So IPX/SPX has become a protocol of choice for many companies, but not because it was an agreed-upon standard endorsed by every huge, multi-alphabet corporation in the world. Quite the opposite — IPX/SPX has become a standard protocol because of the widespread adoption of NetWare and IPX/SPX by hundreds of thousands of customers.

Windows NT actually uses an IPX-compatible protocol named NWLink, although it is called IPX/SPX by most users. NWLink was developed by Microsoft; the company reverse-engineered the IPX protocol. In other words, Microsoft wrote its own version of IPX/SPX by testing true IPX in every possible situation and writing its IPX clone protocol to react the same way as "real IPX." This reverse-engineering allows Microsoft to include IPX in Windows NT without having to pay royalties to Novell. NWLink is functionally equivalent to IPX/SPX; therefore, we use the term IPX/SPX from here on out to indicate both versions of the IPX protocol.

Stellar lineage

No small part of the success of NetWare is due to the fact that IPX/SPX is a terrific protocol for small- to medium-sized networks. IPX is the free-and-easy cousin in the IPX/SPX protocol suite. IPX offers no guarantee that each packet will be received intact at its destination. Instead, it relies on the application that sends the data to perform its own error checking and to guarantee delivery, if that level of service is necessary.

SPX, on the other hand, offers a connection-oriented service to applications in which SPX performs error checking and guarantees successful delivery of all packets, thereby relieving the application of those duties. If SPX sends a packet and fails to receive a positive acknowledgment from the destination computer, SPX will automatically resend that packet until a successful transmission occurs or a timeout is invoked. Some application developers use the features of SPX to guarantee delivery of data without requiring the application to monitor or intervene in the transmission process.

Pluses and minuses

IPX/SPX has a few disadvantages. It is not an efficient protocol across slow, wide area network (WAN) links. Because IPX and SPX require an acknowledgment for each packet transmitted before sending another packet, performance can be very slow: a source computer waits for the packet to traverse the WAN link, then waits for the destination computer to reply, then waits for the reply to traverse a WAN link, and then finally receives the acknowledgment. Because VSAT transmission latency can be as long as 2 seconds per packet, this can add up to round trip times of 4-plus seconds! If an acknowledgment isn't received by the source computer or an acknowledgment indicates a transmission error, the process has to start all over again. For slow links, this can compound delays!

Novell tackled this problem with the introduction of IPX Packet Burst technology. Taking a page from the design documents for the TCP/IP protocol, a Packet Burst-enabled IPX source computer sends multiple packets without waiting for an acknowledgment for each one. The destination computer sends one acknowledgment for the entire group of packets.

If just one of the packets in a group is received incorrectly, the destination computer requests a resend of the single incorrect packet, not the entire group. This process greatly increases the speed of IPX and SPX over WAN links, thereby quieting many of the critics of the IPX/SPX protocol.

Unfortunately, the increasing prevalence of Internet connections and the growing popularity of Windows NT Advanced Server signal that the days of IPX/SPX dominance on corporate networks may be numbered. Although NetWare and NT servers can both support multiple protocols, most network administrators now look long and hard at supporting multiple protocols on local and wide area networks. That's because there's a significant amount of overhead and wasted bandwidth when supporting multiple protocols. As network bandwidth gets squeezed by more computers using more network-intensive applications, one of the first steps administrators can take is to simplify the protocol mix. Lowering the number of protocols makes configuration and troubleshooting easier, too!

TCP/IP: The Little Protocol That Could

TCP/IP is a granddaddy in the protocol world. Actually, TCP/IP is not just a protocol, it's a suite of protocols that originated with the beginning of what we now call the Internet. Where IPX/SPX has become a standard through massive marketplace acceptance, TCP/IP is based on a well-known official standard that has been supported by numerous hardware and software vendors from day one.

The huge popularity of TCP/IP has caused vendors whose product lines were linked to other protocols to add TCP/IP support to their products as well. Novell has finally conceded to market pressures; it now offers a complete set of TCP/IP protocol support for both NetWare server software and NetWare client software. Likewise, Windows NT (both Server and Workstation models) also ship today with built-in TCP/IP support.

Table 17-1	Comparison of TCP/IP and IPX/SPX Protocols	
	IPX/SPX	*TCP/IP*
Origin	Novell for LAN environments	Department of Defense ARPAnet project (forerunner of the Internet)
Routable	Yes	Yes
Standard	De facto	De facto
LAN suitability	Excellent	Good
WAN suitability	Poor; better when running Packet Burst mode	Excellent

TCP/IP emerged from a pressing need to share data and information on the precursor to the Internet, called ARPAnet, in the early 1970s. ARPAnet was a joint network project developed by the U.S. government, many universities around the country, and a select group of research and development companies to allow scientists to communicate and trade information. As more and more computers were interconnected, the TCP/IP protocols began to evolve into the standard we see today.

The TCP/IP standard was officially established in 1982, about the same time that Novell burst onto the network scene with its very first version of NetWare. However, TCP/IP had a huge head start and the backing of both the U.S. government and the research and academic communities. This heritage has left us with a stable, fully defined, and debugged protocol suite well suited for both wide and local area networks.

Without a doubt, TCP/IP is the most widely supported protocol across the largest variety of computers. Everything — from UNIX boxes to assembly-line control computers to LAN servers to mainframes and mid-ranges to network routers — supports and thrives on the TCP/IP protocol.

The key to TCP/IP's popularity rests on its status as an open standard. This means that its specifications are freely available and that there are no impediments — financial or otherwise — to any developer in the world who wants to add TCP/IP support into a product. Although we refer to TCP/IP as a protocol, it's actually a suite that includes different protocols, where each one serves a specific purpose in a TCP/IP network. The TCP/IP suite can be broken down into six distinct categories:

- **Gateway:** Defines how routers communicate with each other on a TCP/IP network. Includes EGP (Exterior Gateway Protocol), GGP (Gateway-to-Gateway Protocol), and IGP (Interior Gateway Protocol).

- **Transport:** Defines how data is transferred between two TCP/IP client computers. Includes TCP (Transmission Control Protocol) and UDP (User Datagram Protocol).

- **Network:** Defines the translation of a common name to a TCP/IP address and addressing in general. This includes ARP (Address Resolution Protocol), RARP (Reserve Address Resolution Protocol), and DNS (Domain Name System).

- **Routing:** Defines how addresses are traced back to the segment to which they are attached. This includes IP (Internet Protocol), OSPF (Open Shortest Path First), RIP (Routing Information Protocol), and ICMP (Internet Control Message Protocol).

- **User services:** These are applications to which users have direct access, including FTP (File Transfer Protocol), Telnet, BOOTP (which allows a diskless workstation to obtain boot-up instructions from a boot server across the network), and TFTP (Trivial File Transfer Protocol).

- **Miscellaneous:** Includes everything else — program-to-program communication across the TCP/IP network, mail handling, network management, and the direct sharing of directories from one machine to another. It also includes SMTP (Simple Mail Transport Protocol), SNMP (Simple Network Management Protocol), NIS (Network Information Service), RPC (Remote Procedure Call), and NFS (Network File System).

DLC with Some TLC

The DLC (Data Link Control) protocol is like a bad check — it just keeps bouncing back. Originally developed by IBM for token-ring-based workstations to connect to IBM mainframes and minicomputers, DLC has also been adopted by printer manufacturers to connect remote printers to print servers.

DLC's primary use today is for connecting to mainframes and minicomputers through a gateway server. The workstation PC talks DLC protocol to the gateway (see Figure 17-1), and the gateway talks SNA (or whatever protocol the mainframe expects to see) to a host computer of some kind. Other gateway products allow a workstation to talk its native protocol — for example, IPX or TCP/IP to the gateway — and the gateway in turn talks SNA (or whatever protocol the mainframe expects to see).

If you have a printer that connects directly to the network, it's probably the source of those strange DLC packets zooming around your network. Windows NT supports DLC for just that reason: so that a Windows NT server can manage and control DLC-based print devices.

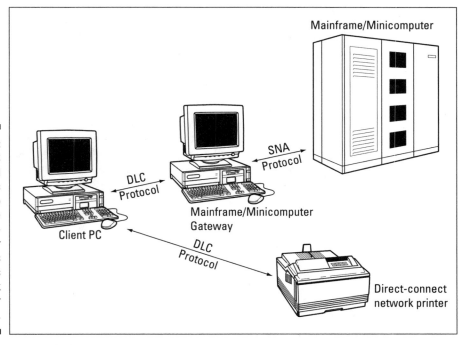

Figure 17-1: The DLC protocol connects PCs to mainframe or mini-computer gateways and handles network printer connections.

Technically, your users could talk directly to the printer's network interface card. However, these network interface cards cannot effectively queue print jobs that arrive at the same time. By using a Windows NT server as a print server, jobs can accumulate in its print queue. The server then acts as printer traffic cop by sending another print job when the current job completes successfully.

Applying AppleTalk

Unless a Macintosh computer or an AppleTalk-based laser printer is in your networking picture, you won't need to think about AppleTalk. But it's included in Windows NT's bag of protocols to cover just those requirements. The Macintosh was one of the first desktop machines to offer its users built-in networking, and it remains one of the easiest machines to network today.

A simple AppleTalk network is self-configuring, more or less. But there are still a few details that you must know (the number of your AppleTalk network or networks and the names of any AppleTalk zones that may be defined thereon). Chances are there's a Mac wizard around your premises. If there isn't and you are clueless, you might want to consider hiring a qualified AppleTalk consultant for a day to help get things going. You should be able to get a referral from a local Apple dealer. (College campuses are hotbeds for the Macintosh; if one is in your vicinity, you can probably find an AppleTalk expert there, too.)

If you're going to mess around with AppleTalk networks yourself, we'd like to recommend two books on the subject. The first, *Inside AppleTalk*, 2nd Edition (Addison-Wesley), was written by one of the architects of AppleTalk, Gursharan S. Sidhu, along with Richard F. Andrews and Alan B. Oppenheimer. The other book by long-time AppleTalk experts Dave Kosiur and Joel Snyder is *The Macworld Networking Bible*, 2nd Edition (IDG Books Worldwide, Inc.). Either of these resources will add significantly to the AppleTalk information provided with Windows NT, and both would make a nice addition to your library!

What To Do?

We recommend TCP/IP as your protocol of choice whenever possible. As corporate networks grow and become connected to the Internet, the usage of TCP/IP is expected to skyrocket. Because TCP/IP is a supported protocol on almost every computer platform, we think that TCP/IP is the obvious choice for a network-wide protocol, including your own network, no matter how small and modest it may be right now.

Particularly now that NetWare servers support TCP/IP as a replacement for their native IPX protocol, there are few remaining situations where you must operate IPX and TCP/IP on the same network. Once you begin to connect your users to the Internet, they will undoubtedly use some version of TCP/IP on their computers. We see no need to stack protocols any more than what's required by applications. (We also think you should carefully weigh the utility of adding to your network any applications that require new protocols.)

IPX/SPX and NetBEUI will certainly continue to enjoy a strong following in small departmental- or workgroup-sized networks — and deservedly so. We wouldn't hesitate to recommend IPX/SPX or NetBEUI for small companies or home networks — though we do think that you should consider a long vacation when you begin to install a network in your home!

DLC will remain a protocol of choice for mainframe and minicomputer gateways for some time. But the future undeniably belongs to the Internet, open standards, and TCP/IP. Be wary of vendors that don't support a standard protocol such as IPX/SPX or TCP/IP. Beware of applications that require a particular version of a particular protocol to operate successfully. Keep an open, standards-compliant mind.

AppleTalk is strictly for the Macintosh, and may be necessary only for those Macs too ancient to support a reasonable TCP/IP stack. Even here, in the sacred precincts of Appledom, we still think TCP/IP is your best bet!

Stacking Protocols: a Virtual Smorgasbord

What if you have to run more than one protocol? You've read our sage advice, but you still need or want to run more than one protocol. You're in luck, friend. Windows NT allows you to install, or stack, any combination of protocols it supports. You can even run all four protocols on each of your network adapters if you need to. So stack to your heart's content!

Remember, Windows NT Server will talk to all comers, as long as the stack they need to use is loaded and running. This feature of Windows NT allows you to connect to every flavor of computer that supports at least one of the four protocols included with Windows NT. Now go forth, conquer, connect, and communicate!

Chapter 18

What's in a Name?

*M*icrosoft NT 4.0 supports several protocols right out of the box. You are left with the task of making all these protocols work together. Even more importantly, you must make these protocols recognize each other to some extent, so that they understand the names you give your computers, users, groups, and network resources. You're in luck, though, because Microsoft provides you with NT utilities that will ease your protocol administration burdens, such as Windows Internet Name Service (WINS), the traditional IP Domain Name Service (DNS), and Dynamic Host Configuration Protocol (DHCP). (If you haven't read Chapter 17 yet, do so before reading this chapter so that you know what we're talking about.)

What's So Keen about Naming Services?

When you issue a command in NT, you're expected to use the proper syntax. Failure to do so might cause the command to execute improperly. For example, when you issue a NET USE command from a command prompt, you must enter the server name and share name, as well as the drive you want to map. So, a simple command such as `NET USE G:\\lanwrights\apps` would map drive G to the APPS share on the LANWRIGHTS server. If you're using the TCP/IP protocol, it doesn't know how to interpret the name LANWRIGHTS as the server. Instead, it understands IP addresses, such as 205.230.248.2.

If you use the TCP/IP protocol on your network, you need a utility to convert IP addresses into names and vice versa. Just as the United Nations requires translators, so do you! In this chapter, we discuss naming considerations and how to get around them. Hold onto your hat — it's going to be a bumpy ride.

NetBIOS names

If you're like the rest of the world, you freeze like a deer in headlights when you hear the word *NetBIOS*. Don't worry: Only a small percentage of people really understand protocols, and even a tinier slice of those people really understand NetBIOS.

A NetBIOS name is often referred to as a computer name. When you install your NT network, you give each workstation and server a unique computer name. Then all your related utilities know the machine by its name. Each time you issue a command that requires the computer name, NT knows which device you're talking about.

If you try to define two devices with the same name, you'll run into trouble. It's like trying to have two identical social security numbers for two different people. That's why you can't have a computer that's connected to a server on the network dial in to that same network through RAS. The workstation registers its computer name on the Ethernet wire. Then, when it dials in to RAS, it tries to register that same name again. The server detects this, reports a duplicate name conflict, and doesn't allow the Ethernet-connected workstation to connect to the RAS server.

Devising meaningful names is important on a network. It's similar to naming your children. You wouldn't call your first born #1 and your second born #2. You give them meaningful names. Okay, so Frank Zappa went a little overboard when he named his kids Dweezil and Moon Unit, but it must have meant something to him!

We think that the best naming scheme is one that is both meaningful and requires the least amount of work. If your organization has a lot of moves, additions, and changes, don't reference the PC's location in the computer name (for example, FL18RM24). Otherwise, you'll be updating it constantly.

What's meaningful in a name to one organization, however, may not mean anything to another. In a listing of all the computer names connected to your system, what would you want to see at a glance to identify computers quickly? What takes the least amount of change in your environment?

You'll probably name workstations differently than servers. When naming workstations, we like to use some derivative of the user's name (for example, LLLLLFM or SMITHJW) or email ID. However, naming a computer based on the user's name doesn't make sense if you have high turnover or play musical chairs in your company. Using people's email addresses or recognizable versions of their names presents a potential security issue; you could lead an "outsider" directly to the machine that he or she wants to snoop into. When security makes a difference, try something less obvious, such as employee ID numbers or some permutation of their telephone extension. And when it comes to servers, we like to name them to indicate their organizational affiliation (for example, Sales).

Don't use lengthy names or put spaces in names. For example, *ThisPCOwnedByMary* is too long and *This PC Owned By Mary* is no good! *MaryTMPC* is better, and perhaps *mmaddenPC* would work, too. NT doesn't care if you use long names or include embedded spaces, but other networking clients and systems may not be able to handle such usages.

TCP/IP names

TCP/IP uses a different scheme for names than NetBIOS/NetBEUI. TCP/IP uses 32-bit numbers to construct IP addresses (for example, 205.230.248.2). Each host or node on a TCP/IP network must have a unique IP address.

IP addresses are not meaningful to most humans and are, therefore, cumbersome to remember. Thus, it's helpful to have a way to convert IP addresses into meaningful names. On an NT network, you use computer names (also known as NetBIOS names). The Internet community uses domain names. Translation methods, such as WINS and DNS, maintain databases for converting an IP address to either a computer name or a domain name.

If you've ever used a Web browser on the Internet, you know that you can type in a URL (Uniform Resource Locator) such as `http://205.230.248.2/default.htm` or `http://www.lanw.com/default.htm` to obtain access to a Web page. That's because the Internet uses DNS to resolve IP addresses to domain names and vice versa. If you type the IP address, your Web browser will go directly to the location. If you type a domain name, your request is routed to a DNS server that resolves the name to an IP address, and then your Web browser goes to the location.

In the IP world, the naming scheme you can use is limited if you plan to connect to the Internet. That's because the Internet Network Information Center (InterNIC) is in charge of approving and maintaining the database of "legal" Internet domain names. You can request any domain name you want, but if someone else is using it or has a legitimate legal claim to a trade or brand name, you won't be able to use it. For example, you probably wouldn't be able to use *mcdonalds.com* or *cocacola.com;* likewise, if the name *xyzcorp.com* is registered to someone else, you wouldn't be able to obtain that name for your own use.

The format of an IP name is host.domainname. The domain name is something you can't guarantee, but typically represents your organization. The host name is usually the name for the computer you attach to when you log on to your network. For example, if your domain name is lanw.com and your computer name is maddemt, your fully qualified domain name (FQDN) is maddemt.lanw.com. To be valid, the FQDM must have a corresponding entry in some DNS server's database that permits it to be translated into a unique IP address; for example, maddemt.lanw.com might resolve into 205.230.248.2.

As long as you're isolated from the Internet, you can assign any names you like on your network. But if you ever connect your network to the Internet, you'll have to go back and change everything. If your network will be — or even might be — connecting to the Internet, obtain and install valid addresses and domain names now. That way, you'll be ready when you get the green light to hook up! For more information, ask your ISP for details on obtaining a domain name. They will probably need to install it and its corresponding IP address in their DNS server, so they're the right source for this information. To learn more about the process of obtaining a domain name in general, visit the Internet Network Information Center's (InterNIC's) Web site at:

```
http://internic.net
```

You'll find details on name registration services as well as the directory and database services that support the Internet's distributed collection of DNS servers.

Understanding addresses

When you send mail, you address the envelope in a particular way. You use the accepted protocol for addressing envelopes so that postal workers will know where and to whom to deliver that message.

If you changed the order of how you address an envelope, your message might not get to its intended recipient. For example, the protocol in the U.S. is to place the recipient's information in the middle of the front of the envelope, the sender's information in the upper-left corner, and the correct postage in the upper-right corner. In addition, you must address the envelope in English.

If you were to rearrange that information, without specifically labeling which address is the sender's and which one the recipient's, the envelope might be sent to you instead of the recipient. But if you want to send a letter to a postal service outside your home country, the protocol for addressing an envelope may differ. This is especially true for details such as the placement of street names, street numbers, and postal codes.

Unique addressing

To send a letter, the recipient must have an address. No two addresses in the United States can be identical; otherwise, the post office wouldn't know where to deliver the envelope. Parts of an address can be identical, such as the city and ZIP, but the entire address must be unique. Likewise, on a network, each node or computer must have a unique identifier, called an address, so that the network knows where to send the packets.

Protocol addressing differences

Different protocols use different addressing schemes. TCP/IP understands numbers (for example, 205.230.248.2). NetBIOS understands computer names (for example, \\myserver). When you install NT, you give it a computer name. If you're using the IP protocol, you also assign an IP address to the server. So now the server has a computer name and an IP address.

Suppose that you're trying to find your server from a workstation. If you're using a utility such as Windows NT Explorer, you type in the server's name rather than its IP address. If you're using a TCP/IP utility such as PING, you type in the server's IP address.

Understanding WINS

WINS is a dynamic database that Microsoft designed to resolve NetBIOS-derived computer names to IP addresses (for example, server name to 205.230.248.2). You enter a computer name and out pops the IP address. The database is dynamic, which means that, as the network changes and names come and go, the database changes right along with it automatically. WINS is something like a multilingual Spanish-English dictionary that's constantly updated as new words are added. You give it a Spanish word, and out pops an English word or translation that means the same thing.

The desired method: automated updates

The best way to implement an address translation service is to automate it and remove the possibility of human error. That's exactly what WINS does for a network. The WINS Server handles the mapping between computer names and IP addresses, and maintains a dynamic database that's automatically updated as computer names or IP addresses change. Systems that query the WINS Server to get the translated information are known as WINS clients.

The manual way — watch out, humans aboard

If you've spent any time around LAN Manager networks, you may be familiar with a text file called LMHosts in the \winnt\system32\ drivers\etc subdirectory. It, too, can provide a source of information for translating between NetBIOS names and IP addresses.

If you want to use LMHosts on your network, you must manually establish and then update the mappings between NetBIOS names (or computer names) to IP addresses yourself. That is, if a computer name or IP address changes on the network, you must update this file by hand. In a large organization, this is impractical or perhaps even impossible. For small networks of 10 addresses or less, it's not unworkable, providing the names on your network don't change too much or too often.

With the LMHosts approach, an oversight or mistake on your part might introduce an addressing error on your network. (Remember, if there's one duplicate name or address on your network or a typo in an address designation, some poor user won't get to his or her data!) We think it's better to let Windows NT handle this job automatically.

WINS servers

A WINS server maintains a database that maps IP addresses to their respective computer names. Rather than sending out broadcasts for address information, which consumes excess network bandwidth, a workstation that's in need of such data makes a request directly to a nearby WINS server. This lets workstations take advantage of well-defined local service and obtain address information more quickly and efficiently. Also, when workstations log on to the network, they will provide information about themselves to the WINS server, so that any changes in their names or addresses will automatically cause the server's database to change accordingly.

WINS clients

When configuring workstations on your network, you'll provide the IP addresses for the WINS Servers on your network. When workstations boot, they provide the WINS Server with their computer names and IP addresses. The server handles everything else. If a workstation needs an IP address that corresponds to a computer name, it asks the WINS server.

Doing the DHCP Thing

Now that you understand why each node on your network needs a unique address, the question arises: "How should you assign IP addresses to your entire network?" That is, should these addresses be assigned manually, which forces them to be assigned statically (or once and for all)? Or should the assignments be made automatically, which means that the addresses are assigned dynamically?

Until the release of Windows NT 4.0, WINS did not make sense for smaller networks. An informal survey of networks based on earlier versions tells us that, for small networks (25 workstations or less), many pre-4.0 NT-based networks relied on manual assignment of static IP addresses. This forced network administrators to practice "network management by walking around" — that is, they had to visit each PC to configure its IP address. Then they had to maintain a list of IP address assignments and update the IP addresses to reflect moves, additions, and changes in the organization. It was a daunting, never-ending task.

Microsoft did a neat thing with NT Server when they included the Dynamic Host Configuration Protocol (DHCP), which automates the assignment of IP addresses to clients. No more manually managing addresses — with DHCP, your server handles this task! You simply tell the server that it's a DHCP server. You can do this during installation, or you can add the service later (DHCP runs as an NT service). After DHCP is installed, you configure it to manage a range (also called pool) of IP addresses, and the DHCP service handles the allocation and assignment of addresses. DHCP even manages variable checkout intervals for individual addresses, so that regular users can obtain permanent assignments, while contractors or short-term users may obtain only limited "leases" on their IP addresses.

You configure your DHCP server service with a range of IP addresses, any addresses within that range that shouldn't be used, and one or more subnet masks. If you're not sure what a subnet mask is, ask your ISP to explain it to you. (Your ISP is probably quite familiar with IP addressing issues, so they should be able to tell you what to put into this field.) You also tell the server how long each assignment should last (the lease). Figure 18-1 shows a configuration screen for a DHCP server.

For example, let's assume you assign the DHCP server the range 205.230.251.60 through 205.230.251.90 with a subnet mask of 255.255.255.224. Based on that assignment, the server knows it can assign any unused address within that range (that is, 205.230.251.60, 205.230.251.61, 205.230.251.62, through 205.230.251.90) to a client that needs an IP address. If you told the DHCP server to exclude certain addresses, it would not assign those addresses under any circumstances.

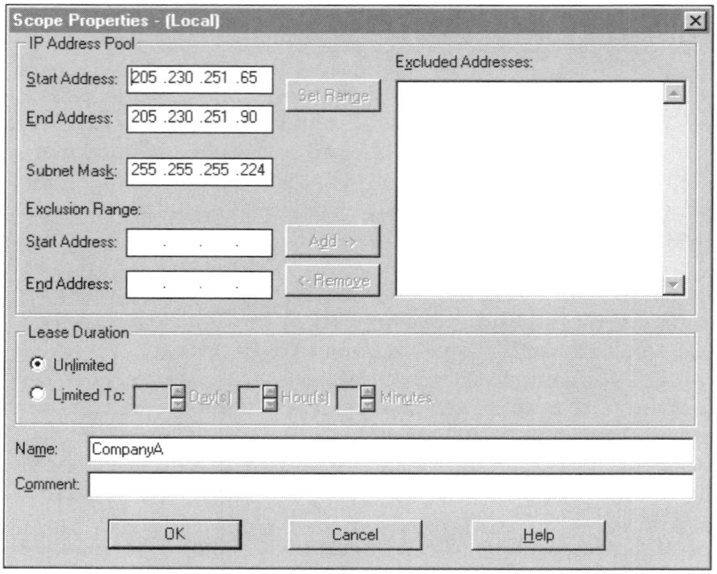

Scope Properties - (Local) ✕

IP Address Pool

Start Address: 205 .230 .251 .65

End Address: 205 .230 .251 .90

Set Range

Excluded Addresses:

Subnet Mask: 255 .255 .255 .224

Exclusion Range:

Start Address: . . .

Add ->

End Address: . . .

<- Remove

Lease Duration

◉ Unlimited

○ Limited To: [ ] Day(s) [ ] Hour(s) [ ] Minutes

Name: CompanyA

Comment:

OK   Cancel   Help

Figure 18-1:
Configuration
choices in a
DHCP
server.

When a client or workstation boots up with the IP protocol installed, it sends out a message saying "Hey, I need an IP address. Can anyone out there give me one?" The DHCP Server responds by sending the workstation an IP address that has a lease period. This means the workstation can use the address for a specified period of time. Administrators can set the lease period to "never expires" or to a finite period of time, such as two months.

DHCP is an easy service to use and very handy. If you use the TCP/IP protocol on your network, install DHCP during the NT installation and use it right away. If your workstations already have IP manually installed, you might need to switch over gradually. If you're planning to connect to the Internet, make sure the addresses you use are valid IP addresses that you can verify with your Internet Service Provider.

If you use DHCP on your network, also use WINS so that you can see the computer names in the WINS database mapping. By itself, DHCP will not tell you anything about NetBIOS computer names.

Serving Up and Replicating Domains

As mentioned, a DNS server resolves IP addresses into domain names and vice versa. For this to work, there has to be a way for DNS servers to receive updates. For example, when Joe Smith's company acquires a new domain name, only his organization knows about it until the rest of the Internet world is given that information (assuming that Joe went through the proper Internet channels to register a valid domain name with the InterNIC).

As you may have guessed, a distributed database handles all the data in a DNS system. No single database on the Internet has enough power to handle a gazillion requests at one time. Therefore, it's appropriate to have many DNS servers that handle this task cooperatively. DNS servers are arranged in a hierarchical fashion, where top-level servers know about second-level servers, and so on. When you acquire an IP domain name, you must also identify the DNS that your domain will use. This domain name will also be placed into a Root Server that knows about next-level servers, and the information propagates downward to the DNS server that you specify (usually, this will be your ISP's DNS server).

When you install workstations or servers to use the IP protocol, you can assign information about which DNS server they should query to resolve addresses. This DNS server can be local or situated elsewhere on the Internet. If you have a small network, it isn't practical to maintain your own DNS server. If you're in a large enterprise, it may be worthwhile, especially if speed is an issue. Placing a DNS server locally provides faster lookups than if the DNS server is on the other side of a communications link.

When you receive a domain name, it has an associated and unique IP address. You typically go through an Internet Service Provider to obtain this name/address pair. (Well, that's the least painful way; you can do it yourself if you're willing to tackle yet another formidable bureaucracy.)

DNS versus NT domain names

The term Domain Name Server is not the same as an NT domain name. NT allows you to organize your network in a few ways depending on how you want to administer the network.

You can group part or all of your network into a single NT domain where administration of the network is centralized and your users need only one account to log on to the domain. You assign one of your servers to act as a Primary Domain Controller (PDC). The PDC maintains a master database called the Security Accounts Manager (SAM), where all updates to user and group information are kept. You then assign other machines to serve as Backup Domain Controllers (BDCs) that can validate user logons so as not to overload the PDC. The PDC replicates its SAM down to the BDCs so they have the latest account validation information. The only similarity between NT domains and DNS servers is that they both work in a hierarchical fashion!

Microsoft includes a great paper on domain planning for enterprises (whether small or large) which you can download from the following site: http://www.microsoft.com.

NT's Trust Relationship

If you have more than one domain on an NT network, the domains won't automatically recognize one another unless you specifically link them. If you want users in domain A to use resources in domain B, you must establish a *trust relationship* between the two. Trust relationships work in only one direction. If you install your network so that domain A trusts domain B, the users in domain B can use the resources in domain A without needing another user account defined in domain A. In this respect, domains A and B function as a single administrative unit. However, users in domain A can't access resources in domain B until a trust relationship has been formed in that direction as well.

This is different from the Internet community. When you're on the Internet, everyone trusts everyone. You can get to any resource on the Internet by simply knowing its IP address or domain name and using the proper IP application. For example, you couldn't use FTP (File Transfer Protocol) to access a Gopher-based resource on the Internet. You'd need to use the proper application (a Gopher client) to reach the right resource (a Gopher server).

Many services on the Internet require that you also enter a logon ID and a password. FTP and certain Web documents, for example, can be password protected. It's one way that organizations can restrict their data on the Internet. If an organization trusts you, they may give you an ID and a password to get to their data. If not, you may be restricted to only the information that the organization chooses to share with the general public (if any).

Chapter 19

The File System: Center of the NT Universe

● ●

In This Chapter

▶ Understanding the NTFS

▶ Exploring the server

▶ Setting up utilities, applications, and more

▶ Using the file system

▶ Defending your server against computer viruses

▶ Taking care of business

● ●

A file system on a network is like the file system in your office. You file documents in alphabetical or chronological order. In addition, you might lock sensitive documents into secure storage. If so, you probably limit the number of keys to those storage cabinets, and you might even want to keep track of who's accessing which files and why.

You'll want to duplicate, for your organization's computer data, all the measures you take with your paper documents. That's where a network operating system can start to show its real prowess.

The file system on a network organizes data, keeps track of where it resides, and checks users' rights to access that data before permitting them to read or write to any files. You've probably heard of file systems such as the DOS File Allocation Table (DOS FAT), the OS/2 High Performance File System (HPFS), or the Macintosh Hierarchical Filing System (HFS).

Microsoft could have designed NT around one of these file systems, but instead it built its own file system. Microsoft engineers designed the NT File System (NTFS) specifically for NT, building in measures to convert other file systems to NTFS.

For a good overview of NTFS, look at the manuals that ship with NT, particularly the section titled "Managing Network Files" in the *Concepts and Planning Guide.*

For a detailed book written solely about NTFS, grab a copy of Helen Custer's *Inside the Windows NT File System.* Helen Custer, who has written other books for Microsoft, works directly with the Microsoft engineers, which is why the book is full of every technical piece of information you'd ever want to know about NTFS.

The NTFS View on Files, Directories, and More

The NTFS design team set out to enhance the old FAT system used on DOS-based computers. The FAT system was designed when PCs were in their infancy. Back then, people didn't store a lot of mission-critical data on their FAT systems, files were smaller, and security wasn't a big issue. Today, as LANs and networks grow in importance, the requirements of a file system are recoverability, reliability, security, and efficiency. NTFS does its best to fulfill all these requirements.

NTFS is a driver that loads into the I/O layer of the NT operating system. After it is loaded, it processes I/O requests pertaining to files, directories, and volumes.

When you install NT, the Setup program gives you the option of which file system to use: FAT or NTFS. If you select FAT, your users can still store and find files on the server, but they won't get any security other than what's already on their PCs. If you choose NTFS, Setup installs this newer, optimized file system. However, you'll no longer be able to simply access all files; instead, you'll have to log on to the server with the proper access rights. It's a tradeoff we think most organizations will be more than willing to make!

If you install NTFS, you can assign security to both directories and files. Thus, if you have two files in a directory, you can assign a different set of security permissions to each. You can also audit who accesses files and directories on the server. If you turn the audit feature on, each access to a file or directory is written to a security log. Subsequent review of that log will tell you exactly who's doing what to which files and directories.

A *disk* is the physical device on which your server stores data. Disks come in varying sizes and shapes, and the standard measurement for disk space has changed over the years. On older disk drives, space is measured in megabytes (MB), or one million bytes. On newer machines, where disk capacity is greater, you find the term gigabytes (GB), or one billion bytes.

You can install more than one disk in your server, or you can carve up one physical disk into multiple logical partitions. A *partition* is created when you logically split the physical disk into two or more parts. The drive functions as though it were two or more physical disks. Many administrators place the system files on the first partition and the program and support files on the next partition. If you have a large drive on your server (perhaps 2GB or larger), it may make sense to carve it up into an A: drive for your system (500MB), a B: drive for applications (1GB), and a C: drive for user data (whatever's left).

A partition may be categorized as either *primary* or *extended.* Primary partitions are for the operating system's use. Each physical disk can contain only four partitions; of that, only one partition can be extended. The extended partition can be further subdivided into logical drives such as F, G, and H. This is useful, for example, if you want to place all your applications on drive F and your data on drive G.

A *volume* is a partition (or grouping of partitions if you have more than one) that has been set aside for use by a file system such as NTFS or FAT. Whew!

You can set up partitions and file systems during or after installation. To modify a disk after you've installed NT on the server, you use the Disk Administrator utility.

There's some debate about whether to split your server's hard disk so that it contains a small FAT partition and a larger NTFS partition. Many network administrators do this on their network servers, and some folks just like the idea of having a "back door" into the server. We don't recommend this because it leaves a way for users to access the server's hard disk, even though it's only a small FAT partition on the disk.

So how in the world does NTFS keep track of your files and the other network users' files? NTFS stores each volume's contents in records in the Master File Table (MFT). Each MFT record typically consists of one data file on the volume. A file can take up more than one record if it's large or has many attributes associated with it. The attributes of a file include the file's name, owner, and security information.

The MFT can increase across your disk as your data storage needs grow. However, it does not decrease if your storage needs decrease. This can cause disk fragmentation on your servers, which can slow down their performance. Symantec's Windows NT Utilities and DiskKeeper from Executive Software include utilities to defragment your disk.

Microsoft will tell you that NTFS reduces fragmentation because it attempts to store files contiguously. But the same folks will also tell you that if a file is already stored and then increases, you should copy it to another drive, and then copy it back again so that NTFS can find a new, contiguous storage location. This is too inconvenient for serious consideration; we recommend that you get a utility such as DiskKeeper to handle these activities automatically.

NTFS supports a *hot fix* feature, which automatically detects any bad spots on a disk and redirects the data so that it's stored on a good area of the disk. After a bad area has been detected, it is cataloged and studiously avoided.

NTFS uses the NT cache manager to read files from and write files to memory, increasing the efficiency of frequently accessed files. As you may already know, accessing files from memory is much faster than accessing them from disk (about three orders of magnitude faster). If you plan to have files up to 16 terabytes in size (NTFS supports that), you'd better plan on having extra memory, too!

As more organizations grow globally, storing information in a uniform file format becomes increasingly necessary. NTFS uses Unicode characters to store all its data; Unicode essentially assigns a unique code to each letter in most of the world's alphabets. This simplifies the exchange of data between countries and permits languages to maintain their own representations.

If you want to go beyond this book and explore the innards of NTFS in extreme detail, get out your trusty TechNet CD-ROM. Perform a query using the keyword *NTFS*. You find plenty of information about NTFS, in varying levels of detail, with lots of graphics!

Navigating the Server

When you're connected to a network, you might choose to save a file to your workstation's local hard drive or to a server's disk where you have the proper access rights. When you save a file to a server, the file is *redirected* from your workstation across the network and onto the server. After the file gets to the server, the file system checks whether you have appropriate rights and then proceeds to process the data for storage.

NT sets up data on the server so that you can view it in a hierarchical manner in the Windows NT Explorer. However, the data is not physically stored that way on the server. Explorer uses a graphical user interface (GUI), so you don't have to look at the "messy" version of the way the data is actually stored. You interact with a logical — and more intelligible — organization of the data instead.

Before you set up NT, you want to lay out the structure of the directories on your server. Some administrators mix system files with data and application files. Others separate system files from data and application files. Others separate all three. It's up to you, but that doesn't mean we don't have some recommendations you might want to consider. So please, read on!

We recommend separating NT system files from the rest of the data on your server. Because the majority of your users need to access only their own data, you can limit their access to that partition. That way, you're less likely to create a security loophole on your system. (If you mix all the network data on a single partition and then accidentally mess up the security rights, the system files on your server might be open to user access. That could lead to disaster!)

If you go one step further and separate user data from application software, you can ensure that you won't accidentally give a user permission to delete software. Imagine coming into work on Monday and finding out that Microsoft Word no longer works on the network. Upon further investigation, you find that you inadvertently gave a user the wrong rights, and the user deleted the application instead of a data file!

You can navigate your way through the server using the Explorer or even the older 3.*x*-style File Manager utility. Shoot, you can even shell out to DOS if you must (use the MS-DOS Command Prompt icon). Explorer is much easier because it's graphical, but if you're an old DOS diehard, you probably feel more comfortable with the DOS prompt. We should warn you that typing *dir* at an NT command prompt results in a UNIX-like directory display (probably because NT emulates DOS; it doesn't really run a true DOS):

```
Date    Time    Type    Size    File/Dir Name
```

Typing *dir* in DOS gives you the following:

```
File/Dir Name    Type    Size    Date    Time
```

Utilities, Applications, and More

We hope you purchase and install only applications and utilities designed to run on your NT server. You never know what you'll get when you try to install something that wasn't specifically designed for NT or for use as a networked application.

Try not to run applications that aren't network-aware. Those programs were written for single users and have no capability to share files. If you place such an application on a server and multiple users access the files, you could get unexpected results. Worst case, the application might not work and the data becomes completely trashed. A less severe case might delude users into thinking the application works, until they discover that the data is inconsistent or incorrect. Either way, everybody loses!

If you use legacy applications, try installing and running them on NT in a test environment before you switch to or install NT on an across-the-board basis. If these applications don't run, you have to go with Plan B! As you may remember, this means finding another, more workable alternative.

Tom Miller, who had a database background, designed NTFS. He knew that databases crash and leave behind a mess of unresolved transactions unless they also implement a recovery strategy. That background helps to explain why he designed NTFS to be able to recover from crashes gracefully — you won't lose your data when the unthinkable becomes all too real!

To make a file system reliable, there has to be some way to track writes to disk. To this end, NTFS uses the log file service (LFS). LFS logs all file and directory updates. This service is used when a crash occurs and the disk must be reconstructed. Pretty handy, huh? You won't find that in a FAT system! By starting from a checkpoint — such as a recent system backup — and applying all changes in order of occurrence since that point, a replay of those transactions should restore NTFS to its most recent working state, just before the crash.

How to Use the File System

Before a user can get to data on the server, that user must be assigned the proper rights and a *share* for a server directory must be set.

When you share a directory, you must give it a name. The name can be the same as the directory's name, or it can be different. If you plan to permit DOS users to access these shares, remember to follow the DOS 8.3 file-naming convention for all share names. To view all the shares on your system, choose Start⇨Administrative Tools⇨Server Manager to start the Server Manager. To identify the default shares that NT creates at installation time, select the target server, and then choose Computer⇨Shared Directories.

Shares adhere to the following syntax:

```
\\ServerName\ShareName
```

After you've shared a directory, users can connect to that shared directory by assigning it a drive letter. The procedure for doing so depends on the operating system at the user's workstation. For example, DOS users would type the following:

```
net use S: \\Austin\Software
```

to map the S drive on their workstation to point to the Software share you created on the Austin server.

Windows 3.1 users can connect a drive on their workstation to a share on the server using File Manager. When networking is enabled on that workstation, File Manager is automatically updated to permit such activity. The same is true for Windows 95 users and the Windows 95 Explorer, and NT Workstation and the Windows NT Explorer.

Your Server versus Computer Viruses

A computer virus can infect an organization's network in no time flat. We heartily recommend that you install virus protection software on your users' PCs and the servers on your network.

A computer virus is a special kind of computer program specifically written to reproduce itself, no matter what havoc it may wreak on your network. A virus can show up on a workstation or a server. It's not uncommon for viruses to infect workstations where there's no virus protection and where there's a regular exchange of floppy disks.

As more organizations connect to the Internet and exchange electronic mail, where file attachments are common, it's equally easy to contract a virus even when no floppies are exchanged! Because email file attachments are encoded, it's particularly important to check your virus software to make sure it can scan encoded files. To make matters more complicated, many of those attachments come across the Internet as zipped or compressed files. Your virus software must be able to scan those types of files, as well.

How often you set your workstations to scan for viruses depends on how lucky you feel! We don't like to take risks, so we prefer to install virus checkers on each workstation and load them into memory so they scan all incoming files all the time.

We also like to see the server's virus software scan all incoming files and file writes continuously. "Oh!" you say, "This could bog down the system." That's true of other operating systems, but NT is a multitasking and multithreaded system, so such a practice has only a minimal effect on performance. Which would you rather have: a fast network full of infected files ready to explode, or a somewhat slower network that's stable, correct, and reliable? Besides, NT handles multiple services with élan; what difference will one more make?

We've seen an entire department's data wiped out because virus protection was unavailable. To make matters worse, that department didn't have a backup of its data either. As a result, forty people lost every piece of data on the server, and had to recreate it from scratch. That's a lot of time and resources taken away from the organization!

Some viruses can take as long as 30 days to emerge if virus detection software is not present. Therefore, it's advisable to store tape backups that span a month's time, in case you need a restore that goes back to before the initial infection.

No Rest for the Weary: Take Care of Business

You probably know the old saying, "A network administrator's job is never done!" And you know it's absolutely true. Even if things run smoothly and fulfill your expectations, you still have daily maintenance and upkeep routines to perform on your network. Your job involves wearing many hats and isn't limited to high-level tasks. Sometimes you even have to pick up a broom and sweep out the computer room!

In case we haven't discussed the topic of backups enough, we take this opportunity to talk about it some more! Think of your organization's data just as you would your family's jewels. You wouldn't store them in a cardboard box at your neighbor's house! Instead, you'd probably insure them, rent a safety deposit box at a bank, and place the jewels there.

Well, the same goes for your network backups. Don't be careless with them, because they represent your organization's data assets in binary form. By backing up these jewels in a safe, regular manner, you're ensuring the integrity of that data!

At a bare minimum, back up the data on the network on a daily basis. At least once a week, store a complete set of backup tapes off-site, at least 20 miles from your office. Use a rotation scheme for your tapes, so that you're don't reuse the same tape over and over again. Validate the previous day's backup on a daily basis, and record that information in a log.

Put a plan in place to rapidly restore your data, should the network ever self-destruct. A mountain of backup tapes will do you no good if you have no server on which to restore them! Many administrators plan for occasional problems such as deleted files, but forget to plan for disasters such as fires, where an entire network could be wiped out in one fell swoop.

You also need to keep an eye on the disk space consumption on your servers, as well as CPU utilization. Letting the disk space become too low without adding additional space or freeing up existing space could crash your server in a heartbeat.

NT provides a Performance Monitor utility to assist you in determining which resources of the server are in use or being taxed (or overtaxed). It's a graphical utility that can help you locate bottlenecks in your system and assist you in planning upgrades to a system's capacity.

You can view the server information in Performance Monitor in real time or opt to send its information to log files. You can chart that information to visualize what's happening on the system.

Performance Monitor permits you to set thresholds for certain values (such as disk space used), and then instructs the system to send an alert when that threshold is exceeded. For example, you might want to know when the server's available disk space drops to 10MB or less.

In addition, when you add third-party utilities, such as American Power Conversion's UPS monitoring software, you can view performance metrics related to that software in Performance Monitor, as well. This lets you extend the reach of this management tool to cover most of the important aspects of your server's capacities and capabilities.

We heartily recommend that you familiarize yourself with this handy utility before launching your system into full-scale production. Open up its Help screen and go through all of its options so you know how to take advantage of this powerful utility. Use it to its fullest!

One last utility that NT provides is the Event Viewer. This is the place to look when weird events occur on your system. *Events* are defined as significant occurrences on the system and are logged to an event log file. It's possible for the system to log events that you deem unnecessary for immediate attention. We recommend that you thoroughly familiarize yourself with this utility to further help you track system problems.

In this chapter, we've covered NT's file system (NTFS) and why you'd want to use it. We also looked at how to access files on the server from an administrative point of view and from the user's point of view. We then examined some administrative utilities that NT provides to keep your network glowing and running. In the following chapter, we cover the ins and outs of the Remote Access Server, a.k.a. RAS.

Chapter 20

Network Security: It's Not a Game!

. . . .

In This Chapter

▶ Setting up the right controls

▶ Being an NTS supervisor

▶ Managing outsiders' access to your network

▶ Creating named groups for specific tasks

▶ Setting permissions

▶ Managing directory, file, and object rights

▶ Controlling and tracking permissions

▶ Assigning effective rights and permissions

▶ Setting NT file and directory attributes

. . . .

Making sure that your organization's data is secure is the single most important function you perform as a network administrator. Security should take precedence as you plan your network's future growth and direction. It probably will take more time than any other function you perform, but you can never be too safe with data!

Just as you lock your car or house, so should you secure your organization's data. Unfortunately, people are lurking out there, just waiting for you to open an access point so that they can get at your data. Imagine if someone steals your organization's price list and broadcasts it across the Internet — your competitors could read it and adjust their prices accordingly. A drop-in business perplexes upper management. By the time anyone realizes what has happened, revenue is irrevocably lost.

Examining this chapter closely is important, even if the material is a little dry. This chapter explains the security structure of NT so that you can make your network as impenetrable as possible. By the time you finish this chapter, you'll feel like you have a moat filled with alligators around your LAN!

Keeping Watch: Setting Up the Right Controls

When you set up accounts for your users, they can log on to the network and see everything on the network. That's why setting the proper permissions for the files and directories to which they need access and restricting them from access to resources that they don't need to see (or even know about) is crucial. You don't want Annie destroying Bill's files, accidentally or otherwise. As network administrator, you must secure Bill's data from Annie and vice versa.

NT includes permissions that you can set on an individual or group basis. In addition, NT enables you to set rights at the file and directory level. To use these capabilities effectively, you need to determine how much security you want to implement.

We've seen small offices (20 people or less) that have a loose security structure. This means that everyone in the office has administrative privileges. In addition, smaller offices tend to allow logon accounts with first names only, and often require no passwords. Although this is the typical security arrangement in small offices, we think it's an invitation to disaster.

This situation often persists because small offices introduce LANs without training their personnel on proper networking techniques. Also, many LAN administrators also have another "real job" in the organization, which may hinder them from becoming properly educated about security. Nevertheless, such education is important, and other responsibilities shouldn't interfere with implementing necessary safeguards.

As more organizations connect their LANs to the Internet, this level of security is unacceptable. Even if you do not feel the need to put your servers behind locked doors, you must make sure that good basic security measures are in place.

It Ain't Easy Being an NTS Supervisor

NT installs with two default accounts: Administrator and Guest. The Administrator account has full access to the NT Server, including the capability to reinstall. The Guest account has fewer privileges, but can wreak havoc on your network if you don't pay close attention to that account's permissions. We talk more about this in the next section, "Visiting Hours."

The Administrator account installs with defaults that give it access to the entire server. Unless you change its name or its rights and privileges, this account can also create pandemonium on the network if misused. Some network administrators like to rename this account to another name to prevent intruders from guessing the password.

The best solution is to endow the Administrator account (or whatever you've changed its name to) with a hard-to-guess password. One suggestion for creating passwords is to go to the library and choose one book, each from different sections (for example, science and geography, or English and gardening). Randomly select a word from each. Then add a number somewhere in between the two words (for example, Istanbul45xray), and you have your new password.

Remember, the Administrator has full access to the server and all its components. The person using this account can shut the server down and restart it, reinstall NT, format the drives, change user permissions and logon scripts, change audit trails, and much, much more. Give access to this account to only one person — that's you! — and guard its password with your life. Instruct anyone else to whom you give an account with the same level of privilege and access to behave the same way.

Visiting Hours

Use the Guest account sparingly, if at all. Typically, you'd use this account when someone visits your office for a few days. You may need to assign that account certain rights and permissions so that that user can get to the files he or she needs while visiting. If two people use the Guest account, they must share those rights. Then you'd have to remember to remove any special access from the Guest account later.

Renaming or disabling the Guest account and creating a named group called Visitors is best. For individual visitors, create an account based on the visitor's name and make them a member of the Visitors group. You can set this account to expire the day after the visitor leaves and then delete that account during your next scheduled maintenance.

Hackers have all the manuals to all the network-operating systems and know which accounts are created by default during installation. Guest is a popular name — it's used in both NetWare and NT. Don't leave a hole in your LAN security. Rename or disable Guest now.

If You Want Help, Do This

If more than one person is designated as an Administrator, don't let them share a single Administrator account. Instead, create an account that identifies each person differently from that person's normal logon account, but gives each one Administrative equivalence (StarnesNL1). Why do this? If you ever need to audit who did what to your system, you'll see names instead of a generic Administrator account. That will let responsibility fall on the right shoulders.

Don't put the word *Admin* in an account name. Doing so alerts hackers to which accounts have administrative privileges. Typically, such Admins have two accounts: an administrative account (StarnesNL1) and a normal user account (StarnesNL).

If Johnny is an administrator on the network but also has to work on his spreadsheets, for example, you'd want him to log on to the network using an account that's appropriate for the function he's performing. When he needs to perform administrative functions, he should log on with his Admin account. Otherwise, he doesn't need administrative access and should behave like the ordinary user he is at the time.

Using Other Empowered Entities

NT includes built-in administrative and operational groups to which you can assign users. These groups are given special permissions during installation to help offload some administrative tasks to others on the network. These groups are shown in Figure 20-1 and are created on a Domain Controller by default during the installation of NT.

At the bottom half of Figure 20-1, you can see a group named Backup Operators. Microsoft's engineers figured that you might not have time to perform backups and restores on the network and might need to designate someone else to handle this task. By adding a user to the Backup Operators group, he or she automatically receives the permissions needed to perform that task. The same holds true for Account Operators: Assigning a user to this group gives the user the rights to add, delete, and modify user accounts.

If you're the only one who's minding the store, you don't need to add yourself to each of these groups; you just log in as the Administrator.

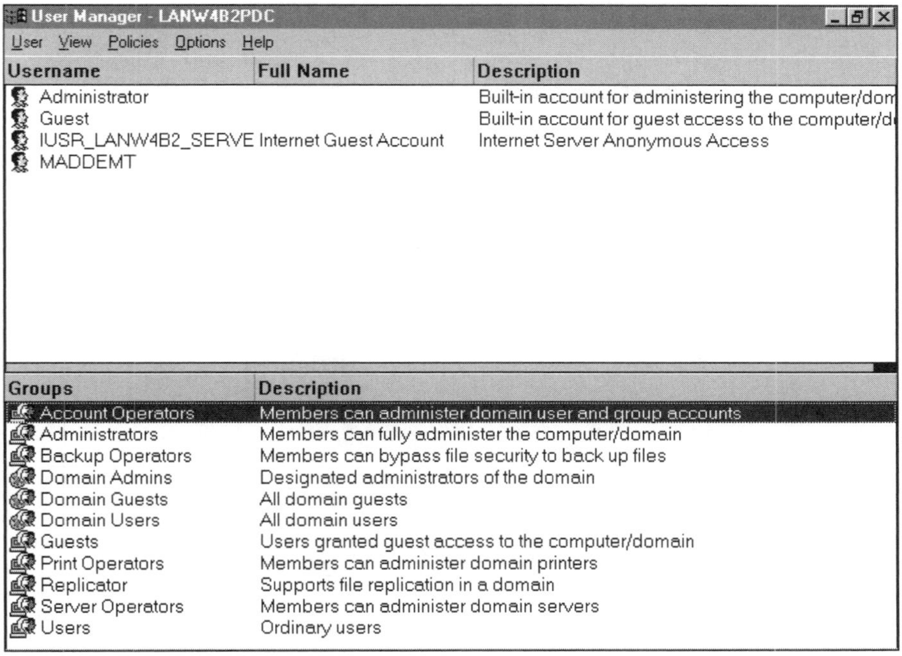

Figure 20-1:
Default
groups and
descriptions
in NT User
Manager.

The Easy Way Out: Tips for Setting Permissions

In versions of NT before 4.0, the File Manager in Windows NT supplied one way to manage file and directory security. NT 4.0 replaces File Manager with Windows NT Explorer, but its features aren't as obvious. The good news is that you can still use File Manager because it's only hidden, not removed. You can even set security permissions simply by browsing from the server's desktop. (However, you should become familiar with Explorer's features instead of reverting to the comfortable File Manager because one day the File Manager will be gone.)

You can set file and directory permissions, activate auditing features, and establish the ownership of files from the Windows NT Explorer by viewing its Properties screen. To activate Explorer, go to the Programs menu and click on Windows NT Explorer. Highlight the directory or file you want to set or view permissions for and right-click to display the Properties screen, as shown in Figure 20-2.

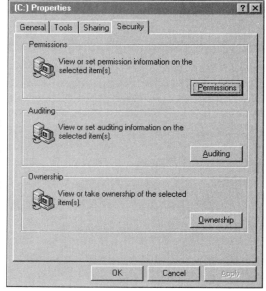

Figure 20-2:
Using NT Explorer to set permissions, shares, ownership, and activate auditing features.

From the Properties menu option, click the Security tab and then click the Permissions button to display the Directory Permissions. At this point, you can associate named accounts or groups with specific access rights, or explicitly deny other named accounts and groups any rights whatsoever.

Stand Up for Your Directory, File, and Object Rights

In Chapter 19, we hound you to use the NT File System (NTFS) and not the old File Allocation Table (FAT) system. NTFS provides an extra layer of security that FAT doesn't. For example, if you're using FAT, you can't set permissions individually at the file and directory level.

We hope you follow our advice and install NTFS on your volume(s); otherwise, much of this chapter won't apply to your system. If you're using the FAT system, you can set permissions at the directory level only if the directory is shared. If a local user obtains unrestricted access to the server console, individual file permissions don't apply.

You should never, ever leave the server unguarded if you've logged on with Administrator privileges. If you must leave, log off before you go!

Setting shares

Setting file and directory permissions in NT is straightforward. On an NTFS volume, you first create a share on a directory and give it a share name so users can connect to it from across the network. The share name can be the same as the directory name or different. For example, if you want your users to be able to access a directory on the root of your server's D drive called Apps (D:\APPS), you would share that directory, probably with the share name of APPS.

Creating a share gives all users in the Everyone group full access to that share and all subdirectories beneath it. Any account added to the domain is also added to the group Everyone, so be careful when setting a share.

If your server is up and running and connected to users, first set file and directory permissions and then set the share. However, we assume that you're setting the server up for the first time and your users aren't connected yet. In that case, you set up user accounts and group names and then tackle access rights and privileges.

When you set permissions on a share, they are in effect only when the share is accessed across the network (not locally). Table 20-1 shows the permissions you can set on a share level by group or user if you are logged on with Administrator equivalence or are a member of the Server Operator group.

Table 20-1	Share Permissions
Permission	*Description*
No Access	User or group can't see the share.
Read	User or group can see the contents of the share but can't save or delete files.
Change	User or group can make changes to this share.
Full Control	User or group can see and access anything in this share.

Permissions for shares operate with file and directory-level permissions. To restrict users or groups from some of the subdirectories and files in D:\Apps in the share associated with that directory, for example, you would set their file and directory permissions as appropriate. Or you might want users to have only read access to that share.

To access the data in a share, your users must connect to that share from their workstation. From NT Workstation, they'd use the Map Network Drive option from the Properties menu of a shared folder icon (likewise for Windows 95). For DOS/Windows or DOS-only workstations, users must employ the NET USE command from DOS, where the following syntax applies:

```
NET USE drive: \\servername\sharename
```

Thus, if the user wanted to assign a drive named G: to the \\myserver\apps share, he or she would type:

```
NET USE G: \\myserver\apps
```

Windows 3.x users who map their drives in DOS before starting Windows can view mapped drives inside File Manager or any other third-party file management software.

Share names on an NT Server can be up to 80 characters long if they are accessed only by NT Server or Workstation machines. If you have DOS users on your network, limit your share names to the DOS 8.3 (filename.ext) naming convention. For file and directory names, Windows NT and 95 support up to 255 characters and also include a name-mapping feature to convert long names to the shorter names that DOS users can see.

You can set, view, and modify shares with the Server Manager utility. After you've set the shares, you use Windows NT Explorer to set permissions on the files and directories.

Who may access what?

The hard part of managing access to files and directories is determining who may access what. After you make that decision, managing access is purely a matter of setting the required permissions. You must decide which files are public (available for everyone on the network to see) and which files and directories are private (visible only to one or more individuals). In addition, you may want some people to be able to read certain files but not delete them.

Individual file and directory permissions

Table 20-2 shows the individual permissions you can set along with a brief description of each one.

Table 20-2		Individual File and Directory Permissions
Permission	*Code*	*Description*
Read	R	User can view the file's name, contents, attributes, owner, and permissions.
Write	W	User can write to the file, change its attributes, or view its attributes.
Delete	D	User can delete the file.
Execute	X	User can run only the EXE or COM file. Used primarily to prevent copying of the file.

Permission	Code	Description
Change Permission	P	User can change the file's permissions.
Take Ownership	O	User can take ownership of the file to set and grant permissions.

You can use these permissions liberally and set them as often as you like. Setting these permissions one at a time, however, can quickly become tedious. The next section explains how to set permissions in groups.

Standard file and directory permissions

Those crafty NT engineers figured that you might want to set some permissions in combinations, without having to add each permission individually. NT includes a standard set of permissions that you can set at the directory level (Table 20-3) or file level (Table 20-4).

Table 20-3	Permission Grouping You Can Set on the Directory Level in One Setting		
Directory Permission	**Individual Permission**	**File Permission**	**Description**
No Access	None	None	User can't access the directory or its files.
List	RX	Not specified	User can list existing files in the directory but not newly created ones. Users can see and navigate through subdirectories of this directory.
Read	RX	RX	User can read and execute files in this directory.
Add	WX	Not specified	User cannot read current files or change them, but can add new files and subdirectories.
Add + Read	RWX	RX	User has same permissions as above, except the user can change the files.
Change	RWXD	RWXD	User can read and change files and add files to the directory.
Full Control	All	All	User can do everything, including read files, change files, add files, delete files, set permissions, and take ownership of files. Use this permission sparingly.

Note: Column 1 in Table 20-3 supplies the names for standard directory permissions, according to Microsoft's standard terminology, as explained in the *Windows NT Concepts and Planning Guide.*

Columns 2 and 3 name the corresponding permissions for existing and new files in a given directory. We distinguish between actual permissions explicitly assigned to existing files (called Individual) and implied permissions to be assigned to new files (called File Permission). The value in column 2 describes the permission granted to an existing file, whereas the value in column 3 describes the permission granted to any new files that might be created in or added to that directory.

Table 20-4 shows the name of the permission in the first column, the collective individual permissions needed in the second column, and a brief description in the last column.

Keep in mind that when you set directory permissions, the setting affects the file permissions for any new files added to that directory. The chosen directory permission doesn't change permissions for existing files unless you specify this explicitly in Windows NT Explorer (by choosing the Replace Permissions on Existing Files option in the Directory Permissions area of the Security tab.) Likewise, the directory permissions you set don't automatically trickle down to their respective subdirectories unless you specify this when setting the permissions in Windows NT Explorer. (Use the Replace Permissions on Subdirectories option in the Directory Permissions area of the Security tab.)

Table 20-4 Single Settings that Assign Multiple Permissions to a File

File Permission	Individual Permission	Description
No Access		User can't see or do anything with the file.
Read	RX	User can read and execute the file.
Change	RWXD	User can read, delete, or change the file.
Full Control	All	User can do everything with the file, including read it, change it, delete it, set permissions, and take ownership.

Permissions are cumulative, except for the No Access permission, which overrides all others. Suppose that JoAnne Holm belongs to two groups, Sales and Marketing. She has the Change permission from the Sales group, she has the Read permission from the Marketing group, and she collectively has the Change permission (which includes the Read permission). However, if she also belongs to the Logistics group, which has No Access, she will be denied access because No Access overrides all other permissions.

Permission to Assign Permissions

You can't go around setting permissions on the server unless you've been given access to do so. As you may have guessed, only the Administrator account and any account assigned administrative equivalence have this privilege.

In addition, if you are the owner of a file or directory, you can change its permissions. Be careful when you assign this right because it lets the person take ownership and then change permissions!

If you give users Full Control or the Change permission, they can also set permissions to a directory or file. As mentioned, use the Full Control right sparingly. Think of it as the "right to wreak havoc" and never place it in the hands of those who don't know what they're doing!

Examining and Changing Access Rights and Permissions

We walk through an example of using Windows NT Explorer to create a new directory on the server and view the defaults that NT sets:

1. **Start Windows NT Explorer and highlight your C drive. Use the menus to access File⇨New⇨Folder.**

   This creates a new folder called New Folder. (Note that NT uses the term *folder* instead of *directory*.)

2. **Highlight New Folder and use the menus to access File⇨Rename. Type** TestDir **and press Enter.**

   You should see your new folder called TestDir in the window.

3. **To view NT's default settings for this new directory, highlight the directory and right-click. Select Properties from the menu.**

   You'll notice that the General tab shows the directory name and share name for that directory if defined. (See Figure 20-3.)

4. **To share this directory on the network, begin by clicking the Sharing tab and then selecting S̲hared As. The rest of the options become available; fill in the screen as shown in Figure 20-4 and then click P̲ermissions.**

   On a default share, NT gives the group Everyone Full Control to this share. You can alter or change this if you want. We'll change permissions on the directory level.

5. **Click Cancel so that you don't change anything yet.**

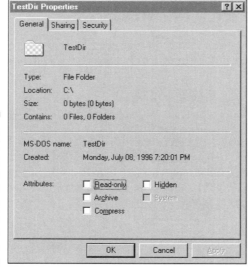

6. **To view or modify permissions, auditing, or ownership of the TempDir directory, first click the Security tab. Click the Permissions button and you'll see the screen shown in Figure 20-5.**

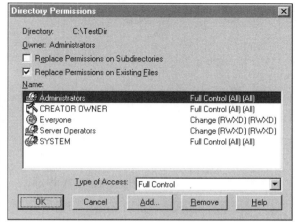

Figure 20-5:
The NT
default
permissions
by group on
a new
folder.

Notice that the group Everyone has Change permissions to this new directory. Every account that's added is added to the group Everyone, including the Guest account. We hope you understand the impact of this: When you set up a new directory (or folder), make sure that you remove rights from those who don't need them, especially the group Everyone. For example, suppose you're setting up a directory for the Sales department and you don't want the Marketing department to access the data. By default, the Marketing department can access this directory unless you delete Full Control from the group Everyone and add Full Control for the Sales group.

You probably noticed a group called System. The operating system uses the System group, so don't mess with this group or its rights. If you change it, you could cause trouble.

Set up your permissions by groups rather than by users because a group-based approach is a lot easier to maintain. Suppose that the Sales Department needs access to expense reports and customer data. You would create a group for them, add the sales folks to that group, and set the permissions to that data on the group level. When new users join the sales force, you would merely add them to the group. Then the new users will have the same rights and permissions to the data as the rest of the group.

File and Directory Attributes

The last thoughts we want to leave you with concern file and directory attributes. You probably saw these in the General tab when we walked through the previous example. Attributes affect the way files and directories are viewed or used. NT has five types of attributes:

- **Read-Only:** The directory or file can't be altered or erased.

- **Hidden:** The directory or file is there, but it can't be listed. DOS users will remember that a file marked with this attribute can't be seen in a DIR command. A user or group can have rights to use the file, but unless they specifically type in the file name or directory name, they can't get to it.

- **Archive:** Used by backup programs to determine when a file or directory needs to be archived.

- **System:** The file or directory is used by the operating system and shouldn't be changed or modified. Doing so could render your system inoperable.

- **Compress:** NT's data compression has reduced the size of the file or directory. When you view the file, NT automatically decompresses the file to its normal size.

Chapter 21

Keeper of the Keys: Managing NTS Security

● ●

In This Chapter

▶ Getting kicked off the LAN

▶ Exposing the ins and outs of logging on and off

▶ Exploring passwords: how to build them, use them, and keep them fresh

▶ Learning that security begins at home — but it doesn't end there

▶ Dealing with audit checks

▶ Making your network intruder-proof

▶ Keeping your servers under lock and key

● ●

A dministrators can take advantage of NT account restrictions when setting up accounts on the network. These options determine when and how a user gains access to the network.

For example, some organizations employ contract workers and need a way to monitor the times that users can log on to the network. In NT, you can restrict the times and days that users are allowed to log on. If you don't want the contractors using the network on the weekends, you can block that time frame from the available logon times.

You can set user accounts to expire on a certain date. This is handy if you know a contract worker needs access to your system only for a limited time. When you set up the account, you can set an expiration date. Assuming that you have a scheduled network maintenance day and time, you could use a third-party utility to print reports on your system that list all expired accounts. Then at that time, you can delete all the accounts with the assurance that the security of your network is still intact.

If you have a contract position that remains the same but the personnel change periodically, you can disable the account instead of expiring it. Then you simply change the account information for each new contractor. This keeps all permissions properly set, but allows you to change the name or password. Or you could establish a named group called Contractors and give each individual contractor his or her own account for as long as they need it. There are many ways to handle user accounts, yet maintain tight security!

Before you set up any user accounts, disable the Guest account and rename the Administrator account. If you can't get up the nerve to disable the Guest account, set a password for it immediately. (You'll also rename it if you're smart; why leave open known entry points into your network?)

The Ins and Outs of Logging On and Off!

After you've built your network, your users may want to climb aboard as fast as possible. Introducing a logon process may annoy some users if you don't educate them about why you require the extra keystrokes. Remember, your network users' main objective in the morning is to turn on their PC and then make a beeline for the coffee pot. They'd rather see their machine up and running — instead of a logon prompt — when they return, beverage in hand.

As the keeper of the keys, you need to design the users' logon process to make it simple and quick, yet safe and secure. Your system should require any user who wants to gain access to the network to have a unique user ID and password. The key word in the last sentence is *unique*. In other words, you don't want to set up a network so that each user logs on under the same name, such as Guest or HeyYou. If you let everyone log on to the network with the same name, you'll never know who's really there.

When a user logs on to the network, it doesn't necessarily mean that they're in the same building as the server. They could dial into the network from outside the office using RAS (Remote Access Service). Regardless of where (and how) users gain access to the system, putting a few controls on the logon process is a good idea. This helps to prevent hackers and wildebeests from gaining undesired entry.

A common trick used by network administrators limits the number of invalid logon attempts to the network for any given account. If any user attempts to log on three times but doesn't get the account name, or password, or both correct, the account is locked for a specified period of time. (If you're one of the truly security conscious, you can also capture potential break-in information to a log file.)

Hackers are notorious for trying to gain access to unsecured systems. How do they do it? Some hackers have specialized programs that run in a loop. Their break-in programs are designed to dial into your system and attach to the network, using known easy accounts and passwords. For instance, easy accounts include first names, first initials plus last names, and other straightforward name permutations. Passwords are the same, except they include birthdays, anniversaries, account numbers, and so on. Stay away from things that are easy to guess!

For example, small offices often set up networks using their users' first names for accounts. Most hackers know that there is probably at least one account named Tom, John, or Mary. And because some of those small offices are lax with their password policies, these hackers know also that there's probably an account named Mot (Tom spelled backwards)!

These specialized hacker programs have associated databases with almost every name you can imagine (and then some) and a complete dictionary. They set their programs to work, looking for any easy points of entry and wait for unprotected networks to crack open like ripe melons.

For an interesting article on "password plucking," point your Web browser to Robert Kane's white paper at the following URL:

```
http://www.intrusion.com/artcl.htm
```

Don't create accounts based on your users' first names, unless you want to expose your network to a hacker attack. Instead, name accounts using a portion of each user's last name but also include the user's initials.

For example, if you set up an account for Ann A. Cin, name that account CINAA. Here, we chose to use the first five letters of the last name, combined with the other initials. Because Ann doesn't have five letters in her last name, we've used all the letters we could.

The reason you would use both initials comes into play when the number of users on your system grows large. What happens if you have one user named John A. Smith and another named Jane P. Smith? If you use only their first initials plus their last names, you wind up with two SMITHJ user names on your system.

Other alternatives for account names and passwords include requiring the use of numbers or special characters. CompuServe, for instance, randomly generates passwords by combining two nouns from a massive dictionary, separated by a punctuation mark (for example, tin#boat or car?pickle). Other schemes include a random number in the string. The possibilities are infinite, which is why the odds of guessing such a password or account name are correspondingly miniscule.

Even if your organization is small today, planning for growth is still smart. If you plan for a more complex naming scheme from the outset, you won't have to scrap your scheme later when the first set of duplicate users shows up! As with other things in life, prevention beats cure every time.

Passwords: How to Build 'Em, Use 'Em, and Keep 'Em Fresh

Now that you know the potential security risks that hackers can pose, you should educate your users about these issues. You don't need to go into the gory details, but a little information won't hurt.

To be a good network administrator, you must stay one step ahead of your users. How can you do this? First and foremost, put yourself in their shoes. Learn to think as they do; don't always look at the world as a network administrator. After you create their logon IDs, it's usually up to your users to create, maintain, and remember their passwords. If your users are smart, it won't surprise you when they come up with clever ways to remember their passwords, such as taping them to their computer monitors. Oops, *that* isn't very secure!

At some point in your budding career, your users will probably want to connect to the Internet. That's another reason why you should instill good password practices early. If you can guess their network passwords easily today, some devious Internet hacker will have no trouble tomorrow!

Although no surefire plan exists for designing passwords exists, making a plan anyway is best. Then educate your users about the plan and strive to enforce it. Here's a simple plan that many network administrators use to design and maintain passwords:

- **Don't allow passwords that contain user names (or portions thereof).** The easiest passwords for a hacker to guess are those derived from a user's first or last name.

- **Force passwords to be a minimum length.** NT defaults to a minimum password length of 6 characters. You can set this anywhere from 0 to 14 characters. We recommend that passwords be at least 8 characters long; in this case, more is better. On the other hand, you don't want users to have to write down lengthy passwords so that they can remember them.

- **Force periodic password changes.** When you create a user account, the NT default is to require users to change their passwords every 42 days. As long as you don't mark the box that reads Password Never Expires when you set up a new user, the NT default should suffice.

✔ **Force passwords to be unique.** After 42 days, users are presented with a prompt to enter a new password. If you force unique passwords, they can't choose the same password again. By default, NT stores the last eight passwords used, thereby forcing the user to cycle through eight different passwords before he or she can reuse the first one.

✔ **Do not allow users to exchange passwords.** This one is hard to prevent. Most of your efforts should be to educate your users about the potential dangers.

Common sense is the order of the day when working with passwords. The real problem is that common sense is so hard to come by. That's why you have to supply as much as possible for your users, through intelligent policies and as much education as you can give them.

Security Begins at Home, but It Doesn't End There

As you struggle to maintain a secure network environment, you should look for as many online freebies that you can get. You'll find as much information as you can handle on CompuServe and the Internet concerning network security. For example, on CompuServe, McAfee Associates, Inc.(GO VIRUS) has a ton of information on the latest viruses and how they can affect your network. McAfee even has a virus hotline that you can call for the latest virus information: 1-888-VIRUS-NO. For more information on how to contact McAfee, consult Appendix C.

If you want to purchase security-oriented products for your network, you'll find more surveys than you can shake a stick at on the Internet. Download the surveys, give them to management, and watch them turn pale at the numbers! If the surveys don't convince management of the need to spend a few wise dollars, you're doomed. The following lists a few pointers on how to find security-related information:

✔ On the Internet, go to any of the search engine locations (that is, http://www.search.com) and type in a keyword, such as security, virus, or audit. You'll find various links to sites with helpful information.

✔ Call, write, or visit the National Security Institute at

National Security Institute
57 East Main Street, Suite 217
Westborough, MA 01581
Telephone: 508-366-5800
Fax: 508-898-0132
URL: http://nsi.org

✔ Visit the following two Web sites for some interesting pointers regarding NT security:

```
http://www.somarsoft.com/security.htm
http://www.telemark.net/~randallg/ntsecure.htm
```

Set aside a specific hour each week to research on-line information regarding network security. If you make research part of your weekly maintenance routine, it will be much easier to stay on top of things.

And at Your Neighbor's, Too!

Some administrators are so concerned about security that they've eliminated floppy drives in workstations (called diskless workstations). Without a floppy, you can't introduce a virus unless you get it from the network.

Viruses are destructive programs coded specifically to sabotage part or all of a PC or network. When a virus is found, its code can be broken down into a pattern of ones and zeros, and labeled. Virus protection software often contains tables of known viruses and can scan your desktops and other systems for their presence. Some newer polymorphic viruses are a little trickier because their code continually changes, which makes it harder to identify them.

Not everyone is able to use diskless workstations, but you can take other measures to protect against viruses. Having virus protection software loaded on each workstation connected to your network is best. In addition, you want to install virus protection software to scan each server in all your domains. Every time users request access to your network, the logon process should scan their machines for viruses.

Although several good products are available, Cheyenne Software, Inc.'s InocuLAN 2.0 stands a head above the rest. It detects most of the known viruses, as certified by the National Software Testing Laboratories (NSTL). The virus detector finds, identifies, and fixes several virus types: boot, file, macro, multipartite, polymorphic, and stealth.

The software's ability to find and fix the virus is crucial, and notifying you in the process is also important. When InocuLAN detects a virus, it sends an alert in a number of ways, depending on your preference. We recommend that you set up your server virus software so that it pages you. However, you can set it up to send you email or send an SNMP alert to your favorite management console. But wait, that's not all: InocuLAN can also send a network broadcast, fax an alert, or print a trouble ticket.

A computer virus bestiary

Although more kinds of viruses than we just mentioned are probably lurking somewhere in cyberspace, here's the skinny on the ones we tell you about in the section "And at Your Neighbor's, Too!"

A *boot sector virus* infects the boot sector on a floppy or hard disk. A boot virus loads into memory before the operating system, takes control of your PC, and can infect any floppy disks that you access.

A *file virus* is one that infects a certain kind of file, usually your .EXE, .COM, or application files. Because of its frequent association with a particular application, it's often called an application virus.

A *macro virus* uses the built-in programming language for some applications (also known as a macro language) to perpetuate itself and possibly cause other side effects, as well.

A *multipartite virus* is both a boot sector virus and a program virus. It can enter your system through an infected application file and then infect your boot sector.

A *polymorphic virus* is one that mutates, or changes form, over time. It cannot be detected through a static signature check and is, thus, more difficult to detect.

A *stealth virus* is one that actively disguises itself from discovery or defends itself against attempts to analyze or remove it. A very nasty customer, this.

So how often should you scan the files on your servers? All the time! A virus takes only a short time to infect an entire network. Set up your software so that it scans all incoming and outgoing files in real time.

Make sure that your virus software can scan compressed files, support long file names, and support Universal Naming Convention (UNC). Also, if it includes the Designed for Microsoft BackOffice logo, consider yourself doubly blessed!

Last, let the software do the rest of the work — logging. You need a record of when the virus software scans your system and how often it finds viruses. InocuLAN records this type of information and sends some of that information to the Windows NT system event log.

Now for Some Audit Checks

You can use the C2 security program utility that ships with the Microsoft Windows NT 3.51 Resource Kit to perform a cursory audit. (When the 4.0 Resource Kit becomes available, use it instead.) It checks for some obvious loopholes, such as problems with the type of file system you're using, and makes suggestions for meeting C2 security levels. C2 is the highest government security level, which signifies that "this network is really, really secure."

You should perform some type of structured audit on your network on a regular basis to make sure that you don't have backdoors through which intruders can enter. Your audit should not stop at the server level; it should include a full audit from the physical layer to the application layer. Unfortunately, no single product can automate this task for you. You can combine a few products, however, and incorporate them into your plan. If your network connects to the Internet, you need to do some extra auditing.

Only a handful of third-party utilities for NT exist because it's the newest kid on the block. A few products are shipping, while some remain in beta form.

Intrusion Detection, Inc., sells Kane Security Analyst for Windows NT for $495 per NT server. It's a network security-assessment tool with a database. Its knowledge base has predefined security information and known NT vulnerability information that it compares to your network. The product checks for all kinds of security loopholes in accounts, domains, permissions, trust relationships, and more, and then advises you. Figure 21-1 shows the result of a Kane security analysis. For more information about this product and company, refer to Appendix C.

Another network audit company is the BindView Development Corporation (formerly the LAN Support Group) of Houston, Texas. Its latest product, BindView EMS (Enterprise Management System), enables you to monitor your NT network from a single console. It also helps you find security breaches within your NT system. This product is still in beta but has received rave reviews.

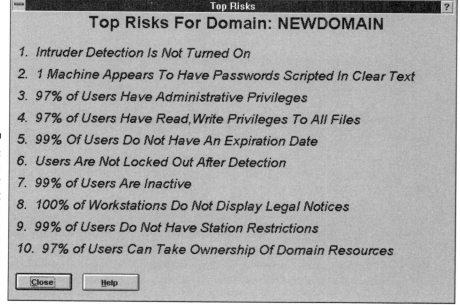

Figure 21-1: Kane Security Analyst analyzes and reports the top risks for a particular domain.

Top Risks

Top Risks For Domain: NEWDOMAIN

1. *Intruder Detection Is Not Turned On*
2. *1 Machine Appears To Have Passwords Scripted In Clear Text*
3. *97% of Users Have Administrative Privileges*
4. *97% of Users Have Read,Write Privileges To All Files*
5. *99% Of Users Do Not Have An Expiration Date*
6. *Users Are Not Locked Out After Detection*
7. *99% of Users Are Inactive*
8. *100% of Workstations Do Not Display Legal Notices*
9. *99% of Users Do Not Have Station Restrictions*
10. *97% of Users Can Take Ownership Of Domain Resources*

Close   Help

Say It Loud and Clear: Intruders Aren't Welcome Here

Set up your network so users get only three chances to connect before their account is locked. Set the account to lock for more than 24 hours. Doing this requires the user to call you before they can log on to the network again. Although this might seem tedious, knowing who's having trouble getting in and why is helpful.

Some administrators who connect their NT network to the Internet like to keep the Guest account active, but delete any permissions tied to that account. This allows them to track the number of logon attempts to that account from the outside. Some also do the same with the Administrator account to keep outsiders from trying to break into that well-known account name. Before you remove all permissions to the Administrator account, however, make sure that you set up another account with equivalent privileges for yourself.

Tracking invalid logon attempts is one of the easiest ways to detect hackers, so monitor this closely. Making this part of your network maintenance routine and checking it frequently is a good idea. Your third-party security analysis tools can help you immensely here.

For Peace of Mind, Keep Servers under Lock and Key

Some network administrators try to save a few dollars by putting the server in a central room where there's a lot of traffic. Then they hang a printer off that server because it's in a good location for users to pick up their print jobs. Although that seems real handy for the users, it's not a good plan.

Look around your office and find a nice, safe, secure location to place your NT server. Ideally, this is a well-ventilated room with limited access that has a special lock on the door. Why, you ask? So that you don't have roaming fingers on the keyboard of your server. The nice part about NT is that it has a Windows 95 look and feel to it. The downside is that your users might think it's a plain old PC that they can mess around with, especially if you leave it out in the open. Imagine the users who think they are doing you a favor by turning the PC off — CRASHHHHHH. We've also heard of servers that have sprouted legs and walked elsewhere when left in open unattended areas.

Put your server in a special room, one where there's little traffic except for the pitter patter of your feet. Put a special lock on this room and limit the number of keys you hand out. Preferably, don't let the housekeeping crew clean that room. Instead, put the trash can outside the room. If you're not handy with a broom, ask housekeeping to clean only on specified days and times when you're available to monitor their actions. This helps to ensure the security and integrity of your network.

If you know who can gain access to that room, you know who can make changes to your server. However, this doesn't mean that changes can't be made to your network.

You also want a well-ventilated room. If you put your server in an air-conditioned but poorly ventilated room, you might come back into the office after a holiday weekend and find that the server's hard disk crashed. That's because the air was cut off for an extra day, and it was enough to build up heat in the room.

Just as you wouldn't leave your pet in a car with the windows rolled up in 90-degree weather, neither should you leave your server in a room that has no air circulating, whether the air conditioner is turned on or off. If you can afford to purchase a temperature monitoring system, you could set up the system to page you if the temperature rises too high.

Chapter 22

Hard Copies: Printing in the NT Environment

. . . .

In This Chapter

▶ Lining up the usual suspects: printers, servers, queues, and users

▶ Printing from Win 3.1, WFW, Win95, and NT Workstation

▶ Using Windows NT printer folders

▶ Setting up and configuring NT Server printers

▶ Sharing local printers on the network

. . . .

*A*ll of the beautiful pictures and documents you can create on your PC are almost worthless if you can't print them easily and efficiently. Can NT Server make network printing easy? Does a one-legged duck swim in a circle? Microsoft is taking another clue from the most oft-heard complaints about Novell NetWare — namely, that network printing is a bear to configure and maintain — by making NT printing as smooth as hot Georgia asphalt.

It's a Small (Printing) World after All

The NT print system has five components: printers, print servers, print queues, print jobs, and the print user. There are two types of printers: physical printers and logical printers. And there are two types of physical printers: server-attached and network-attached. More about printers in a few paragraphs.

Print servers are PCs configured to collect user print jobs and send them to the printers as needed. Print queues are the method print servers use to store, or queue, user print jobs. When a user sends a print job to a print server, the print server stores the print job in the appropriate print queue until the printer is available to accept the print job.

Born to serve: print server to the masses

Almost any of the Microsoft line of Windows operating systems, plus one other odd selection, can be a print server. Most print server PCs share a locally attached printer through one of these operating systems:

- Windows NT Server or Workstation
- Windows 95
- Windows for Workgroups
- Windows 3.1 when running the MS Network Client
- LAN Manager

NT also supports direct network-attached printers that use HP JetDirect cards or a similar network attachment device. These direct-attach printers can receive print jobs directly from users. The smartest way to configure network printers like these, however, is to let an NT server act as the print server, collecting print jobs and sending them to the printer when it is available. This way, no user print jobs are delayed or rejected while the printer is printing another job.

In essence, the print server spools the print jobs in a print queue until the printer is ready. Using print queues and spooling print files is by far the most efficient use of direct network-attached printers. For an NT server to act as a print server for direct network-attached printers, you must load the Microsoft DLC protocol in your NT server's network setup. NT uses the DLC protocol to talk to network-attached printers. Therefore, it's time for Yet Another Protocol (YAP)!

So many printers, so many print queues

The only thing more crucial to the print process than a print user is . . . a printer. As mentioned earlier, there are two types of printers under NT Server and three ways to attach printers to your network. The two types of printers are physical and logical printers. Physical printers are just that: a physical piece of printing hardware. Logical printers are an NT creation that enables you to set up a single print definition that may be serviced by multiple physical printers, or multiple print definitions served by the same physical printers. The three ways to attach printers to your network follow:

- **Network-attached** (a.k.a. network printer): To attach directly to the network, the printer must have a built-in network interface. High-end laser printers commonly include built-in Ethernet interfaces, for instance.

- ✔ **Server-attached** (a.k.a. server printer): You simply use a normal printer cable to connect the printer directly to the Windows NT server.

- ✔ **Workstation-attached** (a.k.a. remote printer): A normal printer cable attaches the printer to a computer, but this time it's to a workstation attached to the network.

Although all three printers are attached to the network differently, they all share the common characteristic of being controlled by the NT Server that manages them.

For example, let's say you have three identical HP LaserJet IVsi printers in the Sales department. You can define a single Sales_Laser logical printer on the NT server. That logical printer can send print jobs to any available HP LaserJet IVsi printer in the Sales department based on which one is not in use.

When you have multiple physical printers served by one logical printer, the physical printers must be identical: the same model, the same features installed, and the same amount of RAM.

Logical printers have another handy feature in the NT Server environment. You can not only assign multiple physical printers to one logical printer, but also assign multiple logical printers to one (or multiple) physical printer. This enables you to create different share names to the same physical printer and, thereby, permits you to assign different access rights, access times, and priority levels to different groups.

Let's say your Customer Service department has a first shift and a second shift. The workers in the first shift can use the share name CS_FIRST_LASER to access the laser printer in their area during their shift. The second shift would use the share name CS_SECOND_LASER to access the same physical printer. The difference between the two shares is the time of use allowed for each share name. This might allow you to better track printer usage and to control who can access which printer at what times.

Line up and sound off: print queues

Now that you understand the difference between logical and physical printers, let's look at where all those print jobs go to wait in line to be printed: the print queue. The print queue is just that: a queue, or line, of jobs waiting to be printed. In Windows NT, the print queue is transparent to both users and administrators. Therefore, we describe queues here mostly for the benefit of those who have used print queues in other network environments.

In Windows NT Server, a print queue is an integral part of each logical printer's definition. If a user sends a print job to a printer that is busy printing, NT Server puts the submitted job into a print queue for that logical printer. When the printer becomes available again, NT sends the next job in the queue to the printer. Under NT, you do not use separate definitions or settings for queues; they are simply there and they simply work. So when users collar you and demand to know where their print jobs went, you can honestly say, "It went to the queue."

What if you don't want your print jobs queued? You certainly have that option, too. When you install the printer on the NT Server, you'll see the option "Print directly to the printer" on the Scheduling tab of the printer's Properties. If you choose this option, print jobs will be passed directly to the physical printer. The downside of this setting is that if the physical device is busy, the user must wait for the physical printer to become available before he or she can continue working.

Can you imagine staring at a print dialog box in Word for Windows for ten or twenty minutes while Karl's 25MB spreadsheet prints on the departmental DinkyJet printer? Now you can see why a print queue is such a good idea. Enable the Print directly to the printer option in the Printer Properties box only if you know that's what you want. (It usually makes sense only when there is a private printer for one person's exclusive use.)

Network print users: the bane of your existence or misunderstood?

We're exaggerating a little about what a pain in the tush those pesky network users can be. Then again, nothing is quite as frustrating as telling someone 107 times how to perform the same simple printing task. Luckily, NT Server makes it much easier to relieve or even avoid that pain.

Depending on the type of operating system your network users use, printing on an NT network ranges from ridiculously easy to only a little harder than blinking. Here's an overview of how to connect to a shared logical printer from various kinds of network clients:

> ✔ **Windows NT:** From the Start menu, double-click the Printers folder. Double-click Add Printer. A wizard pops up to walk you the rest of the way through the printer installation process. Choose Network Print Server from the second screen and click Browse to see the available network printers. Click the network printer you want to add. Indicate at the bottom of the wizard dialog whether you also want to capture print for your MS-DOS applications. Select the correct printer driver from the next screen and you're finished.

✔ **Windows 95:** From the Start menu, double-click the Printers folder. Double-click Add Printer. A wizard pops up to walk you the rest of the way through the printer installation process. Choose Network Printer from the second screen and click Browse to see the available network printers. Click the network printer you want to add. Indicate at the bottom of the wizard dialog whether you also want to capture print for your MS-DOS applications. Select the correct printer driver from the next screen and you're finished.

✔ **Windows for Workgroups:** Open the Control Panel folder. Double-click the Print Manager. Click Add and select the printer driver from the list or choose Unlisted Driver if you have a print driver that's not on the list.

You can easily create an NT server share that contains all available print drivers located on the server's hard drive. Select the print driver and then click Connect. Choose the port you want to assign to this printer and click Network. Select the printer from the list on the bottom of the next box or type the path to the printer share on the NT server.

If you're an NT administrator on a network that uses NT workstations for the client operating systems, those pesky users won't need much of your help when it's time to print. If your users, like most network users today, use a mixture of everything from Windows 1.0 to Windows 95 to Windows for Workgroups, you'll keep yourself plenty busy just assisting users with print definitions and troubleshooting.

Printing without a print driver from an NT workstation

NT's most significant contribution to easy network printing is the radical concept that an NT Workstation client PC isn't required to have the print driver installed locally for the network printer in question. NT Server allows an NT Workstation client to simply route print jobs to a network print queue. From there, the NT Server print driver configures the print job and completes the printing process successfully. Imagine no longer having to install and configure a copy of the printer driver on every PC in your company. If you keep the print drivers up to date on just one machine, the NT server, every user's print jobs should print perfectly. Voilà! Printing is as easy as selecting File⇨Print and then clicking OK from your Windows applications.

The Romaine Domain: Lettuce Define Printers

Now that we know how to define and use printers from the client side, we need to discuss how to define printers from the NT Server side. Here's an all-inclusive list of every single piece of software you'll need to define, share, manage, and delete printers on your NT Server network:

▌ ✔ Printers folder

So much for long lists. Okay, so we didn't include the printer drivers themselves — but you can find printer drivers for all popular modern printers and for most unpopular printers on the NT Server CD-ROM.

Figure 22-1 shows you the NT Server Printers folder screen. Look familiar? It certainly should to anyone who has spent any time with Windows 95. Coincidence? Nope! Microsoft has once again made a smart design decision by making all the administrative tools in NT Server as close to their Windows 95 counterparts as possible. Familiarity may breed contempt, but Microsoft hopes that familiarity also breeds a warm fuzzy feeling as users and administrators upgrade from earlier versions of Windows to Windows NT.

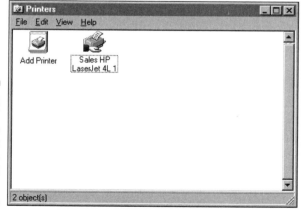

Figure 22-1:
The NT Printers folder from within the Control Panel.

The NT Printers folder should feel like a pair of old shoes, just not as smelly. Here's "How to Define a Printer in Ten Steps or Less":

   1. Double-click the Printers folder in the Control Panel folder.

2. **Double-click Add Printer.**

   The Add Printer Wizard appears.

3. **Choose the type of printer you want to install: one physically attached to this server or one located across the network somewhere. Click Next.**

4. **Mark which port this printer will be attached to and click Next.**

5. **In the left scroll window, select the printer manufacturer (for example, HP). In the right scroll window, select the printer model (for example, HP LaserJet 4L). If you don't see your printer in this screen, click Have Disk and follow the on-screen prompts. Make sure you have the printer driver from the manufacturer handy. Click Next to proceed.**

6. **Choose a name for the printer and tell Setup if you want your Windows-based programs to use this printer as the default printer.**

7. **Tell Setup whether this printer will be shared. If so, type a share name.**

   Make the share name something meaningful, such as Sales_DinkyJet, rather than something obscure, such as Printer1. Setup also wants to know which operating systems will use this printer. This means if you have a Windows 95 workstation that will access this printer, now is the time to tell Setup. If you choose one of these operating systems, Setup will ask you for the pertinent .INF file in a subsequent screen.

8. **Click Next, and then tell Setup whether you want to print a test page after the printer is installed. Click Finish.**

   Setup copies files from your NT Server Installation CD-ROM to your server's hard disk. If you selected an operating system in Step 7, Setup asks you where it can find the Windows 95 .INF file.

9. **Type the proper path or choose Skip File. Click OK or Skip File to proceed.**

   Setup displays the properties you can set for this printer. You'll see tabs such as General, Ports, Scheduling, Sharing, Security, and Device Settings.

10. **To select the port for the printer, select the Ports tab; if the printer is on the LPT1 port, select LPT1 from the list.**

    Go through all the tabs and review the printer's settings. Make appropriate changes or additions. Click OK when you're finished.

Now that wasn't so bad, was it? The process we just described defines a logical printer (see Figure 22-2). Remember, you can create multiple logical printers that point to a single physical printer. To do this, follow the same steps but assign a different name and share name for each logical printer. You can now assign different access rights, access times, and priority levels to each one.

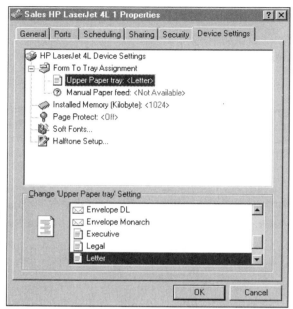

Figure 22-2:
NT's printer
properties
that you
can set.

We also discussed the inverse situation, where you assign multiple identical physical printers to a single logical printer. Print jobs migrate to the first available printer with that logical designation. To assign multiple physical printers to one logical printer (a.k.a. printer pooling), select Properties from the Printers pull-down menu, and then select Additional Ports. Indicate the ports for each printer you want to pool under this name. Remember, you can pool a physical printer that is also shared under its own share name. In other words, multiple logical printers can point to the same physical printer or printer pool.

Local Yokels: Sharing Local Printers

Not all printers on your NT network will be physically connected to your NT server. Your NT server could be the print server for dozens of printers, all connected to other PCs or to the network directly. You can also make your NT server act as a print server for workstation-attached printers shared by your network users.

This helps you maintain control over how locally-shared printers appear on the network at large. Although the general process of sharing a locally-attached printer is similar to creating an NT Server printer, see the system documentation for each version of Windows for details on how to set up and administer locally-shared printers.

Here are the basic high points, sans gory details. Users with printers attached to their machines must create a share for their local printer and assign rights to user name `NTServer` and *no one else*. From the NT server, choose Network Print Server instead of the My Computer option in Step 3 of "How to Define a Printer in Ten Steps or Less" when adding a new printer configuration on the server. Doing this displays a browse of all the available printers on the network for sharing.

Create a printer share as described in the last section and point the port to the share name on the user's local PC. That way, the only user who can access the locally-shared printer across the network is the NT server. (Remember to create a user called NTServer so you can log on to the NT server as that user.) All print jobs will now be spooled to the NT server before reaching the user's PC. You, as network administrator, now have authority over access rights to that printer because your server's ID, NTServer, is the only user authorized for that local share.

It's also simple to make a workstation-attached printer available to the network. Follow the same 10 steps outlined previously in "How to Define a Printer in Ten Steps or Less", except when you get to Step 3, choose Network Print Server instead of My Computer. That is the crucial difference that makes the printer available to the network. Then define a share for that printer to make it available to everyone with rights to that shared resource. Next, select that printer from the list of Network print servers. Continue with Steps 4 through 10 from the list and you're home free.

Cut! It's a Wrap!

That's the inside scoop on printing, NT style. Microsoft has made everything as easy as possible by keeping things consistent among all the various Windows versions. By now, you should be able to sit down with any version of Windows and use a server printer share to share a local printer with the network world (if the version of Windows allows it). Good luck . . . and good printing!

Chapter 23

Got Your Backup against the Wall?

Starting a discussion about backup strategies is akin to starting a discussion about politics or religion: Everybody has an opinion and everybody thinks their opinion is right and everyone else's is wrong. So let's just cut to the chase. Are backups a necessary part of a network? Absolutely. Of the backup strategies and technologies on the market today, which are the best? Most of them. Which strategy is right for you and your network? The one that seems right for you and your network.

Sorry about that. The only backup plan that we don't like is the one that doesn't work. Backup strategies and technologies might not work because of technical issues or internal political issues, or simply because the strategy is too convoluted to follow reliably. Regardless of the reasons why backup strategies fail, you must find a way to provide timely and complete backups.

Choices, We Hear Choices!

There are three basic types of backups: full backups, differential backups, and incremental backups. *Full backups* are just that, a full backup of a server hard drive. *Incremental backups* are when you back up only the files that have changed since the last full or incremental backup. *Differential backups* are when you back up every file that has changed since the most recent full backup (not the most recent incremental backup).

Suppose you implement an incremental backup strategy, and have a disk failure four days after the last full backup. To return the hard drive to its pre-crash contents, you would need to restore five sets of tapes: the last full backup tape set, plus an incremental tape set from each of the four ensuing days. By contrast, a differential backup strategy would require you to restore only two sets of tapes: the last full backup tape set and the differential tape set made the day before the crash.

The correct backup strategy for your network will probably incorporate a mixture of these backup styles, depending on your budget and needs. An incremental backup strategy uses less tape space each day, at the expense of requiring more tapes to successfully complete a restore. Differential backups will back up more files on a daily basis and use more tape space in the process, but always require only two sets of backup tapes for a full recovery (the tapes for the last full backup, plus the tapes for the last differential backup). In a complex, multiserver environment, nightly full backups of every server might not even be possible. You might have enough off hours for only incremental or differential backups.

You'll notice we've been careful to refer to the media for backups, whether full, incremental, or differential, as sets of tapes or tape sets. That's because a backup can require more than one tape, especially for servers with lots of disk space. However, we urge you to purchase a backup unit that can fit an entire full backup on a single tape, if possible, because that's the most convenient and affordable way to automate the backup process. Otherwise, you'll have to buy a tape handling unit (expensive) or manually switch backup tapes yourself (inconvenient).

NT provides an excellent and easy-to-use backup utility called Backup in the Administrative Tools folder. Other, more sophisticated backup utility programs are also available for Windows NT Server. Among these options, you should be able to find a backup program that works in your network environment. Remember, the backup process should be thorough enough to accomplish the job, but not so hard to use that you dread doing backups. NT also provides a predefined user group named Backup to make it easy to define a number of people who will have the privileges and access necessary to participate in the backup process. That way, you can share this responsibility with others!

Why Back Up?

The most obvious question is "Why bother?" That is, why should you spend a lot of time and money doing backups? The easy answer is that it might save your company someday. The data stored on PC hard drives is becoming more important to the day-to-day operations at most companies.

Imagine this: you walk into your office tomorrow, and every single PC is gone. Could your company continue to function? Imagine that you walk in tomorrow and each PC is there, but the hard drives have been erased by a strong electrical surge, compliments of your local power company.

Enter backups. First, let's discuss server backups. Backup devices for networks are, by and large, expensive and large. It makes more sense to train your users to keep critical work-related files in their home directories on the server rather than on their local hard drives. After the company's critical files are on a file server, a single tape drive unit can back up every important file in the company. This makes a tremendous amount of sense.

You also have to cope with the reality that a catastrophic server failure or even minor network outages can render your company as helpless as the stricken PCs in our previous example. The one good thing about a catastrophic server failure in this situation is that *you have a backup of the critical files!* Any type of backup strategy is better than no backup strategy.

Out of Site, but Not Out of Mind

Most modern backup strategies have trickled down from the mainframe world, where backups are an intrinsic part of computer operation. Most large companies have had off-site storage of computer backup tapes for years. You can now find this strategy in all sizes of companies and all types of computer departments.

Off-site storage can be as easy as the network administrator (that's you!) taking home a copy of the previous day's backup tape in his or her briefcase every night. Off-site storage can also cost thousands of dollars yearly for daily or weekly pickups, but guarantees a quick response time in the event of a disaster.

We can't tell you exactly which method is right for you, but consider the following. How much money could your company stand to lose, either directly or indirectly, if your server burned to a crisp and a good backup was unavailable? The answer should tell you a lot about how much time and money you should be spending to make sure your backups are carried off-site at regular intervals.

Backup Strategies of the Rich and Famous

Now that you know how desperately important secure backups are, let's look at some of the strategies we've seen work well in our travels around the computer world. We always schedule our network backups at night, when system utilization is typically low and the majority of files on the server are closed. (Some backup utilities cannot back up open files; fortunately, this does not appear to be true of the built-in Windows NT Backup utility.) Backups in the middle of the work day can slow network operations to a crawl — so can restores, for that matter. In the following tape counts, we assume that you can back up your server to one tape during a full backup procedure. Your mileage may vary, but here's a list of some different backup regimes you might want to consider:

- **Full backup nightly:** If you have a one-server network and enough storage space on your backup device, there is no reason to do anything except a full backup every single night. This way, you'll always need just one tape to perform any type of restore required.

- **Full backup weekly and incremental backup nightly:** This is a good strategy for those on a budget. You perform one full backup, typically on Friday night, followed by incremental backups of only those files that have changed since the last full or incremental backup. This strategy maximizes your tape backup capacity, but also maximizes the amount of tape and trouble required to perform a full restore.

- **Full backup weekly and differential backup nightly:** This strategy is the best of both worlds. Perform a full backup on Friday night. Then perform daily differential backups to back up every file that has changed since the last full backup. Restores are always a two-tape affair.

Money Talks: On-line, Near-line, and Off-line Backups

There are three varieties of backup devices, depending on how "available" you want your backups to be. Here's how they stack up:

- **On-line backups:** Backups that are available immediately, usually in the form of a duplicate hard drive of your server's original hard drive.

- **Near-line backups:** Backups that are kept on devices always connected to your network, but which require some effort or time when you want to restore files.

- **Off-line backups:** Traditional tape backups are considered off-line backups because the restore is removed from the interactive operation of the server.

So, what's the real difference between these three technologies? Money. The closer your data gets to being on-line, the more the backup technology will cost you. Of course, it will also be faster and more convenient, which is what that extra money buys you. Which is right for you? Again, you have to weigh costs against convenience and make some hard choices.

The more expensive your company finds network downtime (the amount of time your network is out of commission), the more inclined it will be to spend money to minimize that time!

On-line and on time

On-line backup data usually depends on a mirrored or duplexed hard drive that always contains the most recent changes to the source data. Being on-line means you can access information directly from the backup server without manual intervention. In other words, on-line backups are available all the time, and you can restore a file from within the Windows NT Explorer. On-line backups are typically on a one-to-one cost ratio with the original data storage device. If you have a $750 3GB hard drive as the main storage device, you'll usually have an identical $750 3GB device for its on-line backup.

Near-line: close, but not quite on-line

Near-line storage is data that is connected to your server and accessible to users, but requires you to perform intervening steps to access the backup data. An example of a near-line backup device is a server-attached hard drive that uses data compression to back up server data. This is almost an on-line device — the hard drive is attached to the server — but the data isn't directly accessible on the backup device.

Hence the name *near-line*. The backup device is always available, but you must decompress some files to restore lost data. Cost ratios for near-line are a function of the amount of compression you use. If your backup software can compress data at a three-to-one ratio, your near-line backup capacity will cost you one-third what your on-line data storage costs. Using an earlier example, the cost per megabyte of a near-line backup device for a $750 hard drive would be $250.

Off-line takes time

The last and most popular option for data backup is off-line. Off-line backup devices are usually traditional tape backup devices that are not on-line at all. You must manually restore backup data to a hard drive to recover data stored on the tape drive unit. Tape backup devices are the slowest way to back up your data, but they are also the least expensive.

Typical tape backup drives offer data compression rates of eight-to-one or ten-to-one. In multiple server network environments, you must take into account the relatively slow speed of tape backup units. You must either buy a tape backup drive capable of backing up all your servers overnight, or adjust your backup strategy so that you do a full backup of at least one server per night, with incremental or differential backups on all other servers.

Hardware That's Hard to Wear

There are more kinds of backup devices than you can shake a stick at — everything from tape drives to WORM drives to erasable CD-ROMs to diskettes. Each type of backup device has an appropriate use. Tape drives are the traditional bastion of backup devices. Tape devices started as the backup device of choice on mainframe computer systems many years ago.

Tape devices come in different sizes and formats: 8mm tape drives, ¼-inch tape drives, ½-inch tape drives, and seemingly every size in between. Within each size, you'll find different encoding and compression methods that offer more or less capacity or speed. Most PC-based network servers today use 8mm tape drives as a happy medium between speed, cost, and reliability.

Changers and exchangers

What do you do if your server capacity exceeds your tape drive's capacity? You have two choices: You can insert another tape into the drive when you get to work the next morning, or you can buy a tape changer for your drive. Most tape drive manufacturers offer tape changers either as add-ons to their higher capacity tape drives or integrated with their top-of-the-line products.

We've had both good and bad luck using tape changers. Reliable technology to automatically change tapes in a drive has been slow to be perfected. Fortunately, most new tape drives and changers seem to work pretty well.

If you own a tape drive to which you want to add a changer, be sure the manufacturer offers the software drivers required to make the tape changer cooperate with your backup software *and* with your server's operating system.

Tape backup and restore operations can cause significant slowdowns on your servers. One of the best uses for tape changers that we've seen is to program your tape drive to automatically load and unload all the tapes you need for an entire week's worth of backups. How's that for making your life easier?

CD-ROMs et al.

WORM stands for Write Once, Read Many. WORM drives are basically CD-ROM drives that you write to once, but can read for a long time. Standard music CD-ROMs could be considered WORM devices: The music is stored on the CD-ROM at the pressing plant and you, the music consumer, can read — or restore — that music as many times as you want.

The heir to the WORM drive is the erasable CD-ROM. These drives are just beginning to show up in the marketplace. They offer, on a compact medium, tremendous capacity — up to 650MB uncompressed in conventional versions, and 2.4 to 4.0GB on some experimental models. As the technology matures and prices fall, erasable CD-ROM technology could easily supplant 8mm tape drive as the backup technology of choice.

There are numerous other hardware solutions for backup devices — one example is the floptical drive (high-capacity floppy optical drive), which is similar to CD-ROM. Another good candidate is a magneto-optical (MO) drive, which uses a combination of magnetic and optical technologies to create rewritable, large-format media. These devices offer the advantages of large capacity and random access. (With random access, it's easy to get to any file stored on the medium. On a tape, you must read everything ahead of any given file to get to that file.) They can be more expensive than tape drives (the units may cost the same, but the media is much more costly), but they're much faster and are easy to transport for use in multiple locations.

Client PC Backups: Can You Afford Not To?

Think about how much critical data resides on your user's local hard drives. Even if you've tried to train your users to store critical data on the server, consider how long it would take for you to rebuild a user's hard drive in the event of a hard drive crash. Maybe it's time to consider backing up your users' local hard drives in addition to your normal server backups.

We believe that client PC backups become more critical as networks grow in size and importance to your company. Of course, server backups are still the most important to a network administrator. You should consider adding client backups to your task list only if your backup device has the capacity. Another important consideration is RAM usage: If a program must be loaded on each PC so that a tape drive can back it up, think long and hard about the ramifications before extending backup services to encompass local hard drives.

Nevertheless, we've come across several valid strategies for backing up user PCs that we'd like to share with you in the sections that follow.

Standard local directory backups

One strategy is to designate a standard local directory name to be backed up at regular intervals. Send out a memo stating that all data stored in each user's C:\BACKUPS directory will be backed up automatically after the close of business every Friday evening. Teach users how to set up their application defaults so that their important documents and data files are automatically stored in C:\BACKUPS.

The only real flaw we see with this strategy is that your users can accomplish the same goal — while making life much easier for you, the network administrator — by saving their documents and critical data to their home directory on the server instead. The only difference is that their local BACKUPS directory will still be available when the server crashes. But, of course, your server will never crash, right?

Full user local hard drive backups

The other option for backing up your users' local hard drives is to buy the biggest, baddest tape drive with tape changer on the market and back up everything in sight once a week. We know of one company that tells users to load their local backup agent software as they leave for lunch according to a division of last names by alphabet, for example, A — F loads the backup agent on Mondays, G — M loads the agent on Tuesdays, and so on. Users are responsible for initiating their own backups, and management has made it clear that each employee is obligated to do weekly backups.

The system works well because of management involvement and because users have been educated about the importance of regular backups. If your job depended on it, you'd probably make backups a higher priority than it is today. Unfortunately, as a network administrator, your job does depend on performing regular backups. So hop to it!

Disaster Prep: Hope for the Best, but Plan for the Worst

The main point of a comprehensive backup strategy is to protect your company's digital assets in case of catastrophe. Always keep this goal in mind: If your company's building burned down to the ground tonight, you'd want to have confidence that you could rebuild your network server (and possibly some of your users' critical data) and restore your operations with no more than one day's data lost.

You might alter this general backup strategy goal to better fit your needs. However, always keep in mind that as the network administrator, management expects you to provide data recovery in just such a catastrophic situation. The good news is that if you are fully prepared at all times for a catastrophe, you'll find it much easier to perform mundane tasks, such as restoring user's files that were accidentally deleted or backing up an old hard drive and restoring it to a new hard drive when users get new PCs. Forewarned is forearmed. And a cohesive backup strategy is your best forearmor!

Chapter 24

Mysteries of the Organism: NTS Configuration

. . . .

In This Chapter

▶ Understanding the basics of installation

▶ Allowing the network to grow — or not

▶ Knowing when to add new software

▶ Using the administrator utilities

▶ Examining the NTS Registry

▶ Setting up groups and users

. . . .

*H*ow do you tie it all together and make your new network work? The only way to begin is to roll up your shirtsleeves and dig in. This chapter walks you through the ins and outs of installing the NT network operating system, examines when to add the latest and greatest software, goes into detail on the NT administrator utilities, and takes a look at some of the more common NT administration exercises, such as setting up the NT Registry and setting up groups and users.

An Overview of Installation Basics

Before you can access anything on the server, you have to install it. Installing NT is a fairly simple and straightforward process. Afterwards, though, you'll need to tweak the system so that it conforms to your organization's requirements. Here are the basic steps that you go through during an NT installation.

1. **Collect the appropriate software needed for the server installation.**

2. **Run the installation program on the server.**

3. **Choose the file system (NTFS or FAT). Format the server's hard disk with that system and partition the drives.**

4. **Let the installation load the system files.**

5. **Tweak the software, add users and groups, create shares, and add security.**

6. **Restart the server.**

7. **Connect the workstations.**

NT's installation manuals and its extensive on-line help will guide you during the installation process. Along the way, you'll have decisions to make — so keep a notebook handy to record what you chose. Name this book your Installation Notebook. You'll want to keep a written record of your server's hardware settings, such as RAM, drive capacity, NIC IRQ and base I/O address (if applicable). In addition to putting this information in the book, you might also want to affix a label with this information to the back of the server, so that you won't have to open it to establish configuration information. (This is especially handy if your boards use jumpers or switches.)

When installing NT, leave the hood off the PC until everything is working. There's nothing more frustrating than plugging everything in and battening down the hatch, only to have to open it up every time you need to view or change a board's configuration.

To grow or not to grow?

Capacity planning should be part of your preinstallation process. Before you buy any server equipment, you'll want to have a general idea on how fast your network will grow. This is sometimes the hardest information to pin down. It's often referred to as trying to hit a moving target while wearing a blindfold.

When you're planning to buy components for your server, think ahead and buy extra. For example, don't buy a server with less than 32MB of RAM installed. Ask your vendor about the difference in cost between a machine whose capacity is 512MB versus one that tops out at 128MB. If the difference is only $200, invest the money to get the extra capacity; you may need it someday!

The same is true for other components on the server. As soon as you add disk space, for example, users find it and use it. That doesn't mean you should let your users run amok on your network and clog it with extraneous data. Your weekly maintenance routine should help you keep a check on that. However, don't limit yourself to a server that can hold only two drive bays.

The prices for hardware and RAM have dropped drastically over the past few years. We recommend that you spend money on your server now and get the most capacity you can so that you don't have to go back to management later. (Repeated financial requests tend to irritate them.)

Don't use proprietary hardware. Otherwise, when a component breaks, you'll have to go back to the same vendor for a replacement. When you're tied to only one vendor, you can't shop around and get the best deal.

Finally, never buy hardware without consulting Microsoft NT's Hardware Compatibility List. And just because something's listed on the HCL doesn't mean it will work. If you add Service Packs to the original installation, you'll probably want to look over the documentation that ships with each pack to make sure there aren't any known bugs with particular hardware. Sending an email inquiry to one of the NT-related mailing lists is another way to find out whether anyone else has experienced hardware problems with Service Packs.

If it ain't broke, don't fix it

Don't add new software just because it's the latest and greatest. If it fills a business need, go ahead. But proceed cautiously: Try the new stuff in a test environment first, and then train your users if necessary. You should also be aware that adding a software upgrade to your system can sometimes cause problems for other packages.

Don't install a Service Pack on your server until you've investigated the list of bugs that it corrects. Some things stop working after a Service Pack is installed, so you could create a problem where none existed just by upgrading.

Perform your upgrades during off-peak hours, notify your users ahead of time, and leave plenty of time to troubleshoot and test any new installations. A poorly planned upgrade is a sure-fire way to anger your user community!

NT Configuration Utilities

NT's User Manager, Server Manager, Event Viewer, Task Manager, and Performance Monitor utilities are probably the most widely used programs for performing administrative tasks. Use these utilities to add groups and users to your network, view server information, check and understand system error messages, examine active tasks on your server, and view the status and health of your server's performance. All of these utilities are located under Programs⇨ Administrative Tools.

NT also provides Administrative Wizards under Programs⇨Administrative Tools⇨Administrative Wizards. For example, the Add User Accounts Wizard will guide you through the process of defining and configuring a new user account.

User Manager

User Manager is a great little graphical utility that you can use to add, delete, or change information related to users and groups. If your server is set up as a Primary Domain Controller, you'll see the name User Manager for Domains (see Figure 24-1). You can add information about new users, and you add an account by simply clicking the Add button when you're finished entering the user information.

You can also modify existing users and add new ones. To add a new user, select User⇨New User from the menu options. The screen shown in Figure 24-2 is displayed. This is where you define information particular to any user. You can customize users' desktops (what they see when they log on) by managing their profiles. If you don't want to set up a separate profile for each user, you can assign a single profile to a group of users. You can also set up a default user template to define new users so you don't have to enter the same information for each one.

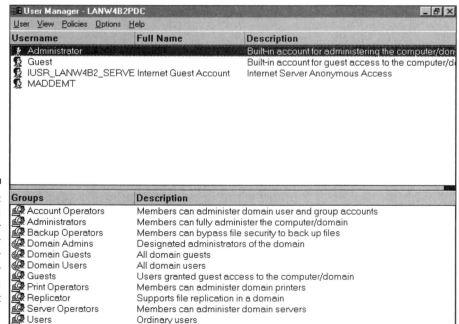

Figure 24-1:
The opening screen for User Manager lists user accounts and default NT groups.

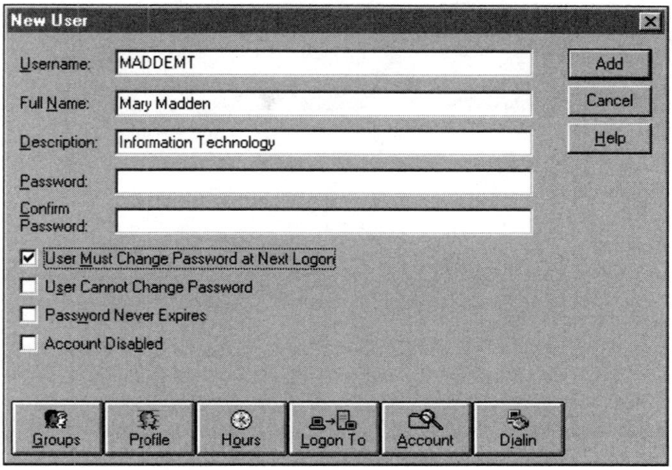

Figure 24-2:
Adding a
new user in
User
Manager.

You'll also use User Manager to define local and global groups. We know, you're asking: "Why doesn't NT include a Group Manager?" Groups are composed of individual accounts, so the two are hand-in-hand. Because these activities are so closely tied to one another, perhaps Microsoft lumped them together in this single utility. If it helps, think of this program as User (and Group) Manager!

Server Manager

Server Manager (see Figure 24-3) is a utility that shows the shares set for a particular server and who's using them. You can also see which users are connected, inspect a list of open files, and determine what services are running (or not running) on that server. You can also send a message to any workstation or server that's connected to this server and inspect the shares defined for workstations on the network.

Event Viewer

NT's Event Viewer (see Figure 24-4) is a great troubleshooting tool. It provides an audit trail of events that may or may not be occurring, with status information for each one. For example, if you're expecting a user to dial into your RAS server and the user can't establish a connection, use the Event Viewer to inspect recent error messages to help determine the causes of any problems.

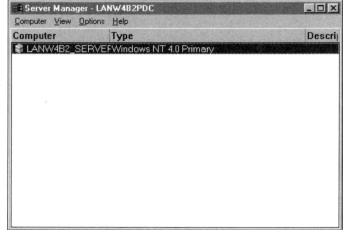

Figure 24-3:
The Server Manager utility lists shares and their users, connections, open files, and more.

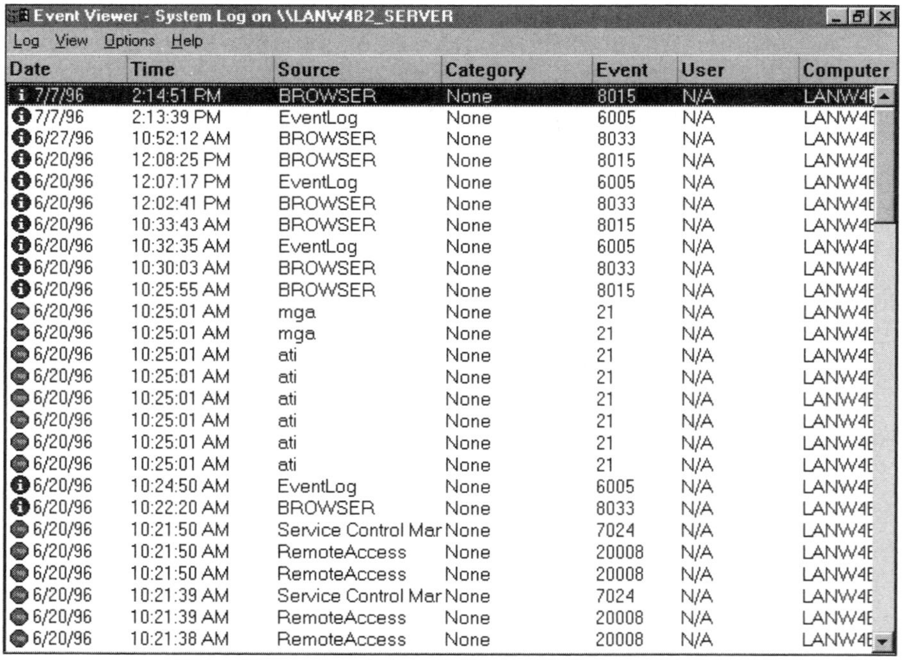

Figure 24-4:
Use NT's Event Viewer while trouble-shooting.

When your NT server boots, events are logged to the Event Viewer. Information recorded about each event resembles a checkbook register consisting of individual line items per event. Each item is time- and date-stamped and includes the following information: source, category, event, user, and computer. Color-coded icons preceding each line item indicate the severity of the event. A red stop sign icon, for example, means that the associated event has a high priority or that there's a potentially serious problem, such as a service that was unable to operate.

When you double-click a line item in the event listing, the Event Viewer describes the event more fully and displays a hexadecimal dump of related system memory data. In Figure 24-5, for instance, the event detail indicates that two drivers are stomping all over each other. We can't remember DOS ever being that helpful!

Figure 24-5:
Double-clicking a line item brings up a detailed event account.

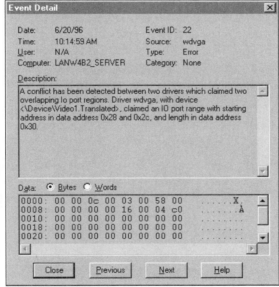

You can customize the Event Viewer log in any of the three main content categories: System, Security, and Application. You can decide what information should be recorded, whether it should be overwritten, and if so, how long it should be kept before it's overwritten. You can even specify how large a log can get to keep them from filling up an entire hard disk!

You can set a viewer filter to exclude events that don't meet certain category and severity requirements so that you're not inundated with screens full of informational events. For example, the blue icons with an *I* in the middle are informational and can be produced by the hundreds in a single boot session. They don't affect the operational status of your server, so you might want to use a filter to skip over them.

You can further define filters to include only certain source devices. For example, if you think your CD-ROM drive is the source of some problem, you can capture only the events where it is the source. For troubleshooting, the Event Viewer is a handy utility, indeed!

Performance Monitor

After your server is installed and your users are connected, you will want to measure your server's performance occasionally. Performance Monitor, shown in Figure 24-6, enables you to chart performance graphically along a number of dimensions. (There's no activity because we haven't chosen any counters to display.)

Click the Plus button on the toolbar, and then select the activity to monitor. Figure 24-7 shows the screen after we selected several processes to follow and chart.

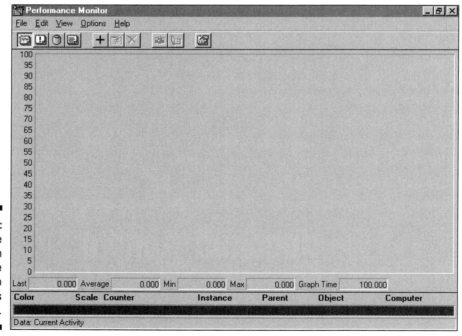

Figure 24-6: Performance Monitor in its idle state with no processes chosen.

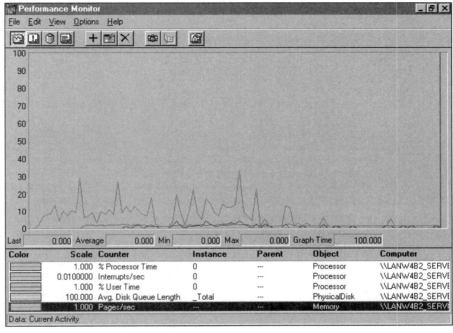

Figure 24-7:
Selecting
one or more
processes
displays
graphical
data.

The NTS Registry Hierarchy

The NTS Registry is a database of configuration information about your server, its applications, and its users. If you're familiar with earlier versions of Windows, you'll remember all those .INI, .SYS, and .BAT configuration files. The Registry works in conjunction with these files and even makes those old DOS stalwarts (AUTOEXEC.BAT and CONFIG.SYS) more or less unnecessary. When you make a configuration change on the server, it will usually be recorded in the Registry database.

Some NT Server configuration information isn't available in menu format. Instead, you must manually edit the Registry to make changes. This can be very dangerous if you don't know what you're doing — you can render your system inoperable with the wrong changes. We recommend that you don't edit your Registry unless you absolutely have to and have investigated it thoroughly. Furthermore, we urge you to make a backup of the Registry if you plan to make changes, so that you can get back to where you started if anything goes wrong.

To edit the Registry, you must run the Registry Editor utility (\WINNT\SYSTEM32\regedt32.exe). You can launch the Registry Editor by selecting Start⇨Run and then typing regedt32. This pulls up a hierarchical tree with four components called *subtrees*. We cover these and other important Registry components next.

Subtrees

The following is a list of subtrees and their descriptions:

- **HKEY_LOCAL_MACHINE:** Contains the configuration data for the local computer. The information in this database is used by applications, device drivers, and the Windows NT system to establish configuration data for the local computer, regardless of who's logged on and what software is in use.

  Also included is information about the operating system. (Do you see why it can be dangerous to edit the Registry?)

- **HKEY_CLASSES_ROOT:** Holds information about object linking and embedding (OLE) plus information about file associations.

- **HKEY_CURRENT_USER:** Holds information about users who are currently logged on.

- **HKEY_USERS:** Contains information on currently loaded user profiles.

Hives

Below each subtree is a collection of hives and files. If you're wondering why Microsoft picked the name hives, it's because the structure resembles a beehive (or so they think)! Below the HKEY_LOCAL_MACHINE subtree, for example, you'll typically find the following hives:

- **HARDWARE:** Contains information about the system's hardware and configuration.

- **SAM:** Contains information about the Security Account Manager (SAM) which houses domain, user, and group security information.

- **SECURITY:** Contains information about the local security information that this machine's security subsystem uses.

- **SOFTWARE:** Contains information about the local software and its configuration.

- **SYSTEM:** Contains information about the operating system and related information.

Values

Progressing down the Registry tree, below the hives you'll find Registry keys, which contain items called value entries. This is typically where you edit, add, or delete values. Be sure you know what you're doing (and have a backup)!

Where to learn more

In addition to the Registry Editor, NT 4.0 includes a program called the System Policy Editor. Choose Start⇨Programs⇨Administrative Tools⇨System Policy Editor. When that program has started, choose File⇨Open Registry to see some of the icons NT provides. This utility allows you to change Registry settings on a limited basis for only HKEY_CURRENT_USER and HKEY_LOCAL_MACHINE. (And NT changed their icon names to confuse you a little.)

If you want to stay on the safe side and only view information, use the Windows NT Diagnostics program, WINMSD.EXE (Programs⇨Administrative Tools⇨ Windows NT Diagnostics). Think of it as a way to inspect the Registry's configuration information in read-only mode.

We've only introduced you to the basic concepts of the NT Registry. Before you make any changes manually, read Microsoft's in-depth discussion of the Registry in Appendix A of their *Concepts and Planning Guide*.

Setting Up Groups and Users

It's much simpler and less tedious to define permissions on groups instead of users. Groups enable you to collect user accounts into a single batch and to set permissions once instead of for each user. If a user moves into a different department, you don't need to define a new set of rights for that user. You simply delete the user from Group A and add the account name to Group B.

You should still set up a unique account for each user who logs on to your network. After you define an account with the basics, add it to the applicable group.

Not all users fit neatly into a group. You'll probably have a few stray users for whom you must set rights individually. When you do this, make a note in your documentation binder. We usually add this type of information below a heading called Exceptions. Then, whenever we do maintenance or upgrades, we go to the Exception heading and it jogs our memory about the users who must be managed on a case-by-case basis.

If you have a small network, setting up users and groups is simple and best accomplished in User Manager. If your organization is medium to large-sized, administration can become time consuming if everything is a special case. You want to manage users in bulk; that's why groups are so handy.

In this chapter, you learned about some of NT's installation basics, and what to expect when you install your own server. You learned about the built-in utilities found in NT to help make your administrative tasks a little easier. In the next chapter, you'll learn about the other utilities and third-party NT applications that are available.

Chapter 25

File, Information, and Management Utilities

- -

- -

*N*T has many useful utilities. You probably use (or will use) some of these programs daily; others might be useful only when you're troubleshooting.

Most NT utilities are GUI-based, but NT also provides some command-line utilities in case you're an old DOS stickler. (Some people find a GUI interface hard to contend with and can more quickly navigate a server with DOS-based commands.)

In this chapter, we list both types of utilities in alphabetical order, so you can dog-ear this chapter to use later as a reference. We hope it provides the introduction you need to help you boost your productivity!

The NET Word

The word *NET* has been around a long time in Microsoft networks. It's your ticket to the DOS world if that's what you prefer. If you're not sure which commands you can use, type NET ? and you'll be presented with a list of commands that can be used with the word NET.

For example, we found that you can use the command NET ACCOUNTS. We weren't sure what options were available with that command, so we typed NET ACCOUNTS ? and received the syntax with a list of parameters, but not much more.

We wanted more help on these commands, so we typed NET HELP. We received some more good information, but the information didn't tell us what each command did. It told us if we wanted information on each command, we'd have to type NET HELP command. So we did. We typed NET HELP ACCOUNTS and received a lot of information on what that command does, its syntax, and a breakdown of each parameter in the command. You might want to try this approach, too.

Common Keyboard Gotchas You Need to Know

Trying to navigate NT's command prompt can be daunting if you don't know some of the secrets buried in its myriad manuals. If you're an old-timer with Microsoft networking products (such as PC LAN and LAN Manager), you might already know some of these helpful hints:

- ✔ If you don't know the full syntax when issuing a command, type the command followed by a question mark. For example, typing NET USE ? provides the syntax and all parameters (optional or required) for that command.

- ✔ Some command-line syntax includes symbols such as brackets ([]). Anything inside the brackets is optional information.

- ✔ If you see *domainname*, supply the domain name assigned to the domain you're trying to access. In small organizations, there's usually just one domain name. In larger organizations, there could be several.

- ✔ If you see *devicename*, supply a drive designator (for example, G:).

- ✔ If you see *computername*, supply a NetBIOS computer name (for example, maddemt).

- ✔ If you see *sharename*, supply the name of the share set by the Administrator. You can view available shares in Server Manager.

- ✔ If you see */persistent:(yes | no)*, NT is asking whether you want this mapping or command to remain in effect after the system reboots. For example, when you issue a NET USE command and map a drive, answering yes means that the drive mapping should remain in effect after a reboot. Answering no means the drive mapping is for that session only.

- ✔ If you see |, enter either what's before or what's after the character. (For example, in the preceding item, you would answer either yes or no, but not both.)

NT also enables you to use keystroke combinations to access the pull-down menus inside the GUI-based utilities. You can find most of these utilities from Start⇨Programs⇨Administrative Tools. Here are some tips for using those keystrokes to navigate NT:

✔ Use the Alt key to access the pull-down menu from the title bar area of your screens.

✔ Use the Alt key plus the underlined letter shown on your screen to access the menu item directly (for example, ALT+U displays the New Uesr option in User Manager for Domains).

✔ After you access some menu options, you can press a single key to access their menu choices. For example, F8 in User Manager for Domains enables you to copy existing user information to a new user name. (Please note: If the menu bar is activated, you can't press F8 to perform such a copy; you'd have to exit the menu by pressing the Esc key until all the menus clear the screen.)

A Road Map to the NTS Utilities

Here, we give you an at-a-glance look at some of NT's powerful utilities. You can find most of these utilities by clicking on Start⇨Programs⇨Administrative Tools.

Getting your bearings: file, directory, and disk utilities

NT has a few utilities that tell you about the files you own on the network, which permissions are set on those files and directories, which shares are set, and more.

chkdsk

If you're an old DOS user, you'll remember the chkdsk utility. You can use this command with the /F option to check the disk for errors, as well as correct errors. If you have a workstation that you don't use too much, you may want to practice using chkdsk there first.

Disk Administrator

You use the Disk Administrator tool to manage disks on your NT server. It shows you a graphical representation of how your disks are formatted, partitioned, and labeled. It's like the DOS-based FDISK on steroids.

You can add and delete new partitions, create and delete logical drives, create and delete stripe sets, and create and delete volume sets. You can view a host of other information about your disks and their configurations. If you want to do anything with your server's disks, this is the best place to start — after you've performed a backup!

Emergency Repair Disk

We hope you never have to use the Emergency Repair Disk (RDISK.EXE) utility. As the name suggests, you use it to correct something that has gone awry. When you install NT, it asks whether you want to create an Emergency Repair Disk. If you didn't create one then, ask yourself why. If you wanted to shave a few minutes off the install time, shame on you! Don't cut corners with anything that contains the words *Emergency Repair*. You can still create one using the RDISK.EXE utility. Read all the online help for this utility because it's an important one that could help you restore your system.

Windows NT Backup

NT Backup isn't really a utility; it's a necessity. But Microsoft did place it under the Administrative Tools section. (Plus, by including it here, you get to see the word *backup* again.)

NT permits you to back up and restore files on your server to a tape drive. You can use all kinds of bells and whistles, such as selecting the type of backup (normal, incremental, daily, and so on) and appending backups on tapes. Most tape drives come with their own software; you may or may not choose to use NT's. Typically, software that ships with a drive has more features and can recognize its own hardware very well.

Windows NT Explorer

NT Explorer isn't really a utility. It's more like a browser that lets you navigate your way through the network and your workstation. Don't confuse this Explorer with NT's Internet Explorer. They are both browser-like, but Internet Explorer allows you to browse the Internet's World Wide Web.

Information, please

Some NT utilities provide you with information and viewing material for network performance, audit logs, licensing, and more.

Event Viewer

An *event* is something that takes place or something that should have taken place, but didn't. For example, a service starting, not starting, or stopping is considered an event, and its status information can be captured and viewed. The Event Viewer provides an audit trail of events that includes error and information messages, with status information for each event.

License Manager

License Manager is a handy little utility that helps you keep track of the number of licenses you've purchased for NT and BackOffice. Licensing is a serious matter. This utility probably isn't sophisticated enough to shield you from inadvertently not buying enough licenses. It does, however, help you input information from your purchase orders. It also provides a server browser so you can view the network as you're filling in information.

The online help and Microsoft's manuals do a good job of helping you understand the complex licensing issues. Remember that manuals are quickly outdated, and it's your responsibility to protect your organization from prosecution by the Software Publishers Association (SPA), which oversees licensing issues and can prosecute organizations for software misuse.

Performance Monitor

Once a year, you get a performance review from your boss. He or she tells you all the wonderful things you've accomplished and which areas need improvement. Performance Monitor does the same for your NT Server. It tells you which pieces need fine-tuning or more capacity. You can look at information such as processor utilization and packet transmission. Performance Monitor presents the information in a chart format; you can select several items to view at once, each with a different color. The view can be in real time or recorded over time. You can make changes to the system and see the effects. You can also set thresholds on the system and configure the utility to send you alerts when those thresholds are exceeded.

Windows NT Diagnostics

Use the Windows NT Diagnostics utility if you want to view or print the configuration information for your server. It's like a beefed-up Microsoft Diagnostics (MSD) program. Microsoft took out the DOS-based look and feel and added a GUI interface. You can still view the same type of diagnostics information for BIOS, memory, IRQs, ports, drivers, services, devices, and much more.

Administrative Wizards

Use the Administrative Wizards utility when you want someone to hold your hand while performing administrative tasks. For example, you can select the Add User Accounts Wizard to walk you through setting up a new user. This utility is a great place to begin your adventures in the NT world because it can help you set up printers, licensing, client disks, groups, programs, and more.

DHCP Manager

The DHCP Manager helps you dynamically allocate and manage IP addresses. Without it, you'd have to go to each node and manually enter a unique IP address. Then if the node moved to another subnet, you'd have to go back and manually change the address. This can be tedious, so why not let the DHCP Manager handle this pesky task for you? The less human intervention involved in typing in IP addresses, the better. This utility also lets you decide how long a node can keep an assigned IP address before it has to request a new one.

Dr. Watson

When an application causes an error, the built-in Windows NT error diagnosis tool, Dr. Watson (drwtsn32.exe, also known as the Windows NT Post Mortem Debugger), pops up and writes the error information to disk so you can view it later. You can use the information to help you determine what's causing a problem. To start the utility from the command prompt, use the Run command from the Start menu. Then press F1 for help in setting it up.

Under Windows NT, Dr. Watson is configured to automatically catch any 32-bit application errors and generate a log file that contains information about the offending application. The following data appears in the Dr. Watson log file:

- ✔ Exception information, including the exception number and name. (You can use the name or number to look up an explanation of the error in the Windows NT Help system, or in Volume 3 of the *Windows NT Resource Kit.*)

- ✔ System information, including the machine name, user name, NT version, and other descriptive information about the machine where the error occurred.

- ✔ The Windows NT task list, which lists all active tasks on the system at the time the error occurred.

- ✔ A state dump for each execution thread, including a register dump, disassembly, stack walk, and symbol table. Unless you're a real system wizard, this will be gibberish.

You'll find the Dr. Watson log file, which is named DRWTSN32.LOG, in the \WINNT\directory, unless you directed it somewhere else when you installed the program. In addition to the information in the Dr. Watson log, the Windows NT application log (which can be viewed through Event Viewer) also contains a record about the error. You'll find this information useful if you need help from a technical support person, or if you need to learn more about possible causes (and cures) for errors on your system.

Network Client Administrator

The Network Client Administrator utility guides you through setting up network clients. If you have DOS- or Windows-based clients, you can create client disks from this utility that you'd use to install the client software on workstations elsewhere on your network. (For more information on this topic, please consult Chapter 16.) There are several options for installing your workstations (for example, across the network or from diskettes).

Network Monitor

Network Monitor is by far the coolest built-in NT utility. If you've been around the Ethernet a few times and have held (or shelled out cash for) a protocol analyzer, you'll understand the value of this utility.

Network Monitor captures packets as they travel across the wire. You can then analyze those packets to troubleshoot hardware and software problems (such as tracking down a faulty NIC). If you can't figure out the problem, you can send a captured trace to someone that can read it. You could accidentally capture the President's email messages this way, so be careful who's minding the store!

This utility allows you to view data down to the protocol level, so you might not want to start here if you're learning about networks. Go to the User Manager utility first, and come back here after you know how to add a few users.

Remote Boot

You use the Remote Boot utility to configure DOS, Windows, and Windows 95 workstations on your network to boot from your server instead of from the hard disk. Those workstations must have a NIC with a Remote Initial Program Load chip. This type of boot situation is found most often in networks with diskless workstations. Some places require a remote boot for security purposes.

ScanDisk

ScanDisk is a full 32-bit low-level disk repair and analysis utility. It repairs problems with long filenames (LFNs), works on FAT- and NTFS-based volumes, repairs damaged file and directory structures, and can even deal with the internal structure of compressed volumes. It can handle both diskettes and hard drives, or even virtual disk drives created in RAM. To start ScanDisk, right-click on a drive icon in a Window, choose Properties, click the Tools tab, and then click Check Now. This produces a ScanDisk dialog box, where you'll be able to launch diagnosis and repair routines.

Server Manager

The Server Manager utility displays which shares have been set on which servers, which trusts are in effect, which users are connected, and what files they're using. If you want to replicate directories on the server, this is the place to visit. You can also set a filter to send all administrative alerts to a specific computer or user (most likely you). Finally, you can also use the Server Manager to scope out what's happening on any Windows NT Workstation machines on your network.

User Manager

The User Manager utility enables you to add, delete, or modify user and group account information easily. You can restrict the times that users can log on to the network, restrict workstations that users log on from, and assign profiles to users.

WINS Manager

The WINS Manager utility enables you to configure WINS servers and view the database mappings they contain to resolve NetBIOS names to IP addresses. You can rearrange the data any way you want (for example, IP address order or name order).

Beyond the NTS planet

NT doesn't stop at the network level. It also provides utilities in case you extend your LAN to the rest of the world through the Internet. You can use some of the following utilities to troubleshoot your LAN and to extend your problem-solving abilities.

RAS Admin

NT provides the RAS Admin utility to help you decide which users can remotely access your network. We discussed RAS in detail in Chapters 15 and 16.

TRACERT

If you're experiencing problems connecting from point A to point B on the Internet, you can use TRACERT to trace the routes a packet takes as it traverses the wires. You'll see a screen dump of all the routers the packet travels through, the routers' names, and the time it takes to reach those routers.

Sometimes TRACERT is useful when selecting an ISP, because you can trace the route between the ISP's router and another point to see how many hops are in between and how long it takes to send a transmission between the two. If the ISP routes your packets all over the world before reaching its destination, you'll want to avoid that ISP. Accessing this utility is as simple as typing `TRACERT host` (for example, TRACERT io.com).

PING

PING is a TCP/IP utility. Using PING is like sending a Western Union telegram to someone and asking "Hey, are you there?" If you get a reply telegram, you know the person is there and you can talk with them. If you don't get a response, you know there's a problem and you won't be able to communicate.

PING does the same type of telegram thing with IP hosts. From your workstation, you can PING another host and wait for a response. The syntax is `PING IP Address` or `PING host` (for example, PING 205.230.247.2 or PING microsoft.com).

IPCONFIG

IPCONFIG with the /ALL option lists all the TCP/IP information about your NT server or workstation. This is especially useful if you're using RAS and connecting to the Internet. Sometimes RAS is assigned one IP number that's no good, and you can track it down this way. IPCONFIG provides information, such as the IP address for each interface device and subnet masks.

NETSTAT

The NETSTAT utility provides statistics in the TCP/IP world. If you're running a TCP/IP application on another host, it gives you stats on the IP address and port number of local and remote computers. Typing `NETSTAT host` will produce the statistics information.

Chapter 26
Shooting Trouble

*W*indows NT is a fantastic product and Microsoft has gone to great lengths to make sure that you never have problems installing and using the product. You can rest easy, secure in the fact that thousands of programmers and beta testers around the globe spent countless hours making sure that nothing will ever go wrong with your Windows NT Server or Workstation.

Okay, now back to the real world. We can expect to experience the occasional glitch with any product this complicated which is designed to run on such a diverse group of hardware. We've put together our Top 30 troubleshooting tips, compiled from the experiences of network administrators in three countries (actually, four countries, counting Texas). But first, a few hints and how-to's for troubleshooting all kinds of Windows NT problems.

Common Troubleshooting for Uncommon Problems

The following list gives you some places to check out when you need help with NT.

✔ The first place to check is the Troubleshooting section in the Windows NT on-line Help facility. It appears as a topic in the Topics list (available by clicking the Contents tab in the Help main window).

✔ Get on the Internet and use the Microsoft NT home page as your source of insight into many NT problems. You can search the Microsoft Knowledge Base on-line at the Microsoft Web site (www.microsoft.com). The MS Knowledge Base is the same information repository used by the Microsoft technical support staff to answer user inquiries. Microsoft also includes access to its file updates, patches, and driver libraries on the NT home page. You will likely find mention of common or "popular" NT problems on the NT Troubleshooting FAQ (Frequently Asked Questions).

✔ Use the tools Microsoft provides with the product itself. The Event Viewer gives you quick access to the various system information and error logs. When a strange error pops up on the screen, chances are good that the Event Viewer will show the error (if you have error logging turned on for that component) as well as offer details on the meaning of the error. Microsoft also includes on-line documentation for the entire NT product on the NT CD-ROM. The Help system's search and index features are very useful.

✔ Use third-party technical support resources. Most manufacturers who are developing hardware or software for use with Windows NT have had contact with the NT product long enough to know quite a bit about how their product meshes with NT. All large developers and manufacturers already have a home page on the World Wide Web where they store their own FAQs. Most smaller developers are following suit.

✔ Make sure that the suspect hardware is on the Windows NT Hardware Compatibility List (HCL). You can waste a lot of time trying to get untested hardware to work under Windows NT. If you stick to the NT HCL, the hardware should work under normal circumstances. If you call Microsoft to complain about the problem you're having with your new DinkyJet printer that isn't on the NT HCL, you're up the proverbial waterway without a suitable hand-held propulsion device.

Installation Can Be a Breeze or a Hurricane

The following deals with some common problems that can occur when you install Windows NT Server:

✔ No video or the video is distorted. This is usually the result of a problem with resetting the video adapter on boot up or a shared IRQ conflict. Try a cold boot of your PC. If this corrects the video problem, you will probably have to do a cold boot each time you restart Windows NT. You may have a system BIOS conflict with the video adapter if you can't get the video to initialize properly even after a cold boot. Possible solutions: Move the device that conflicts with your video adapter to an unused IRQ. Avoid video adapters on IRQs 12, 9, and 2 on PCI-based PCs.

✔ During setup, you get an error message stating "NT Cannot Find the Temporary Directory." This error indicates that you are using the setup diskettes from a diskette-based Windows NT installation on a CD-ROM-based installation. Possible solutions: Use the entire set of installation diskettes instead of the CD-ROM, make a new set of setup boot disks by issuing the command WINNT/OX, or use the original CD-ROM boot disks.

✔ Is it really necessary to create an emergency repair disk? Face it. It's not called "a boot diskette for when everything is going fine." It's for *emergency* use. Every server has emergencies, so you'd better have an emergency repair disk handy. Solution: Splurge on a few blank diskettes and create an emergency repair disk.

✔ Random system lockups after Setup enters the GUI-mode phase of installation. Possible solutions: Update your system BIOS, look for possible interrupt conflicts, or look for possible SCSI addressing or termination problems.

✔ During setup, you get an error message stating "Insert Windows NT (Workstation/Server) Diskette #." This message is usually caused by multiple CD-ROM drives installed in one PC. Possible solution: Insert the Windows NT CD-ROM in the primary CD-ROM drive. Which one is the primary drive? It's very hard to tell. Try inserting the NT CD-ROM in every CD-ROM drive until the message goes away.

Hardware Configuration Problems

The following details some common hardware problems and solutions:

✔ If you suspect a hardware problem, run the diagnostic programs that came with the suspect component.

✔ Remove and re-seat all add-in boards and RAM modules in your PC.

✔ If you have SCSI devices in your PC, be sure that they are properly terminated.

✔ Make sure all your hardware is on the Windows NT Hardware Compatibility List.

✔ Remove one add-in adapter at a time to pinpoint possible configuration conflicts.

✔ If possible, swap RAM modules, disk controllers, modems, and video boards with other, known good adapters.

✔ Always look at the Event Log to check for hardware warnings or errors.

Disk Controller Problems

Moving hard drives from one disk controller to another can make it difficult for NT to recognize the partitions. If the partition problems are on an NT boot drive, you may not even be able to boot your NT system. Possible solutions: Always be careful when moving hard drives around. Keep a detailed list of your original, working configuration in case you have to restore the drives to their original positions. The only other solution is to do a full and verified backup and be prepared to repartition every hard drive on your system after you begin to move hard drives.

CHKDSK and Check Dat

This section concentrates on problems specific to CHKDSK. Before you spend too much time troubleshooting, try ScanDisk first (covered in Chapter 25). Use CHKDSK only if ScanDisk can't help you. Here's the list, now that you've read our disclaimer:

✔ CHKDSK won't run at all. Solution: No files can be open for CHKDSK/F to properly run. If CHKDSK detects any open files, even system files, it will offer to check your disk on the next reboot. You can also boot from NT boot diskettes to run CHKDSK.

✔ CHKDSK runs but does not complete. This is usually caused by not having enough memory. This typically happens on memory-constrained PCs — those with less than 16MB installed — because there is no virtual memory available on boot up. Possible solution: Add more RAM to your NT PC.

✔ CHKDSK runs but gives strange errors. CHKDSK without the /F parameter does not stop other applications from making file system calls while CHKDSK is running. (If you constantly had other changes to your work while you were working on it, you might spit out an error or two yourself.) Possible solution: Be sure to close all other applications and services before running CHKDSK.

✔ CHKDSK always runs as my machine is booting. This is usually an indication that the system was not properly shut down, had problems while shutting down, or otherwise didn't get a chance to flush its cache buffers before the power was turned off. Possible solution: Go buy a little patience. Always wait for NT to tell you that it is now safe to turn off your PC before you flick off the big red switch.

File System Errors

Question: Why can't I access one of my drives? Answer: This problem has multiple causes. The following details some of the possible causes and solutions:

✔ Your system files may not be loading properly or may be corrupt. Make sure that these files are in the C:\SYSTEM32\DRIVERS directory: NTFS.SYS, FASTFAT.SYS, and FTDISK.SYS (if you're using software fault tolerance). If you think these files are missing or corrupt, reinstall them from your setup diskettes.

✔ There are various system errors when trying to access files. It is not unheard of for the file system to occasionally corrupt some files. Possible solution: Run CHKDSK/F on the affected drive.

✔ Corrupt FAT or NTFS volumes. FAT volumes are susceptible to file corruption due to system errors. Microsoft had the foresight to remedy many of these problems with NTFS. NTFS is a robust file system that can dynamically recover from minor file corruption and many common file allocation problems. NTFS does this by keeping redundant copies of the disk's directory structure and key files at various different physical locations on the disk. Possible solution: Run the Windows NT Repair utility, available from the Start➪Programs➪Administrative Tools Window.

✔ There could be a bug in Windows NT! Yes, a file corruption error or system lockup could be caused by a bug. Possible solution: Contact the Microsoft technical support and verify that your problem is a unique and reproducible problem. The next release of the NT service pack could correct a bug with your name on it!

Virus corruption of a boot sector

Windows NT is pretty virus-resistant. As NT's popularity continues to grow, however, it will undoubtedly become the target of more virus hackers. An infected NT boot disk drive will probably not boot properly. Be sure to check all your hard drives — not just your Windows NT drives — on a regular basis for boot viruses or viruses of any kind. We recommend any of the popular virus scan utilities designed for Windows NT. Even virus scanning programs designed for DOS Master Boot Record scanning, however, can detect an MBR virus on an NT hard drive.

If you do not have a virus scan program, you may be able to correct some MBR viruses by booting from a DOS boot diskette and running FDISK /MBR. Unfortunately, this method works in only some cases; in other cases, it may make the hard drive unreadable. Use this method with extreme caution or in absolute desperation.

Poor System Performance

If your NT system runs slower than Granny's old dog on a winter's morn, there are many possible culprits. Here are just a few:

✔ **File fragmentation.** Files are usually written in contiguous blocks on the hard drive. As the hard drive fills up, there are fewer and fewer contiguous spaces big enough to contain whole files, so NT (and every other major operating system) begins to store files in noncontiguous blocks. It takes much longer to read a file stored in noncontiguous blocks than to read one stored contiguously. NTFS avoids file fragmentation as much as possible, but some fragmentation is inevitable. Possible solution: Buy a commercial utility that defragments NT hard drives. Run it once a month to keep file fragmentation to a minimum.

✔ **Too many files in one directory.** Every file system slows down as more files are stored in each directory. Although NTFS handles large directories better than FAT-based (and most other) file systems, even NTFS begins to slow down when you have thousands of files in a directory. Possible solution: Use subdirectories to segment files into logical organizations to reduce the number of files in one directory.

✔ **Too many files on one volume.** Similar to the previous problem, even NTFS can bog down with more than a million files stored on a single volume. Possible solution: Add more volumes to keep from having too many files on one volume.

Printing and Not Printing Problems

Here comes everyone's favorite: printing problems. Answer these quick trouble-shooting questions and you're on your way to printing bliss:

✔ Is there a pattern to the print errors? If only certain applications or certain user names or certain PCs have the errors, you most likely have a configuration error. Always try to print the same print job while logged in as Administrator to verify that the problem isn't rights-related.

✔ Are you using the correct print driver? The correct printer driver is crucial for printing success. Download the latest version from the manufacturer's home page if you have any doubts about the problem being driver-related.

✔ Does the printer setup match the driver setup? Make sure that all printer options are accurately reflected in the print driver settings. Settings include paper trays, duplex features, and amount of memory installed.

✔ Maybe you're just forgetting to print. Check your memory. Actually, you should check your printer's memory to be sure that enough is installed to print the jobs being sent. You might have more documents than your printer has memory.

Here are some common boo-boos involving NT:

✔ If you still have printing problems after following the previous recommendations, you might be running out of local hard drive space or the server may not have enough room to spool very big print jobs. Possible solutions: Simplify your print job so that it is smaller, or clean off unused programs from the client and server hard drive.

✔ Corrupted printer driver. Your print driver may have spent too many nights in smoky bars. It may now be . . . corrupt! Possible solution: If you suspect that the print driver is the root problem, or if you run out of ideas as to what could be the root problem, reinstall the printer driver.

Here are a few tips to remedy the problem of very slow printing:

✔ As you know, Windows NT is multitasking; maybe another task is eating up all CPU time. Close every application possible to see whether the slow print problem is the result of another application hogging the limelight.

✔ Be sure that the printer driver and the printer agree on things, such as the amount of memory installed on the printer. You might think your printer is slow now, but wait until you have a memory mismatch between print driver and printer. Some of your print will never come out.

Troubleshooting RAS Hardware Problems

RAS can cause a few unforeseen problems. Here are some common pitfalls and solutions:

✔ The most common port problems you may encounter on a PC have to do with the mapping of COM1: and COM3: to the same port, and COM2: and COM4: likewise. Thus, if you try to use a mouse on COM1: and a modem on COM3:, you're headed for trouble. Check this possibility first!

✔ Check the Control Panel PORTS application. If PORTS can't see your modem, it's probably not correctly configured.

✔ Check the Event Viewer for any serial-type problems.

✔ Hardware conflicts: If you suspect an interrupt or address port conflict, change the interrupt or port used by either the modem or the other conflicting device.

✔ Always use the standard assignments for the interrupts and port addresses for your modems:

COM Port	IRQ	Base I/O Address
1	4	3F8
2	3	2F8
3	4	3E8
4	3	2E8

✔ Error 692: Hardware failure in port or attached device. This error message means that RAS either sent an incorrect initialization string to the modem or that your modem, serial port, or modem cable is misbehaving.

That's it for troubleshooting, pardner. Hang tough and you can generally find out what's ailing your system. If you can't figure out the problem on your own, check the resources we listed. Good luck, and good shootin'!

Part IV
The Part of Tens

The 5th Wave   By Rich Tennant

"OH SURE, $1.8 MILLION SEEMS LIKE A LOT RIGHT NOW, BUT WHAT ABOUT RANDY? WHAT ABOUT HIS FUTURE? THINK WHAT A COMPUTER LIKE THIS WILL DO FOR HIS S.A.T. SCORE SOMEDAY."

In this part . . .

When Moses came down from the mount, how many commandments did he have? Ten. How many fingers do most people have? Ten. How did Bo Derek rate in the movie of the same name? Ten! We're not sure how all this stuff relates, but that number keeps popping up everywhere we look. Maybe that's why there's a Part of Tens in this and all other . . .*For Dummies* books.

Each chapter in this part includes a list of admonitions, commandments, guidelines, suggestions, ideas, or other stuff worth considering when it comes to networking with Windows NT Server. We'd like to claim divine inspiration, but we're pretty sure that Redmond's reach, while long, has yet to extend into the hallways of Heaven!

The chapters have been carefully formulated to save you time, steer you around common networking potholes, and arm you to cope with everyday weirdness on your Windows NT Server network. The best part of tens, however, is the part where you *count to ten* when you're losing your cool. You might want to get in the habit of trying that one before you consult any of the part of tens in this book!

Chapter 27

Dealing with a Dead Network

. . . .

In This Chapter

▶ Knowing what to do when the network goes down

▶ Examining why the network slows to a crawl

▶ Losing servers or workstations (a sure sign of trouble)

▶ Running out of disk space

▶ Minimizing the impact of power failures and other electrical difficulties

▶ Staying within the recommended cable lengths

▶ Catching the intermittent glitch

▶ Logging on to the network — if it will let you!

. . . .

Okay, so things don't always work as they're supposed to. Sometimes they go completely astray. Don't panic — even perfect networks fail from time to time. Check out our pantheon of common networking problems. You'll probably see all of these malefactors firsthand during your illustrious networking career!

At least seven out of every ten networking problems occur because of loose cables or connections. Always check the wiring first!

Is Anybody Home?

The most disconcerting problem for network users occurs when the whole thing fails. Nobody can access the network, let alone log on or do something useful. What can you do when the network vanishes?

The most common cause of *network interruptus* is a break in the cable. For that reason, this condition is far more likely to occur on a bus than on a star topology. A bus links everyone, so a failure affects the whole cable segment.

When a star topology fails, go immediately to the hub that services the users affected; most likely, you'll be at the source of the problem.

When a bus topology fails, the usual culprit is a break or interruption somewhere on the cable. Look for a user who's moving from one office to another, or for people messing around near the cable. If you're lucky, somebody unplugged a cable; if you're unlucky, you'll have to repair or replace a damaged cable. If you're really cursed, the break is in a hole in the ground somewhere on your premises. (That is, a backhoe has used its unique capability to find and break your network!)

Whoa! "Server Unavailable"

"Server unavailable" is a typical symptom encountered by users who have altered their configurations, particularly if they've misspelled a server's name or omitted some crucial details. If things worked before, but have unexpectedly quit working, first inspect what has changed between then and now. It might be anything from problems in the Windows NT Registry or with the Network applet in the Control Panel to forgetting to reconnect a NIC card or cable from the PC to the network. When you get the "server unavailable" message, start with the cabling and work your way up to the software: Check the cable, the interface card, and the network software configuration in that order. Sooner or later, you'll discover the cause of the problem.

Suddenly, Slow Networking

Sometimes, your network will run very slowly. Even if you don't notice this yourself, your users will rush to let you know. Curiously, nothing stimulates the need for speed like a slow network. Could the grass be that much greener elsewhere?

The most common culprits for excessively slow networks include the following:

- ✔ A short in the cable, which can make the network work only intermittently
- ✔ Server problems that exhaust or deplete important resources, such as disk space or available memory
- ✔ Excessive server usage

When your network is unacceptably slow, go straight to the slow server and check the Server Manager, or double-click the Network icon in the Control Panel to check the server. Check any network-related settings to see what's what. If you browse through the various displays, especially those that cover network utilization, server memory, and network configuration, you should find the cause of the problem right away.

It's abnormal to have more than 2 percent of total traffic for errors (that is, the number of packets with errors as a percentage of all traffic on a given cable segment). When this happens, a bad cable is most often at fault! You'll need a protocol analyzer or a traffic capture program to obtain this kind of data. There are many such products available; we've had good luck with Novell's Windows-based LANalyzer for Windows product.

Can't Get from Point A to Point B

On networks with multiple servers, especially those using WAN links, the day may come when you can't get there from here. First, check the link between "here" and "there." Typically, the link will be down or the router that manages communications between both locations is out of commission. Checking that link is the first step; ensuring that traffic can traverse the link is the second step. It's not uncommon to be forced to reset the devices on both sides of the "problem link" — especially where modems are in use. It never hurts to reset the routers, either (if applicable).

Out of Disk Space

Running out of storage space calls for better system maintenance, as we argued throughout Part 3. After you examine the full drive and throw out the old and moldy stuff, remove those unessential files that build up like plaque on your teeth. Then reread Chapter 19: It shows how to practice prevention rather than find a cure!

Dealing with a full disk requires that you free some space. Survey your file system, identify the space hogs, and make them slim down their holdings. Another easy target is email, which has a way of sprouting tons of files (even better, you can clean these up yourself). Better still, use the Windows NT Server disk compression utility to squeeze down files and directories to free up space on your drives. You can compress, at your discretion, files or entire volumes. Finally, NT Server volumes sometimes benefit from defragmentation, in which you rewrite a volume to store all its files contiguously. This frees up so-called "slack space," which represents the tail ends of disk blocks left over when a chunk of a file doesn't consume the whole block. If you employ one or more of these tools or techniques, you'll create free space on your drive. You might decide to lower disk allocations for your space hogs, too.

It's dangerous to run a Windows NT Server with less than 10 percent disk space free. The server needs room to maneuver — for print files, temporary files, virtual memory, and so on. Without some workspace, things can bog down in a hurry. Double this requirement if you run a DBMS or use a RAS server, because both consume appreciable amounts of disk space.

Beating the Blackout Blues

Okay, the power was out for some reason and it's just come back. NT Servers would rather be shut down gracefully than have their plugs pulled. To recover from this insult, you must restart the server and perform any necessary file system repair. If the server has been *really* hosed, however, you may have to restore from a recent backup and break the news to your users that today's work is gone forever. Be prepared to be unpopular.

That's why we recommend purchasing an uninterruptible power supply (UPS) for your servers. When the power goes out, a UPS gives you enough juice to shut down the server properly, thereby avoiding file system damage. At a minimum, install a good surge suppresser and spike arrester on your server; this will protect you from outright damage if lightning strikes nearby.

Networks Have Rules for Good Reasons

You can break the rules of networking in lots of interesting ways, from excessive cable lengths or connection violations to trying to support more log ons than your NT Server license allows. Rules were made to be broken, but you must suffer the consequences.

The closer to the physical layer that such violations occur, the more severe the consequences. For instance, the eleventh user who tries to log on to an NT Server with a ten-user limit is politely rejected with an error message indicating that no additional user connections are available. This might offend that user, but has no other consequences for other folks on the network. By contrast, over-long cables can cause intermittent problems if the cables are not too far over the limit, and total network failure if they are way over the line.

Here again, staying legal beats correcting a violation. If you follow the rules, you are safe. If you don't, you have to find the straw that broke your network's back. Unless a problem is obvious, start at the wire and work up to the software. After a few of these drills, we think you'll agree that staying legal beats troubleshooting every time!

Correcting Intermittent Problems

Problems that come and go are the trickiest to catch, which makes them even trickier to correct. Intermittent glitches are usually caused by hardware, especially cable shorts or loose connections. (However, that is a tendency, not an absolute rule.)

When faced with an intermittent problem, first perform a survey — that is, determine the problem's scope. Figure out who's affected and where they are, and catalog the symptoms. Pay attention to everything odd, no matter how unrelated the elements appear. For example, the strangest intermittent problem we ever encountered was at a site where the network backbone ran up and down a building's elevator shaft. The only time the backbone failed was when the elevator came within a floor of the cable. Proximity caused it to interfere with the signals on the cable; otherwise, everything worked. The solution: We rerouted the backbone through a heavily shielded coaxial cable in a metal conduit.

We've heard wonderful stories about similar problems caused by industrial vacuum cleaners, servers being moved to mop beneath them, and other strange and unlikely events. If you're lucky, you won't have a story to tell yourself. Just keep your eyes peeled for out-of-the-ordinary situations and round up the usual suspects.

Losing Your Log On

An inability to log on to the network covers a multitude of causes. Fortunately, this problem usually affects only one workstation at a time. Start at the cable, and then work your way through the NIC to the software. Users who have made recent changes to their desktops may have inadvertently altered their Registry database to leave out the network directory, or they may not be loading the right software.

When you're troubleshooting user workstations, it's a good idea to bring a set of bootup disks that include working network software. That way, you can boot the workstation with a clean, controlled environment. This makes it perfectly clear when something's out of whack with the workstation's software.

If you have a portable or laptop with a network connection, bring that and connect it to the network in place of the suspect machine. This will help identify whether the culprit is the machine or the network connection. The biggest difference between this and the diskette approach is size and weight. You decide what's best.

In General

Whenever you're troubleshooting, adopt a positive attitude and make sure you see your problem-solving through to its inevitable conclusion. If things look hopelessly fouled up, take a break: Go for a walk, call a friend, have a cup of coffee. When you become wound up decoding symptoms, clues right in front of you can elude you. If you become too wound up, you miss them. A little relaxation sets your creative juices flowing and restores your detective skills. If Edison's best hours were spent daydreaming, why not yours?

The 5th Wave   By Rich Tennant

"WE SORT OF HAVE OUR OWN WAY OF PREDICTING NETWORK PROBLEMS"

Chapter 28

What You Should Know about Your Network

. . . .

In This Chapter

▶ Identifying all cables

▶ Keeping track of connections

▶ Watching out for cable-length violations

▶ Mapping out equipment

▶ Listing which NICs go where

▶ Keeping inventories of all machines on the network

▶ Knowing who to call when the network gets weird

▶ Keeping records for support calls

▶ Mapping out your network

▶ Stocking spares (and other arrangements)

. . . .

Chapter 6 extols the virtues of a network map (and a database of information about machines, links, software, and more to go with it). This chapter provides a checklist to remind you what your map and database should include.

Where's the Wiring?

Vital wiring data includes the location of cable ends and how they are color-coded or labeled (especially critical for twisted-pair wiring, where cables run in packs and often look alike). For a complete reference, record the code on the outside of the cable (typically printed on the insulation) and the name of the vendor, when available.

Where Are Your Connections?

For wiring schemes, such as coaxial cable, that involve taps, knowing the location (and number) of connections is important for staying on the right side of the rules. Likewise, the locations of punchdown blocks or other termination points are crucial.

How Long Is Each Cable?

You can get information about the length of each cable in two ways — the easy way and the expensive way. If you measure as you go, you can record how long each cable is as it is installed. If you're measuring cable that's already in place (or if you didn't keep track along the way), rent a Time-Domain Reflectometer (TDR) and use it to measure each cable. Especially when dealing with twisted-pair, don't be surprised when you encounter unexpectedly long segments: Cabling folklore is full of stories about cables that include a whole spool of wire hidden somewhere in a ceiling. Because you can't always see these wires, the only way to size them is to measure them electronically. Go ahead, rent a TDR. (You'll feel like a real network professional then!)

Where's the Gear, and What Do You Have?

When you know the location of every hub, router, concentrator, or other piece of networking gear, you know where to look when you need to find any of it again. Keep track of network addresses, used and unused ports, and other configuration information about these devices, too. This information comes in handy. While you're at it, record the manufacturer, model, and serial number for each item. (You may be able to get some of this information from the purchase records, but you need the serial number or asset tag number to identify individual items.)

Know Your NICs

Be sure to keep at least one manual for each kind of NIC in the network. Find a source for the latest and greatest drivers for each one, too. A manual's best feature is usually the phone number for the manufacturer's technical-support hotline. They can tell you everything you need to know about a NIC and its software. Be sure to download the Windows NT Hardware Compatibility List on a regular basis, too — it includes useful information on NICs (and other server gear).

For each NIC that's installed, be it on a server or a workstation, record all the current settings (such as IRQ, memory base, I/O port, and DMA channel). If it's okay to gum up the back of your PCs a little, record this information on a small label on the back of the case. That way, you don't have to open the PC and remove the NIC to check its settings. It's even better to record this in your configuration database.

Your Nodes Know, but Do You?

For reasons lost in the mists of time, any machine attached to a network is called a *node.* (Maybe they're called nodes because topologists refer to each point on a connected graph as a node.) For each node, record and maintain a description of its hardware and software configuration, and keep an inventory of the software that's installed. This information has a rightful place in your configuration database.

Dealing with Vendors

Over time, you buy parts of your network from various sources: mail order, local computer stores, or maybe even a vendor's own sales rep. You also buy stuff from different vendors. We recommend that you build and maintain a vendor file that includes the following information:

- ✔ Name and model number for each item
- ✔ Purchase information (a copy of the invoice or purchase order is a good idea, and is often required to talk to the folks in tech support)
- ✔ Serial number and other identification information
- ✔ Vendor's address and phone numbers for sales and technical support

If you assemble all this information in one place, you're ready to call for help whenever you need it. You also have all the information you need to convince the person on the other end of the phone that you have a legitimate claim to their assistance.

Contact Logging

No, "contact logging" is not an obscure timber sport. Every time you call a vendor (or a reseller, a professional support organization, or anyone else about your network), log the call. Write down the date, time, and the names of the people you talk to. If they promise anything or advise you to do something, write that down too.

Your contact log is valuable for at least two reasons: If things get really weird, you have a way to reconstruct (and validate) your side of the story. Better still, you can use the log to identify who's worth talking to, and ask for them by name when next you call.

The Map's the Thing!

Obtain the engineering or architect's plans for your building or office or barn or whatever. Use a copy to record cable placement, cable length, and machine placement. This helps you locate things; it also helps you figure out how big your problem might be when you suspect the cause to be a shared cable or hub.

Never mark up originals — check your local Yellow Pages for a drafting or architectural supply store. Most will copy blue lines or other architectural drawings for you. Then when you've built your network map, make some working copies so you can mark up a copy without defacing your original. You'll probably want to supply copies to building management and to the facilities staff — they can use it to forewarn outside contractors before they mess with your network. Remember: It's easier to avoid trouble than to fix something after it breaks!

Stockpiling Spares . . .

Over time, you acquire a collection of spare parts and unused cable. If you keep track of what you have and where it's stored, the person who replaces you will be able to find stuff. Follow the golden rule — if you had to take over for somebody else, you'd want the same treatment, wouldn't you?

As the eminent cyberneticist and mathematician Alfred Korzybski so poignantly remarked, "The map is not the territory." True though that statement may be, it's the best tool we know of for finding your way around your networking territory. All the best networks have one — why not yours?

Chapter 29

Ten Things You Must Know Before Anyone Can Help You

S ometimes you'll become stuck on a networking problem and you won't be able to solve it without outside help. A good rule of thumb to follow is to guess how long a particular job should take before you start. If half your estimate has expired and you're not halfway there, it's time to bring out the heavy artillery — tech support!

To deal effectively with another person, whether it's somebody from tech support or just plain old Fred, the Windows NT guru next door (or down the hall), follow the guidelines in this chapter first.

Assemble the Facts

Most technical support departments or companies require you to identify yourself as a legitimate owner of a product or system before gaining access to their services. It's like checking into a hospital: Before they admit you, you must identify yourself and provide proof of insurance (or at least an ability to pay). Here, you must demonstrate a legitimate claim.

To obtain technical support from most vendors, you must know the name of the product in question and its serial number, and be able to provide proof of purchase. If you've built the network database we suggested as part of your network mapping efforts (see Chapter 28), you have this material at hand. If not, start digging; some technical support operations won't talk to you until you can provide this information, so it's best to be prepared to rattle it off when asked. At the very least, you'll be asked to provide proof of purchase (such as an invoice or receipt) or a serial number for the product you want supported. Don't be surprised if they ask you for a credit card or purchase order number — an increasing number of companies offer only pay-as-you-go tech support!

Sometimes you won't be able to get help from tech support until you've provided them with a filled-out registration card. If this happens to you, ask them whether you can fax the card to them.

Describe the Problem and its Symptoms

Write down everything you can about the system that has the problem. If it's a workstation, record information about every interface and its settings, the kind of CPU, the amount of RAM, the disk drive and controller, the operating system type and version, and copies of relevant files. (For DOS or Windows 3.x, you'll need the AUTOEXEC.BAT and CONFIG.SYS files. Windows for Workgroups will probably require the PROTOCOL.INI file. For Windows 95 and Windows NT, the contents of the Registry will probably be required.)

If it's a server, write down everything we already mentioned, plus the version of Windows NT Server. It's a good idea to dump the contents of the Windows NT Registry and print copies of its configuration files.

The idea is to be able to completely document what you're dealing with.

What's Showing?

Give an accurate description of the problem, including any error messages that crop up. (It's important to copy them down verbatim, especially if numeric error codes or other obscure messages appear. Even though they may not mean much to you, they might to somebody else!)

What's New or Changed?

If your system was working fine until you made a change or addition, it's extremely important to describe what has changed and why you can't get back to where you started.

What Have You Tried?

If you've tried to correct the problem yourself, recount what you've tried and the results you obtained. If you tell tech support all about it, you may be able to save yourself and the other party to your call some time and energy. Ask the support person if he or she is interested in knowing about the blind alleys you've already explored. If the answer is "No," don't insist on telling them anyway.

What Happened?

If you've suffered a power outage or if someone accidentally disconnected your server, please tell your support contact about it. Make sure that you test the A/C outlet to be sure there's power in that receptacle. Also, see whether the PC is capable of powering up. No power or a dead unit is a different problem than a unit you can at least turn on.

Does the Problem Have a History?

Sometimes a badly damaged file system or a failing disk drive starts off with small, occasional faults that worsen over time until the system fails completely. If your problem has been building for a while, let the other person know how long this has been going on, how it began, and what's happened as the symptoms have progressed.

Be Clear, Concise, and Polite

It's disconcerting for a system or network to go down in flames. But the people who are trying to help you can't fix your feelings. They can deal only with your problem. Take a deep breath and do your best to calm down. Stick with facts, and keep the emotional content to a minimum, if you can.

If you're clear and direct when describing your problem and when providing information they request, things will go much faster. If you did your homework and built a configuration database, you should be able to tell them everything they want to know as soon as they ask. This will help keep you calm, but it will help them even more!

Send Information through Other Channels

If the help you're after isn't immediately available, tell the technical support people what information you've already gathered. Ask if you can upload or fax it to them (assuming that you still can). Especially when the contents of configuration files or other computer information are involved, providing a copy for the person on the other end of the conversation can be a real time-saver.

Can You Do Anything Else?

It's easy to become upset when things are broken. Focus on how effectively you're communicating and keep checking in with the other party to see how you're doing. This helps you be more objective and get the information across. The more good information you give, the better (and faster) the results will flow. A positive attitude works wonders, too.

Getting good help requires giving good information. This usually means going through the process of recreating your computing environment and describing the causes of whatever problem led to your plea for help. The more you can do to document the circumstances accurately and objectively, the better your support person can do his or her job. Just remember that you both share the same goal — to get things working as quickly as possible.

Chapter 30

Keeping the Peerage Pleased with the Network

*J*ust because NT Workstation supports peer-to-peer networking, that doesn't mean you can set up a network and never think about it again. Setting up an NT Workstation network may be straightforward, but it still takes some planning and hard work to make things fly. If you follow a few basic rules of prudent networking practice, you can keep things up and running — and available for everybody. Peer-to-peer means that all users become part-time network administrators, whether or not they care to admit it.

Users Must Be Responsible to Each Other

In Windows NT Workstation workgroups, PCs are both clients and servers. Anyone whose machine offers a shared service has to be educated about what that means — namely, that other users will depend on the services that the machine provides. Therefore, users should no longer reboot their machines whenever they want. They also shouldn't turn their machines off during lunch. To remain useful, a shared resource must be available to all who want to share it! You may want to consider leaving some machines up and running 24 hours a day (for example, machines that handle the network printer or RAS dial-in access to the network).

If you can make your users understand that they depend on each other and on each other's machines, they'll feel more responsible to each other. This responsibility makes for safer computing and a more workable Windows NT Workstation network.

Define a Naming Scheme and Use It Hard!

If users share disk drives or printers on multiple machines around the network, try to create and organize names so that they make some kind of sense.

For example, LASERP could be the name of your laser printer, and DOTP the name of the dot-matrix printer. Or you could call the laser printer HP4M and the fax/printer Lexmark4SX, to reflect machine types. Make the directories where shared applications reside reflect their type: Call the spreadsheet SHARE SPREAD or EXCEL, for example, and the word processing program SHARE WORD.

If names communicate what a resource does or is, or what a shared drive contains, users can find their way around pretty easily. Even so, build a map of the network's shared resources, name the file NETWORK.MAP, put a copy on every network drive, and keep the map current.

Dedication Supports Heavy Sharing

For heavily used network drives or printers, the poor user whose machine plays host will suffer from the traffic. If you have a heavily used resource, beg, borrow, or invent a separate machine to put it on. The poor user will thank you, and the rest of the users will get better service. You can leave Windows NT Workstation on the dedicated server for smaller networks, but you'll want to consider switching to Windows NT Server if the server's user pool becomes bigger than 15 or 20 users.

Don't Be a File Hog

Just because there's free space on a network drive doesn't mean that you have to fill it up. Exercise some restraint. The rule of thumb is to store on network drives only things that must be shared or that require public access. Anything more is just plain piggish.

Common Rules Promote Common Courtesy

Bring your users together before you turn on the network (and once a quarter or so, thereafter, to give newbies a chance to hear your story). Tell them what they can expect from the network. Emphasize the responsible role that all individual users must play. Be clear and firm on this topic: Users whose machines host shares must respect others' needs for those resources. Indicate the normal hours of operation for each machine, including those that must be left on all the time. Users must also make sure that someone else knows how to boot up their machines and make their network resources available for the days when they are sick or on vacation. (Of course, if it's an NT machine, all they need to know is how to find the power switch.) Our final word on the subject is: "Make some policies, make them clear, and make them stick!"

Dealing with Error Messages

Although Windows NT Workstation works pretty well, things do go wrong occasionally. You'll certainly have opportunities to observe error messages from the system firsthand, and you should expect to hear similar experiences from your users.

When responding to an error message, the most important task is to try to understand what it means. Volume 4 of the *Windows NT Resource Kit* from Microsoft Press is an invaluable resource in this regard; entitled *Windows NT Messages*, it devotes more than 700 pages to an alphabetized list of NT system messages. Because it's such a handy tool, you might want to pick up a copy for your network! You can use it to help you understand what a message means and to figure out what action, if any, to take in response.

Back Up Shared Resources!

Anything worth sharing is worth keeping around. That's why it's essential to establish a backup routine for all machines with shared resources and perform regular backups at least once a week. The more valuable the data, the more often you'll want to back it up. Don't forget that a backup may be all that stands between you and unemployment!

Smart Users Use Secure Networks

Windows NT Workstation supports domain names, user accounts, user passwords, and named groups. If any data on your network is confidential, or if the network is exposed to outsiders, you should make hard-to-guess account names and passwords mandatory. Teach your users to be secure. They'll not only feel better about the network, but also help you protect its valuable assets.

Maintenance Is the Key to Network Salvation

Regular tune-ups of your NT Workstation machines aren't a bad idea, just to keep your network working at top performance. But we're talking about computers, not cars, so let's talk about software upgrades and file system cleanup instead of carburetors and oil changes. You'll want to keep your eyes peeled for new Service Packs for Windows NT and install them before a weekly full system backup if you decide to use them. You'll also want to inspect shared machines from time to time and delete stale, unnecessary files (such as .TMP and .BAK) and obsolete files. That way, you'll get the best use from the disk space your users must share. In addition, you'll be assured that everyone's using the latest and greatest software.

Keeping a Windows NT Workstation network running isn't that much work. It simply requires developing good habits and practices, and then sticking to them. Anything less is simply unacceptable!

Chapter 31

What You Should Know Before Making Changes to a Windows NT Server

- -

In This Chapter

▶ Backing up before changing — anything!

▶ Getting acquainted with the file system's layout and contents

▶ Documenting the server's hardware configuration

▶ Understanding your system's services and applications

▶ Documenting special network addresses

▶ Mapping routers and where your server fits

▶ Mapping print servers, queues, and network printers

▶ Surveying your server's situation

▶ Understanding user accounts, defined groups, trust relationships, and supervisory rights

▶ Researching your server's Windows NT version and whether the installation is up to date

- -

*T*he power of common practice is strong, but the power of common expectations is even stronger. Although the setup of many servers is similar, each has its own quirks. You must understand these things when you take over a Windows NT server, especially before you begin changing things to fit your own ideas of good structure and organization. This chapter presents a checklist so that you can become familiar with what you have — and get back to where you started should you need to reverse your course.

Make Two Complete Backups?

A complete backup means that you copy everything. Why would you want two? For insurance. If anything goes wrong with one backup, the other one should still be okay. If you make changes and the changes don't work or don't work in the way you want them to, these backups could be your only lifeline back to a known working system configuration.

Inspect and Survey the File System

Print directory structures for all the volumes on your server, especially WINNT\SYSTEM and WINNT\SYSTEM32. Try to understand how the pieces fit: Does the file system follow conventional Windows NT structures, or does it do its own thing? The answer to that question will help you find your way around and figure out what, if anything, must change.

While you're poking around, inspect the files to see whether the system has been cleaned up. Look for outdated files, unnecessary duplicates, and .TMP or .BAK files in mass profusion. Check the contents of email directories and their user subdirectories. Avoid the temptation to clean as you go — you're building a survey, remember?

Document the System

Unless you're lucky enough to inherit a server from someone who's already made a network map and a configuration database, you'll have to do some sleuthing to document the system. Examine the boot sequence for your server; pay special attention to the AUTOEXEC.BAT and CONFIG.SYS files, where applicable. Print a dump of the NT Registry and review it carefully. You'll also want to check out all configuration information for the services and applications that load as System Services when the server boots up. This information is a good start for most of what you need to know.

Map Network Addresses and Configurations

You have to understand the protocols and network addresses that pertain to your server. (Typically, there is one additional network address per protocol for every NIC installed on your server.) The list of protocols for which you must obtain names and addresses includes all of the following: NetBIOS/NetBEUI, TCP/IP, AppleTalk, DLC, IPX, or whatever else might be installed.

Master Your Network's Routing

If you're running Windows NT Server 3.51 or better, the server can act as a router. Check to see which protocols, if any, are being routed. If your network includes a dedicated or stand alone router, map all the networks serviced. Build a routing map that shows the network addresses involved and the routers that link individual network segments. This map shows you how data moves around on your internetwork, and it tells you how address ranges are assigned.

Map Your Print Services

Create a list of the printers, print queues, and print servers on the network. Add locations for print servers and printers to your network map. This will make the devices easy to locate. Figure out what kinds of special service queues have been set up and how the currently available print services are used. If everybody is happy with the way things work, leave your print services alone until you understand them fully.

Check the Server Situation

Examine your server's physical situation. Is it in a secure area or out in the open? Does it have a UPS or a surge suppresser (to handle lightning or power sags and surges)? Does it have adequate cooling and ventilation? Dubious answers to any of these questions should lead to improved conditions, at the very least. If everything is okay, move on to other concerns. Don't be afraid to spend some time and money analyzing and improving your server's situation, though — it's well worth it in the long run. Remember: A happy server situation leads to happy users!

Know Your User Community

It's vital that you understand who uses your servers, what they use them for, and when they use them. This will help you schedule backups and system maintenance at off-peak hours. Observe and understand your user community's usage patterns and behavior. Find out which users are the power users and heavy system consumers. Find out what they like and don't like about the network in its current incarnation. (This group is usually vocal and will be happy to tell you what's in need of adjustment, tweaking, or replacement too.)

Familiarize yourself with your local NT Domain Services and get to know the defined user groups, domains, and trust relationships from your server's perspective. Find out who has administrative permissions and who has access to the NT Server Security Accounts Manager and other vital configuration and security control programs. For your own protection, enable access to such utilities only to your administrative account. When others complain about "losing their rights," you'll be able to decide whether they really need administrative access.

Version and Service Pack Check

Your final check investigates the currency of your NT Server installation. First, find out the version number (which is reported as the server boots and is also available from the My Computer⇨Help⇨About Windows NT menu entry). Next, investigate which Service Packs have been installed. Remember, a Service Pack is a downloadable collection of files with patches, fixes, and enhancements to Windows NT Server available through CompuServe (GO MSOFT) or on the Internet (from `http://www.microsoft.com`).

Here's where an investigation of the Help About information pays a dividend: Because it lists the latest Service Pack installed, it also indicates how up to date your server is. We recommend that you install Service Packs only if they include important updates or bug fixes or supply functionality for your Windows NT machine that's otherwise unavailable. Nevertheless, knowing what revisions your machine already has installed will help you decide whether you should install the latest Service Pack on your system.

When you take over an existing server, become as familiar with it as though you had put it together yourself. If you're lucky, it will be laid out along familiar lines — and use the well-worn defaults and directory structures. If not, you must perform a detailed inspection and investigation. This takes time, but the effort is always rewarded!

Chapter 32

The Paths to Print Perfection

Sometimes, printing on a network can seem like a challenge. Maybe it's because so many kinds of printers exist, each with its own eccentricities. Maybe it's because providing perfection for print services is difficult. Nevertheless, Windows NT Server does a terrific job with print services (especially if you're accustomed to other networking environments).

As long as you have an NT driver for your particular printer, the rest is pretty darn easy! Difficult printing problems usually manifest themselves only when you can't find a driver for a printer you already own. (Remember to check the Hardware Compatibility List, if the NT built-in printer wizard can't help you find the driver or drivers you need.) In this chapter, we warn you about some printing pitfalls and point out some practices that ensure perfect printing every time!

You've Gotta Have Drivers

If you want Windows NT Server (and other Windows implementations) to handle printing, you must have a driver for your particular printer to make the all-important connection between the Printer folder and the physical device. Without boring you to distraction with the details, suffice it to say that a driver performs some magic on the contents of a general output file to tailor it to a specific device.

If you're lucky, your DinkyJet printer's driver is included with the Windows NT Server distribution media. In that case, the printer wizard selects the driver for you, and all you need to do is name that device. If you're not so lucky, try using one of the generic drivers or an emulation mode (such as PCL5, PostScript, or Epson LQ100) before launching a full-scale search for the exact driver you need.

If you need to go hunting, try the printer manufacturer on-line first. You can probably find what you need on CompuServe or at the manufacturer's Web or FTP site. If you strike out, call their tech support number next and ask for help. It may take some doing, but you can find drivers for most equipment if it isn't too ancient. If you can't find a driver, you need to be in the market for a new printer.

After you find what you need (or buy another printer), make sure that the printer works before you tell your users that it's available. The only thing worse than not having what you need is being told that you have it and then finding out that it doesn't work!

Make Printer Names Self-Documenting

When you create printer definitions in the Printer folder, printer names can be up to 127 characters long. This gives you lots of room to maneuver, so try not to be too cryptic when naming printers. It's easier for users to understand that HPLJ4-2ndFloor means "the HP LaserJet 4 on the second floor" than to guess that H2 means the same thing. We know you want to maximize your efficiency and, therefore, keep keystrokes to a minimum, but there's a tradeoff between efficiency and intelligibility. In other words, be careful not to be too efficient!

If you can design a naming scheme that takes all the important variables into account, so much the better. In most organizations, this includes department, location, and device type. So you might want to name that printer Sales-HPLJ4-2ndFloor instead of simply HPLJ4-2ndFloor. Likewise, if you designate multiple logical printers for specific services — such as printing envelopes, letterhead, or forms — you want to add a function field to the name, for example, Sales-HPLJ4-2ndFloor-Env. You get the idea.

But no matter what kind of naming scheme you use, be sure to explain it to your users. Put together a network description for your users and be sure to explain how network printer names work. Include a list of names, with explanations for each one, and you can always tell users to "read the description file" when they call looking for information!

Creating the Right Mix of Logical and Physical

In Chapter 22, you find that, in the Windows NT Server environment, multiple logical printers can talk to a single physical printer, or multiple physical printers can be driven by a single logical printer. When might you want to do either or both? Here are some ideas:

✔ When a large group of users wants to do a lot of printing, or there's a high-volume output operation, a single logical printer works well with multiple physical printers. This arrangement ships the next print job in the queue to the first available physical printer in the group. This greatly increases the output capacity of that logical printer at the same time. And, as long as all the printers are in the same location, users won't care exactly which printer produces their output, assuming they can find it easily.

✔ When a single printer must handle multiple kinds of output — for instance, envelopes, letterhead, plain paper, and legal paper — setting up multiple logical devices for that printer makes a lot of sense. If you make plain paper the default device, and require manual intervention for print jobs to the other logical printers, you can explain to your users that they have to go to the printer and change the paper bin or manually feed an envelope, for example, to get their job going.

Putting a Windows workstation right next to the printer when you require users to operate a printer manually is a good idea. That way, when users make a mistake (and it will happen, even to you), they can restart their print job on the spot, without having to walk back to their desks to fire it off again!

Direct Printing

The Printer folder in Windows NT Server gives the option of directing output to a printer directly or through a queue. Queues let users fire off print jobs and get on with the rest of their lives. With direct printing, users have to wait for the printer to become available and then print the requested job. We can't think of too many reasons why anybody would want to use direct printing.

The only way direct printing makes sense is if the printer is the exclusive possession of one person. Then the person can wait for stuff to finish if he or she wants. Explain the tradeoff to your users carefully — most will prefer queues to waiting, every time!

Separating User Communities

Most modern printers can handle output from all kinds of workstations by using the same driver or by switching among drivers automatically. This means the printers can handle a mixed bag of print jobs — from UNIX, Macintosh, and PC users — with panache and aplomb. But some older printers, which are still quite capable and ready for many years of further service, may not be so accommodating. That's when defining separate, but equal, logical printers may make sense.

If a device must reload drivers for specific print job types or user platforms, setting up multiple logical printers so that jobs can queue for each specific service type may be worth it. You then have two options. You can schedule times when particular drivers are loaded, so users know when they can pick up their output. Alternately, you can poll the queues for each service type and handling those that either have jobs in them or have the most jobs in them (if more than one queue contains pending print jobs).

The Print Job Must Die!

Every now and then, users send something to the printer, only to find out that they need to make more changes before a hard copy is worthwhile. Occasionally, they even send a badly formatted job that must be killed, lest it consume the contents of the world's forests. It's important that you and your users know how to kill a print job, so that it won't continue wasting paper when further output is no longer required.

You have two basic approaches to killing a print job:

✔ Users can kill the job from their local workstation, provided their print management functions work with the NT Server Print Manager. For PC users running Windows, this is a snap: They use their own desktop Printer folder, select the offending job, and simply delete that sucker. For Macintosh or UNIX users, their ability to kill print jobs depends on the version of software they're running and its capability to communicate with the Printer folder on the server. That's where the second approach comes in handy.

✔ You can kill print jobs from the NT Server's Printer folder, but that means you must either do the job yourself or trust others to use their server access properly without mucking up other queues and printers. If you're the trusting type, you could set up a group named PrtMgr with permissions to access the server's Printer folder and assign membership to your user community. This is pretty easy, but it may expose your printing environment to a bit of horseplay or outright monkey business.

Or you can set a relatively high page count limit on print jobs (100 pages seems fair) and simply absorb the costs of paper that will be wasted when the occasional formatting problems occur. *Note:* If you take this approach, users with legitimate print jobs longer than 100 pages will have to bug you for help to get those jobs printed.

The paperless office remains more of a mirage than a vision of the future. As long as hard copy is needed, printers will be necessary on your networks. That will make it easy for you to appreciate how simple and straightforward the NT printing services can be!

Chapter 33

Backups Benefit Everybody

· ·

· ·

*I*t's sad to report, but less than half of all network servers are backed up regularly. We can only speculate how this blissfully ignorant majority can justify living with the possibility that a system failure means a total loss of all data and applications. This only proves what we've always thought — there's no guarantee that the majority is right!

If you want to risk everything you have on your system, we can't stop you. But if you're even half-smart, you'll establish a good backup routine. When things go wrong, you are ready to deal with Murphy as he manifests himself on your server. (Murphy's Law: What can go wrong, will.)

Buy Enough Capacity

The mainstay of a good backup process is that it is applied regularly and frequently. The more data you own, the longer backing it up takes. Likewise, the more stuff you back up, the more media you need to store it.

Don't try to save money with a cheap, low-capacity backup system if yours is an expensive, high-capacity server. If you can back up everything on a single tape or magneto-optical (MO) disk, that's good. If you can back up to a single tape or MO disk several times, that's better yet.

Here's why: Backups are normally scheduled during off-peak hours, so they usually happen on weekends or during the wee hours. If you can fit everything you need on a single tape or disk, you won't have to be around to swap tapes, cartridges, disks, or whatever. You can get your rest. If the data is too big to fit on a single platter, cartridge, or whatever, consider buying a stacker, changer, or jukebox instead of a single-play unit. (For more details, please visit Chapter 23.) When calculating how much capacity you need, be sure to leave room for growth, too!

Automatic Pilot Is the Only Way to Go

The safest way to make sure that your system is backed up regularly is to let the computer do the work. The only good backup is a fresh backup, and you can make the computer create a new one every day. If you insist on doing it yourself, however, excuses won't make up for the data that become lost as a consequence! So automate your backup process completely and let the system follow a rigid backup schedule.

If You Miss It, You Lose It!

When setting backup intervals, you have an important trade-off between frequency versus time and expense. On the one hand, the more often you back up, the more productive time you lose on your system. On the other hand, the less often you back up, the more data will be lost as a result. The key is to figure out how much data you can lose before your business really hurts.

Most operations decide that a day's work is about all that they can lose. That decision has as much to do with the scheduling of backups at night as it does with damage control. Think long and hard before you exceed that cut-off point. What would the loss of several days or a week of work cost you and your company? If you can live with the answer, you won't need to back up as often.

Store a Backup Off-site

If you think backing up is a good idea, please take the next logical step: Make arrangements to store a set of backups off-site. You can probably find companies that offer secure, underground, temperature- and humidity-controlled data storage environments in your area. (Try the Yellow Pages, under Storage.) This may sound like overkill, but if your building goes up in flames, your off-site backup won't be barbecued along with it.

Most organizations deliver backup copies to storage facilities weekly rather than daily. You have to decide which is best for you.

Disaster Planning?

Beyond off-site backup storage, the ultimate backup strategy is to arrange for a redundant site where you could install your off-site backup in a (very expensive) pinch. If your company can't function without a network, obtaining guaranteed access to an equivalent system is probably worth the money if yours is ever put completely out of service. This process is called disaster recovery. Ask management (and yourself) this question: "How long can we do without our network before we are out of business?" If the answer is less than a week or two, you want to consider this option carefully. Think about how long finding and buying everything you'd need to rebuild your network would take; you'll quickly see what we mean.

Practice, Practice, Practice!

A fresh backup and the best backup system in the world aren't worth squat unless you know how to use them. In other words, if you can't make your backup system work, your backup is worthless.

The only way to figure out how things work is to try them and see what happens. The only way to become good at restoring data from a backup is to restore some data from a backup. In other words — practice with what you store!

If you schedule a restoration drill once every three months or so, you stay reasonably familiar with your system's restore capabilities. Then when a crisis happens, you can concentrate on restoring your network instead of relearning how to use your backup system!

What about Workstation Backups?

After you establish a good backup habit for your servers, the next hurdle you face is deciding what to do about workstations. If you can train your users to keep their important files on a server, you don't have to back up workstations, period. If you can't, you must decide whether backing them up is worth the extra time, expense, and effort.

Typically, the only people who merit this kind of consideration are your bosses. Sometimes, covering your assets means covering theirs, too!

Rotating Media by the Book

As you get your backups in gear, adding new media to your pool from time to time is important. Chapter 23 covers several media rotation schemes in detail. The important thing is to not wear out the tapes, cartridges, or whatever you use to capture your data. Worn media can make backups unreadable and, therefore, useless.

Choose a rotation scheme and schedule and stick with it. Be sure to budget for media expenses and related expenses, too — nothing is worse than losing data because you can't spend the money to get the media you need for your backups.

Mixing Backup and Routine Maintenance

Another reason to back up your server can be easy to overlook: Whenever something changes, be it hardware or software, some danger of a failure always exists. If you don't time system upgrades or changes right after a regular, complete system backup, you take the chance of losing important data. That's why backing up first and making changes second is so important.

Choosing a Suitable Backup System

If you purchase a backup system, you have to weigh a whole slew of considerations (which we cover in Chapter 23). The following list covers the top three:

✔ **File-by-file restore:** Users lose files, and Windows NT (both Server and Workstation) doesn't support an undelete capability. Although NT does save deleted files in the Recycle bin, that will be no help if the bin's been purged recently. File-by-file restoration lets you restore only what you need and saves time and frustration.

✔ **Automatic backup scheduling:** If the package you're looking at doesn't let you automate regular full or incremental backups, don't even *think* about buying it! Ideally, the package will have a flexible, usable built-in scheduler as well.

✔ **Native NT Windows support:** If you need to back up Windows NT, choose a solution that supports the product. Such products are usually branded with a special logo that includes the Windows icon plus the words "Microsoft Windows Compatible 32-bit Application." Otherwise, you risk missing crucial system configuration information that might leave you with a system that doesn't work after you restore your files.

Get the most effective backup package that meets your needs. Remember, backing up is the cheapest form of insurance for your company's investment in the systems it uses.

Chapter 34

Success Means Growing Pains Lie Ahead

● ●

In This Chapter

▶ Dealing with erratic network performance

▶ Worsening network response times

▶ Exceeding the license limits

▶ Running out of disk space

▶ Overcrowding your media

▶ Growing pains for users means growing pains for you!

▶ Growing on its own: networks run amok

▶ Crashing regularly is a definite symptom

▶ Backing up requires multiple media

▶ Burning sensations tell you something's amiss

● ●

*Y*our network's finally humming along; everything appears to be working. Does this sound like the calm before the storm?

"Nothing succeeds like success," so growing pains must be the reward for doing your job so well. Just as your pants became a little too short when you were outgrowing them as a youth, the fabric of your network can begin to lose the capability to cover all the action. This time, though, your ankles are showing because you're running around like crazy, putting out fires.

In this chapter, we describe some common symptoms of network growing pains. If you watch out for them, you can begin planning for growth before things start bursting at the seams.

Flaky Is as Flaky Does

If all your users show up at their desks at about the same time and fire up their workstations right away, that's about the toughest test your network will have. If the network falls to its knees as a result, you're approaching the limits of your server or network's carrying capacity.

If only one NIC is installed on your server, you can get an immediate performance boost by installing a second NIC. Then split the cable layout in two and attach half the users to each one. If you already have two NICs, consider adding one or two more, and so on.

If your server's running low on running room, the cure is more drastic. It might be time to buy a second server (and a second Windows NT Server license, plus more disk drives, NICs, and all the other stuff) and split up your user community. When you're running out of capacity, something has to give!

When Delays Become Normal

It's one thing if your server starts out slow and then speeds up. It's another if your server starts out slow and becomes even slower. The most common cause of server slowdown is cramped RAM or an overfull hard disk, so the first things to try require that you add some more memory or disk space.

You can buy 16MB of RAM for $120 and $170 (depending on speed, parity, and other bells and whistles). A 2GB Fast, Wide SCSI disk drive costs between $320 and $500. These prices are about as cheap as it ever gets when improving performance on a Windows NT server.

More Users Than Logons

Because buying extra licenses costs more money, the temptation to save money by scrimping on NT-user licenses is nearly irresistible. Users begin their relationship with most networks by keeping their distance and not staying logged on all the time. One of the major effects of networking success, however, is an increased dependency on the network. This, in turn, means users stay logged on throughout their working hours.

An easy cure exists if more users want to use the server than the number permitted by your Windows NT Server license. You can upgrade a Windows NT license from a lower to a higher number of users whenever you like, for about 50 percent of the difference between the price you paid for your license and the cost of a new license for that higher number. If you don't have to upgrade your hardware at the same time, this approach is affordable.

Chronic Disk Space Shortages

Disk capacity is what servers run out of first, and it's one of the shortages that's easiest to correct. All you need is funding to pay for more disk drives (and possibly another disk controller). Before you rush out to buy more disks, check out the Windows NT disk compression feature first: You may be able to make more room on your server's disks without spending any money!

Regular Network Traffic Jams

If the Windows NT Performance Monitor reports excessive transmission errors on your network, you may be overloading your network's carrying capacity (or you have a loose cable or malfunctioning device somewhere). This probably means that you're asking the cables to carry more traffic than they can handle.

This is another situation where adding more NICs to your server and splitting the wiring into subsets can reduce the traffic that any one cable segment must handle. This technique is most likely to help when your server utilization consistently stays below 30 to 40 percent but when the network stays congested anyway.

Dirty Looks in the Hallway

Users may not always tell you how they feel about network performance. If you start catching lots of dirty looks, however, consider it a warning that things are getting out of hand. Take action fast.

Mystery Guests on Your Network?

When mysterious printers, workstations, and other stuff — perhaps even mystery servers — start to appear on your network, it's often a sign that more resources will be needed soon. First examine the network for signs of congestion. Second, go out and resurvey your network to identify what's new and interesting out there.

Chronic Crashes Signal Imminent Danger

Any server failure or hang is a sure sign of trouble. But if this begins to happen regularly — perhaps at month end, when accounting is running the numbers, or during other peak loads — it's the network's way of telling you that something is being stretched beyond its capacity. Again, the rule is to identify the bottleneck, and then divide, duplicate, and conquer the related resource problem.

The Backup Won't Fit!

A sure sign of growing pains is when your backup system can no longer accommodate all the hard disk storage on your server on a single tape, cartridge, or MO disk. When this happens, you'll want to upgrade your backup system immediately. (Think about the effect of having to stay up and hand-feed the current system.) Shop around for a system with a capacity at least double your current needs; that way, you won't have to go through this process again too soon.

Burned in Effigy

You must have missed those dirty looks in the hallway, but hey, now you know! Get cracking on increasing resources, or they may burn *you!*

Growing pains are good because they tell you that you're doing a good job. But increasing demand for your network's services means planning for and providing increased capacity. If you can stay ahead of the users and add capacity before things get too weird, you'll be a hero. Watch for the warning signs and take appropriate action!

Appendix A

Technical Assistance: When and How to Get It

● ●

*T*his appendix tells you how to be effective when you interact with technical support organizations. It also explains the kind of help you can expect from these groups and what to do if your expectations aren't met.

Build a List and Check It Twice

When you organize a network or the applications that use it, keep a list of the equipment and applications that you own. Build a map and configuration database, as Chapter 6 outlines. You can use an inventory package, but plain paper and pencil are often enough. Although taking inventory is a boring task, it's also critically important. Be sure to include the following equipment and software in your inventory:

- Cable plant (type, length, location, end-labels)
- Network server(s)
- Network server software
- Workstations
- Software running on each workstation
- Tape-backup unit
- Disk storage (amount, type, make, model)

For your file server, you must know its vital statistics, such as the amount of RAM and disk space, as well as the type of network adapters, disk controllers, and display hardware. Write all this information down in the following questionnaire, or store it in a database or spreadsheet program. (If you do keep it on-line, print a hard copy just in case.) Keep this information where you can find it.

File server

File server manufacturer: _____

_____

File server model: _____

Processor

Processor type (286, 386, 486, Pentium, Pentium Pro, PowerPC): _____

Processor speed (66 MHz, 75 MHz, 90 MHz, 100 MHz, 120 MH, etc.): _____

Bus type(s) (ISA, EISA, Micro Channel, PCI, VLB): _____

Type of disk controller (SCSI, IDE): _____

Drive 1

Drive manufacturer: _____

_____

Drive model: _____

Drive capacity (in megabytes): _____

Disk drives: _____

Other stuff: _____

_____

_____

Drive (for more than one)

Drive manufacturer: _____

_____

Drive model: _____

Drive capacity (in megabytes): _____

Disk drives: _____

Other stuff: _____

_____

_____

_____

Drive (for more than two)

Drive manufacturer: _____

_____

Drive model: _____

Drive capacity (in megabytes): _____

Disk drives: _____

Other stuff: _____

_____

_____

_____

Display

Display manufacturer: _____

_____

Display type (monochrome, VGA, SVGA): __

_____

Display resolution: _____

Storage and RAM

Base memory address: _____

Amount of RAM (in megabytes): _____

Amount of disk storage (in megabytes): __

_____

Network adapter

Network adapter manufacturer: _____

_____

Type of adapter (Ethernet, token ring, and so on): _____

Model number: _____

Interrupt set at: _____

DMA set at: _____

Speed set at (if token ring): _____

Base memory address: _____

Network adapter (for more than one)

Network adapter manufacturer: _____

_____

Type of adapter: _____

Model number: _____

Interrupt set at: _____

DMA set at: _____

Speed set at (if token ring): _____

Base memory address: _____

Network adapter (for more than two)

Network adapter manufacturer: _____

_____

Type of adapter: _____

Model number: _____

Interrupt set at: _____

DMA set at: _____

Speed set at (if token ring): _____

Base memory address: _____

Tape backup

Tape backup manufacturer: _____

_____

Tape backup model: _____

Tape backup type (QIC, DAT, 8mm): _____

Tape backup capacity: _____

Location of off-site storage: _____

Location of on-site storage: _____

_____

Preferred tape type: _____

Software

OS name: _____

OS version: _____

_____

Application: _____

Version: _____

Application: _____

Version: _____

Application: _____

Version _____

Application: _____

Version _____

Application: _____

Version _____

Other stuff: _____

_____

Now you have to record the same kind of information for each workstation on the LAN (lucky for you, most workstations have only a single NIC). While you're at it, add the contents of the workstation's AUTOEXEC.BAT and CONFIG.SYS files to the list, if applicable. (These files are typically empty on machines that run Windows NT Workstation; in that case, you want a dump of their Registry databases.) Are you getting tired yet?

After you finish these lists, you need to know more about the software configuration of the workgroup. You need a listing of your server's Registry database and its various .INI files, and you have to put together lists of the following items, too:

- ✔ User names and their network addresses
- ✔ Groups and domains on the network
- ✔ File and directory access rights for each user and group
- ✔ Directory structure on the server
- ✔ Drive and other device shares

Write This Down Before Making the Call

When you encounter a problem, document what happened before the problem occurred. List any changes you made to files or the hardware. Write down any error messages you received. Trust us: When you call the technical-support number, you will be asked for this information.

Talk the Talk, Walk the Walk

Now that you have all this information written down, you're ready to combat the vendor's technical support line when something goes wrong. Before you call, gather your lists together. Better yet, get close to the troublesome PC so that you can lead the tech support person through the problem (by trying to duplicate it, for example).

When you make the call, be prepared for one of five things to happen:

- ✔ You're put on hold for what seems like forever. When you do get through, you can only leave voicemail.
- ✔ You are told that it is an operator error, which is a catch-all term that technical support people use when somebody has made a mistake. This term is also used when they don't want to deal with the question or they don't have the answer.

> ✔ You are told that no one has ever done anything this stupid. Hold your ground. Even if you've pioneered new realms of the absurd, it's still the responsibility of the technical support person to help you out.
>
> ✔ The person you talk to doesn't have the answer to the problem but will have someone else get back to you to solve the problem.
>
> ✔ A nice person on the telephone helps you work through the problem.

Be prepared to answer all the technical support person's questions, no matter how stupid they may sound. Tech support people don't read minds. If they did, they would make BIG bucks.

Escalation — Not Just for Department Stores

If you get someone on the phone who doesn't want to help, act just as you do when you have a problem with your electric bill. Ask to speak to a supervisor. In the lingo of the business, this is called escalating the call. After all, you paid good money for the product and you should get satisfaction.

The same applies to technical support people who don't call you back in a timely manner — 24 hours should be the maximum amount of time to wait for a return call. If you don't hear from them in that time, they should hear from you shortly thereafter!

Some vendors offer technical support 24 hours a day, seven days a week. When you buy products, find out about the vendor's technical support line. Paying a little more up front to get good support later may be worth it. For network hardware especially, 24-hour support is critical — you won't be taking the LAN down during working hours to insert a new network adapter in the server.

One-Stop Shopping: the TSA

In 1992, Novell organized the Technical Support Alliance (TSA) to provide better support for users. The TSA, a group of 42 vendors (including Microsoft), cross-train each other in the use of their products. When you call a TSA member about a problem that may involve several vendors' products, you can get an answer with just one phone call. Sounds neat, huh? Well, it is!

Let Your Fingers Do the Walking

There are other places to get help. Your best avenue is the Internet, where Microsoft is staking out one of the largest chunks of cyberspace under their main home page:

```
http://www.microsoft.com
```

This is now Microsoft's primary on-line presence and should be the first place you go to look for information on Windows NT or other Microsoft products, news, and technologies. (We provide information about what's available on the Internet in Appendix B.) Another avenue is CompuServe, which hosts a large number of Microsoft-focused forums and libraries. Lots of other vendors that provide networking products also have forums on CompuServe.

America OnLine (AOL) also offers a wealth of network-related information and Q&A support. In addition, many companies also operate their own bulletin board systems, where you can leave questions or download copies of new adapter drivers, bug fixes, and other stuff.

Training for the Pros

Books and classes on Windows NT are also available. Check the computer and networking magazines, and look around in your local bookstore. In particular, we recommend the following publications:

- ✔ *Networking Essentials,* Microsoft Press, 1996. List price: $99.95. This book and CD-ROM combination prepares its readers to support Windows NT networks and helps them get ready for the MCP exam. It's part of Microsoft's official Windows NT curriculum.

- ✔ *The Windows NT Resource Kit* (4 volumes, plus 2 CDs), Microsoft Press, 1995. List price: $149.95. This massive collection of Windows NT information remains valuable, even though it is getting out-of-date. Two add-on volumes are currently in print: *The Windows NT Resource Kit Version 3.51 Update* and *The Windows NT Resource Kit Version 3.51 Update 2*, Copyright 1995 and 1996, respectively. List price $39.95 (same for both books). These two slim volumes, each of which also includes a CD, provide essential updates to the original *Resource Kit*. All of these books are worth owning, but keep your eyes peeled for a new edition for NT 4.0 in early 1997.

- ✔ Rathbone, Andy: *Windows NT For Dummies*, IDG Books Worldwide, 1996. List price: $19.95. The *...For Dummies* companion to this book, it concentrates more on using Windows NT as a desktop operating system, and less on networking. (It makes an excellent complement to the coverage herein.)

- ✔ Hilley, Valda: *Windows NT Server 4.0 SECRETS,* IDG Books Worldwide, Inc., 1996. List price: $49.99.

- ✔ *Windows NT Magazine,* published monthly by Duke Communications International, Inc., P.O. Box 447, Loveland, Colorado, 80539-0447. Phone: 800-621-1544 or 970-663-4700. An excellent source of hands-on information about Windows NT and related software, hardware, and services. Note: Two of this book's authors are columnists for this magazine.

You can also attend Microsoft training centers; check the networking magazines for the list of centers in your state.

After attending a Microsoft training center, you might decide that you want to be a Certified Microsoft Technician (CMT). If you're simply a user on the LAN, this certification probably isn't for you. If you're responsible for the LAN, however, consider it seriously. The required courses necessary for certification cover Windows NT Workstation and Server, Windows 95, and network administration and configuration. It involves several courses, as well as tests. Without too much effort, you could make a career out of this!

Appendix B

An Incredibly Concise Guide to On-line Information

• •

*O*ur goal in this appendix is not to tell you how to use the Internet or CompuServe, or the Microsoft Forums, or World Wide Web, in particular. Rather, we just want to tell you what information is available on Windows NT on-line and why you might find it interesting. In addition, we offer suggestions on the most effective way to interact with CompuServe and the Internet: what to look for, what questions to ask, and what answers you're likely to receive.

Whither the Internet?

A veritable feast of resources are on the Internet that contain Windows NT information. Microsoft itself maintains a fleet of World Wide Web servers and FTP servers that you can reach from any location. But the treasure trove doesn't even begin to stop there: A quick visit to any of your favorite Web-based search engines with "Windows NT" as your target will turn up thousands of potential leads. (For the ultimate Web search tool, please visit http://www.metacrawler.com.) The real problem quickly becomes finding exactly what you need rather than anything at all!

Because more people are using the Internet than any other on-line community, we assume that you know the basics of navigating the Internet. If not, look for a copy of John R. Levine and Carol Baroudi's *Internet For Dummies,* 2nd Edition, from IDG Books Worldwide, Inc., at your local bookstore and brush up. If you're hungry for more, try John R. Levine's and Margaret Levine Young's *MORE Internet For Dummies*!

Information please

The best source of Windows NT information on the Internet is the Microsoft World Wide Web server. Located at www.microsoft.com, it contains all kinds of Windows NT-related information. If, for example, you try the home page's search engine (under the Search button, natch; be sure to narrow your scope to

Windows NT Server), you'll turn up thousands of pages to visit. You can find all types of product information, descriptions of service packs, lists of trade shows that Microsoft will be attending, and a range of multimedia product demos. With a WWW browser, such as the Microsoft Internet Explorer or the Netscape Communications Navigator, use

```
http://www.microsoft.com
```

as the uniform resource locator (URL) for this server. Be sure to tune in, because the Microsoft home page is *the* source for late-breaking news and up-to-the-minute information on Windows NT.

Microsoft is in the process of reinventing its Internet presence in the wake of a June 1996 announcement of their intention to discontinue direct technical support through CompuServe and switch their offerings to the Internet. Unfortunately, this means their site is still in a state of flux, so we can't be too specific about how it's organized or what you'll find there. We can tell you with confidence, however, that you'll find it well worth a visit, whether for software, technical information, or access to an on-line presence fielded by Microsoft Technical Support.

Remaining anonymous

Perhaps the easiest way to download Microsoft files from the Internet is by using simple, old-fashioned FTP (File Transfer Protocol). The Microsoft FTP address is `ftp.microsoft.com`.

Underneath this capacious umbrella, you find all kinds of interesting stuff. We recommend checking out the following files and directories:

/.../README.TXT	In any given subdirectory, you'll find this text file, which explains what's going on and what's inside other subdirectories or files
/download	A set of subdirectories for all kinds of Microsoft products and technologies, from ActiveX to webpost, chock-full of interesting download files
/peropsys/GEN_INFO/KB	The full set of articles from the Microsoft Knowledge Base (file names represent article numbers)
/Win_News	News articles, information, and an archive of the files from the excellent Windows NT News mailing list
/dirmap.htm	Point your Web browser to `ftp:/ftp.microsoft.com/dirmap.htm`, and you can download whatever you want from this site

USENET newsgroups

The USENET news hierarchy is a great way to obtain quick, informative responses to particular questions, even if you simply read the traffic without posting any queries of your own. Of the 17,000-plus newsgroups currently in existence, far too many of them touch on Windows NT to cover them all here. Nevertheless, we recommend checking out the groups beneath these two hierarchies:

```
comp.os.ms-windows.nt.
microsoft.public.windowsnt.
```

We recommend also obtaining a list of the newsgroups (your newsreader will usually store it as a text file, or you can obtain a copy from any ISP that maintains a USENET service) and using ".nt." or ".windowsnt." as a search string. It should turn up all relevant newsgroups for your perusal. (Our most recent search turned up such newsgroups, plus another 112 with "windows" in the group's name.) You may not be able to get the `microsoft.public.hierarchy` through the news server at your ISP; you may need to sign up with the Microsoft Internet service to get access to this information. Set your newsreader's NNTP server to this domain name:

```
msnews.microsoft.com
```

You may have to reset your newsreader to regain access to your normal newsfeed; just to be on the safe side, write down your original NNTP server's domain name before you point your newsreader at the address listed above.

The best NT mailing list

Beverly Hills Software, itself an excellent resource for Windows NT software and information, is also the home of the Microsoft WinNTNews Electronic Newsletter. This list gets a message once every week to 10 days, and always includes interesting information: the scoop on betas, upgrades, and Service Packs, and access to all kinds of early-bird information about Windows NT. To join this mailing list, point your Web browser to

```
http://www.bhs.com/microsoft.winntnews
```

and fill out the form there. The underlying CGI program does the rest.

To subscribe by email, send the command `subscribe winntnews` as the first line of your message to

```
winntnews-admin@microsoft.bhs.com
```

This signs you up and produces a message that explains how to unsubscribe should you ever want to leave the mailing list. (Make a copy of this message and keep it where you can find it again — you may need it someday!)

Welcome to CompuServe

The CompuServe Information Service (CIS) offers thousands of topics for your perusal. To access CompuServe, you need an individual account (called a membership number) with an accompanying password. You can obtain trial access at no charge in many ways, but if you want to play on CompuServe, sooner or later you have to pay. CompuServe charges a monthly membership fee in addition to connection charges. (Some services on CompuServe have additional charges as well.) Spending time and money on CompuServe is easy.

Forums for conversation and investigation

When you access CompuServe, you need to select an area of interest to focus your exploration. Information on CompuServe is organized into forums. A *forum* is an area dedicated to a particular subject or a collection of related subjects. Each forum contains one or more of the following:

- **Message board:** Features electronic conversations organized by specific subjects into sections related to particular topics. (Ethernet issues, for instance, are a topic, as are token-ring issues. In the Ethernet section, you would expect to find discussions of frame types, drivers for particular NICs, and the like.) A given sequence of messages, chained together by a common subject or by replies to an original message, is called a *thread.* It's important to note that threads may read like conversations but that messages in a thread can be separated by hours or days.

- **Conference room:** An electronic analog to the real thing, it brings individuals together to exchange ideas and information in real time. Conference rooms can be frustrating for those with limited touch-typing skills.

- **File library:** A collection of files organized by subject that can be copied, or downloaded, for further use. Examples of file types in CompuServe libraries are archived collections of threads, documents of all kinds, and a variety of software ranging from program patches and fixes to entire programs.

CompuServe represents an "electronic information warehouse" and offers an absorbing source of information, gossip, software, and activity.

Obtaining a CompuServe membership

You request an account by telephone or by writing to CompuServe. For telephone inquiries, ask for Representative 200. Use these numbers:

- ✔ Within the U.S. (except Ohio), including Alaska, Hawaii, Puerto Rico, and the American Virgin Islands, call toll free at 800-848-8199.
- ✔ Outside the U.S., in Canada, and in Ohio, call 614-457-8650.

Telephone hours are 8 A.M. to 10 P.M. Eastern time Monday through Friday and from noon to 5 P.M. on Saturday.

Direct written inquiries to:

> CompuServe, Inc.
> Attn: Customer Service
> P.O. Box 20212
> 5000 Arlington Centre Boulevard
> Columbus, OH 43220
> U.S.A.

Accessing CompuServe

To access CompuServe, you must equip your computer with a modem and attach that modem to a telephone line. You also need a communications program to let your computer talk to CompuServe. Finally, you have to obtain a telephone number for CompuServe — most numbers are local, especially in the U.S.

Connection-time charges are based on your modem speed. Although faster modems do incur higher connection charges, the higher price is offset by faster transfer speeds. (The faster the transmission, the less time you're on-line paying for the connection.) If your CompuServe bill is more than $30 a month, a high-speed modem will normally pay for itself in six months or less.

After you connect to CompuServe, enter your membership number and your password. First-time users should follow the instructions provided by your CompuServe representative or in the *CompuServe Starter Kit* that's available from CompuServe (for an additional fee). After you're logged on, it's easy to get to the Microsoft on-line forums, collected under the name "the Microsoft Connection." Type `GO MSOFT` or `GO MICROSOFT` from the CompuServe prompt, and you are presented with a menu of additional choices for Microsoft products and information, including Windows NT.

What Is the Microsoft Connection?

The Microsoft Connection is a collection of CompuServe forums all dedicated to Microsoft technologies, products, support groups, and databases, many of which focus on Microsoft networking products and related information. The Microsoft Connection is a great alternative to using the company's telephone hotline for technical support. This is one of the busiest collections of forums on CompuServe, with over 40,000 users daily. At the time this overview was written, there were more than 40 Microsoft-related CompuServe forums.

Reaping rewards from the Microsoft Connection

The benefits of using the Microsoft Connection are hard to overstate but easy to understand. The most important benefit is the help that's available. This on-line universe is staffed by volunteer system operators (sysops); they're not Microsoft employees, but many are extremely knowledgeable about Microsoft and Windows NT topics.

Together with other power users, the sysops and their colleagues are an invaluable source of information, help, and advice about networking topics. As a bonus, almost all questions are answered within 24 hours of being posted. You will want to log on at least once a day, when you are waiting for replies to questions. (The *scroll rate,* the speed at which messages age and are deleted from the Microsoft forums, is about two days.)

The Microsoft Connection is also the place to go for the latest and greatest patches and fixes for Windows NT and other Microsoft products. The libraries that contain the files available for downloading are uploaded daily and documented extensively in catalogs of information available on-line. Lots of third-party applications and utilities are available for your perusal.

The Microsoft Connection is also a place where Windows NT users of the world congregate. It puts you in touch with thousands of other users, most of whom are eager to share what they have learned — and the mistakes they have made. Messages are posted in public forums so that all who access the Microsoft forums can see and add to the growing collection of information. As a side effect, the Microsoft Connection is also the premier source of contacts for consulting, sales, and business opportunities for the Windows NT community.

"About Microsoft Connection"

The only thing you need to know from this section is that an on-line roadmap to the Microsoft Connection is always available. The on-line universe is nothing if not mutable, so visiting the on-line section named "About Microsoft Connection" is the best place to orient yourself whenever you drop into this collection of CompuServe forums.

The sections that follow are subject to radical change and rearrangement at a moment's notice.

Microsoft File Finder (GO MSFF)

If you want to download any Microsoft-related files, go to Microsoft File Finder. It includes instructions for searching and a special list of *CompuServe Magazine* feature files from the current issue. If you know the name of a download file, or can make some educated guesses about keywords to identify what you're looking for, MSFF is a very handy tool.

Windows Forum Directory

The Windows Forum Directory takes you to a directory of over 20 Windows-related forums that cover topics as diverse as Accounting/Tax Information to Word Processing. You'll probably be most interested in Communications/Networking and Operating Systems, both of which provide ample coverage of Windows NT Workstation and Server.

Windows shareware forums

The Windows shareware forums are a collection of forums devoted to Windows shareware, covering topics from productivity software to business applications. This is a good place to go prospecting for add-ons to the basic capabilities delivered "in the box" with Windows NT Workstation or Server.

Download customized Microsoft WinCIM

WinCIM stands for Windows CompuServe Information Manager, a Windows CompuServe browsing tool. The customized version makes accessing any of the Microsoft stuff we cover easy. If you use CompuServe primarily for Microsoft information and downloads, the customized Microsoft version of WinCIM is probably worth downloading and installing on your system.

Surf the libraries

After familiarizing yourself with the forums, you probably will end up checking out the libraries (that of Microsoft and third-party uploads, respectively). The new stuff hits here first, and these areas seldom require as much reading to find what you need as others do.

Whatever your level of interest, we're sure that a trip to the Microsoft Connection will be well worth it. If you want to be a real Windows NT professional, it's a good place to visit!

Appendix C
Vendor List

· ·

Adaptec, Inc.
691 S. Milpitas Boulevard
Milpitas, CA 95035
800-934-2766; 408-945-8600
Direct sales: 800-442-SCSI
FAX: 408-262-2533
http://www.adaptec.com

America Online, Inc.
8619 Westwood Center Drive
Vienna, VA 22182-2285
800-827-6364; 703-448-8700
FAX: 800-827-4595
http://www.aol.com

**American National Standards
Institute (ANSI)**
11 West 42nd Street
New York, NY 10036
212-642-4900
FAX: 212-398-0023
http://www.ansi.org

**American Power Conversion
Corp.**
132 Fairgrounds Road
West Kingston, RI 02892-9906
800-800-4272; 401-789-0204
FAX: 401-789-3710
http://www.apcc.com

Apple Computer, Inc.
1 Infinite Loop
Cupertino, CA 95014
800-776-2333; 408-996-1010
Direct sales: 800-538-9696
(Hardware); 800-325-2747
(Software/Claris Corp.)
FAX: 408-996-0275
http://www.apple.com

Banyan Systems, Inc.
120 Flanders Road
Westborough, MA 01581-5013
800-222-6926; 508-898-1000
FAX: 508-898-1755
http://www.banyan.com

BindView Development Corp.
3355 W. Alabama, Suite 1200
Houston, TX 77098
800-749-8439; 713-881-9100
FAX: 713-881-9200
http://www.bindview.com

**BusLogic Inc. (subsidiary of
Mylex Corp.)**
4151 Burton Drive
Santa Clara, CA 95054-1564
800-707-7274; 408-492-9090
FAX: 408-492-1542
Tech support: 408-654-0760
Tech support BBS: 408-492-1984
http://www.buslogic.com

Cheyenne Software, Inc.
630 Pleasant Hill Road,
Suite 180-200
Atlanta, GA 30136-5287
800-395-1812; 770-682-7004
FAX: 770-339-1812
http://www.cheyenne.com

Compaq Computer Corp.
20555 State Highway 249
Houston, TX 77070-2698
800-345-1518; 713-514-0484
Direct sales: 800-888-5925
(Compaq DirectPlus)
FAX: 713-514-4583
http://www.compaq.com

Compaq IPG (formerly Thomas-Conrad Corp.)
12301 Technology Boulevard
Austin, TX 78727
800-332-8683; 512-433-6000
FAX: 512-433-6029
http://www.tci.com

CompuServe, Inc.
5000 Arlington Centre Boulevard
P.O. Box 20212
Columbus, OH 43220
800-848-8199; 614-457-8600
FAX: 614-457-0348
Tech support: 800-848-8990
http://www.compuserve.com

Datapoint Corp.
8400 Datapoint Drive
San Antonio, TX 78229-8500
800-733-1500; 210-593-7000
FAX: 210-593-7601

Dell Computer Corp.
2300 Greenlawn Boulevard
Round Rock, TX 78664-7098
800-289-3355; 512-338-4400
FAX: 512-728-3653
http://www.dell.com

Digital Equipment Corp. (DEC)
146 Main Street
Maynard, MA 01754-2571
800-344-4825; 508-493-5111
Direct sales: 800-642-4532
(Digital PC/PCs Compleat)
FAX: 508-493-8780
http://www.dec.com

Distributed Processing Technology (DPT)
140 Candace Drive
Maitland, FL 32751
800-322-4DPT; 407-830-5522
FAX: 407-260-5366
http://www.dpt.com

Frye Computer Systems (division of Seagate Technology, Inc.)
31 Saint James Avenue
Boston, MA 02116
800-234-3793; 617-368-3300
FAX: 617-753-0484

Hewlett-Packard Co.
3000 Hanover Street
Palo Alto, CA 94304
800-752-0900; 800-387-3867 (CD);
415-857-1501
Direct sales: 800-637-7740
(HP Direct)
http://www.hp.com

Horizons Technology, Inc.
3990 Ruffin Road
San Diego, CA 92123-1826
800-828-3808; 619-292-8331
FAX: 619-292-9439
http://www.horizons.com

IBM
Old Orchard Road
Armonk, NY 10504
800-426-3333; 914-765-1900
Direct sales: 800-426-7255
(IBM PC Direct)
http://www.ibm.com

Intel Corp.
2200 Mission College Boulevard
Santa Clara, CA 95051
800-548-4725; 408-765-8080
FAX: 408-765-1821
http://www.intel.com

International Standards Organization (ISO)
1, rue de Varembé
Case postale 56
CH-1211 Genève 20
Switzerland
41-22-749-01-11
FAX: 41-22-733-34-30
http://www.iso.ch

Internet Engineering Task Force (IETF)
c/o Corporation for National Research Initiatives
1895 Preston White Drive, Suite 100
Reston, VA 22091
703-620-8990
FAX: 703-758-5913
http://www.ietf.org

InterNIC
800-862-0677; 908-668-6587
admin@ds.internic.net
http://www.internic.net

Intrusion Detection, Inc.
217 East 86th Street, Suite 213
New York, NY 10028
800-408-6104; 212-360-6104
Direct sales: 212-348-8900
FAX: 212-427-9185
http://www.intrusion.com

LANWrights, Inc.
5810 Lookout Mountain Drive
Austin, TX 78731
512-452-3768; 512-452-5670
FAX: 512-452-8018
http://www.lanw.com

Lexmark International, Inc.
740 New Circle Road, NW
Lexington, KY 40511-1876
800-358-5835; 606-232-2000
Direct sales: 800-438-2468
FAX: 606-232-2403
http://www.lexmark.com

McAfee Associates, Inc.
2710 Walsh Avenue, Suite 200
Santa Clara, CA 95051-0963
800-866-6585; 408-988-3832
Direct sales: 800-332-9966
FAX: 408-970-9727
http://www.mcafee.com

Microsoft Corp.
One Microsoft Way
Redmond, WA 98052-6399
800-426-9400; 206-882-8080
Direct sales: 800-MSPRESS
FAX: 206-93-MSFAX
http://www.microsoft.com

National Security Institute
57 East Main Street, Suite 217
Westborough, MA 01581
Telephone: 508-366-5800
Fax: 508-898-0132
http://www.nsi.org

National Software Testing Laboratories
A division of The McGraw-Hill Companies
Plymouth Corporate Center
625 Ridge Pike
Conshohocken, PA 19428
610-941-9600
FAX: 610-941-9952
http://www.nstl.com

Network General Corp.
4200 Bohannon Drive
Menlo Park, CA 94025
800-764-3337; 415-473-2000
FAX: 415-321-0855
http://www.ngc.com

Novell, Inc.
1555 N. Technology Way
Orem, UT 84757
800-453-1267; 801-222-6000
FAX: 800-NOVLFAX
http://www.novell.com

**Software Publishers
Association (SPA)**
1730 M Street, NW, Suite 700
Washington, DC 20036-4510
202-452-1600
Anti-Piracy Hotline: 800-388-7478
FAX: 202-223-8756
Fax On Demand Service:
800-637-6823
http://www.spa.org

Symantec Corp.
10201 Torre Avenue
Cupertino, CA 95014-2132
800-441-7234; 408-253-9600
Direct sales: 800-453-1193
FAX: 408-253-3968
http://www.symantec.com

Thomas-Conrad Corp.
(See Compaq IPG)

Xerox Corp.
100 S. Clinton Avenue,
Xerox Square
Rochester, NY 14644
800-ASK-XEROX; 716-423-5090
FAX: 716-427-5400
http://www.xerox.com

Index